THE PHILOSOPHICAL DEFENCE
OF PSYCHIATRY

PHILOSOPHICAL ISSUES IN SCIENCE

General Editor
W. H. Newton-Smith

THE RATIONAL AND THE SOCIAL
James Robert Brown

THE NATURE OF DISEASE
Lawrie Reznek

INFERENCE TO THE BEST EXPLANATION
Peter Lipton

forthcoming

TIME, SPACE AND PHILOSOPHY
Christopher Ray

MATHEMATICS AND THE IMAGE OF REASON
Mary Tiles

THE PHILOSOPHICAL DEFENCE OF PSYCHIATRY

Lawrie Reznek

London and New York

First Published 1991
by Routledge
11 New Fetter Lane, London EC4P 4EE

Simultaneously published in the USA and Canada
by Routledge
a division of Routledge, Chapman and Hall, Inc.
29 West 35th Street, New York, NY 10001

© 1991 Lawrie Reznek
Phototypeset in 10/12 Bembo by
Input Typesetting Ltd, London
Printed in Great Britain by
T. J. Press (Padstow) Ltd, Padstow, Cornwall

British Library Cataloguing in Publication Data
Reznek, Lawrie.
The philosophical defence of psychiatry. – (Philosophical issues in
science).
1. Medicine. Psychiatry
I. Title   II. Series
616.89

Library of Congress Cataloging in Publication Data
Reznek, Lawrie.
The philosophical defence of psychiatry / Lawrie Reznek.
p.   cm. — (Philosophical issues in science)
Includes bibliographical references.
Includes index.
1. Mental illness—Philosophy.   2. Psychiatry—Philosophy.
I. Title.   II. Series.
[DNLM: 1. Philosophy, Medical.   2 Psychiatry.   WM 100 R4667p]
RC437.5.R49   1991
616.89′001—dc20
DNLM/DLC
for Library of Congress
90–8823
CIP

ISBN 0–415–03593–7

To my wife,
Eleanor,
For more than I can say

CONTENTS

PREFACE

This book aims to provide psychiatry with philosophical foundations. Because I believe that the essence of philosophy is *argument*, I will concentrate on arguments throughout the book, especially the conceptual premises of those arguments. For those unfamiliar with philosophy, the boundaries of our concepts will be mapped by describing situations that have not yet occurred. We do not have to wait for these events to see how our concepts will behave – we can imagine them.

The first half of the book examines many challenges to the concept of mental illness. I will show that these attacks on the heart of psychiatry are based on philosophical assumptions – e.g. on the nature of disease, the nature of mind, the relationship between cause and reason, the nature of responsibility, etc. – that are mistaken. This will reinforce my thesis that philosophy is necessary in order to understand psychiatry. I will reconstruct and analyse the arguments made. Here two caveats are in order. First, I will be more concerned with the arguments themselves than with the issue of whether they can be correctly attributed to the authors in question. This is a work of philosophy and not of the history of ideas. And second, space limits both the number and depth of critics I can examine.

The second half of the book will be an attempt to provide a coherent account of mental illness and the nature of psychiatry which answers objections examined in the first half. In this connection, I must add a third caveat. Because the book hopes to examine a wide variety of philosophical issues raised by psychiatry, it cannot hope to deal with each issue in the depth that it merits. Every issue no doubt requires a separate book, but I hope that this single book will provide a consistent picture of psychiatry that escapes the criticisms levelled against her. Finally, although this book is intended to stand on its own, some of the issues are covered in more detail in my book, *The Nature of Disease*.

This book has been written while continuing my psychiatry training at the Royal Edinburgh Hospital. I would like to thank members of the Edinburgh University Department of Psychiatry for their help, especially Eve Johnstone, who read an early draft and gave many useful suggestions, and Robert Kendell, who read a number of chapters and made valuable comments. Bill Newton-Smith and Paul Harrison also read the penultimate draft with great care and gave invaluable assistance. My thanks also go to Derek Chiswick, Cathy Adams, Anthony Pelosi, and David Ryan who helped with individual chapters. I must, however, take full responsibility for all the views in this book. Finally, I would like to thank my wife who put up with being a computer-widow for over a year while the book was being written. It is to her that it is dedicated.

INTRODUCTION: PSYCHIATRY IN CRISIS

The foundations of psychiatry are shaking. As a branch of medicine, it is firmly committed to the existence of mental illnesses, but there is little consensus as to their existence. As a branch of medical science, it presumes to discover the truth about the causes of abnormal human behaviour using scientific methodology, but there is a question mark against the scientific status of psychiatric knowledge. As a science over two thousand years old, one expects some agreement as to the basic form of psychiatric explanation, but instead there is a plethora of conflicting theoretical perspectives or paradigms. In short, as a theoretical enterprise, psychiatry is in a bad way.

THE CLASH OF PARADIGMS

Psychiatry is in a theoretical mess. As two commentators observe:

> There is no indication that psychiatry has a common theoretical base and each practitioner seems to have an idiosyncratic approach which is often at complete variance from that of his colleagues. It is often said that if you want five different opinions on any aspect of mental health you just need to ask five psychiatrists.
>
> (Tyrer and Steinberg, 1987, p. 1)

In what follows, I will illustrate this clash of paradigms with the example of depression.

The standard medical view sees depression as a disease of the neurotransmitter systems of the brain:

A given affective state may represent a balance between

1

central cholinergic and adrenergic neurotransmitter activity in those areas of the brain which regulate affect, with depression being a disease of cholinergic dominance and mania being the converse.

(Janowsky *et al.*, 1972, p. 632)

On this view, depression is the consequence of some underlying biological abnormality.

Others argue that there is no disease of depression. For Sigmund Freud and other psychoanalysts, depression or melancholia is the product of psychodynamic forces:

We have discovered that the self-reproaches, with which these melancholic patients torment themselves in the most merciless fashion, in fact apply to another person, the sexual object which they have lost. . . . From this we can conclude that the melancholic has, it is true, withdrawn his libido from the object, but that, by a process which we must call 'narcissistic identification', the object has been set up in the ego itself. . . . The subject's own ego is then treated to all the acts of aggression and expressions of vengefulness which have been aimed at the object. A melancholic's propensity to suicide is also made more intelligible if we consider that the patient's embitterment strikes with a single blow at his own ego and at the loved and hated object.

(Freud, 1973, pp. 477–8)

A loss, real or imagined, of a loved one produces anger towards the abandoning person. When this anger is turned inward on to the self, depression is the result. This inner-directed anger is seen as explaining the clinical features, like the self-torment and suicidal tendency, of the syndrome of depression.

Some see the mental state of depression as the result of forces of conditioning. If a person is subjected to unpleasant events such as failures, frustrations, and rejections, his behaviour will be negatively reinforced:

These are the types of events bearing a critical relationship to the occurrence of depression. When the good ones occur at low rates and the negative ones occur at high rates, the individual is likely to feel depressed. We also hypothesize that these are the major types of events that act as reinforcers for people; occurrence of the ones that are negatively associated with dysphoria serve to maintain our behaviour, and the occurrence of events that are positively associated with dysphoria reduces our rates of behaviour.

(Lewinsohn, Youngren and Grosscup, 1979, p. 313)

By seeing behaviour as the product of schedules of conditioning, this view is able to explain the clinical features, like the inactivity, of depressed patients.

Aaron Beck sees the mental state of depression as the product of faulty cognitive processes. Depressed patients react to loss in a negative way, inferring that they are failures, that the world is full of obstacles, etc. Distorted inferences lead to a negative view of the self, the world, and the future, and this 'cognitive triad' explains the symptoms of depression:

> The cognitive model offers a hypothesis about predisposition to depression. Briefly, the theory proposes that early experiences provide the basis for forming negative concepts about one's self, the future, and the external world. These negative concepts may be latent but can be activated by specific circumstances which are analogous to experiences initially responsible for embedding the negative attitude. . . . In response to traumatic situations the average person will still maintain interest in and realistically appraise other nontraumatic aspects of his life. On the other hand, the thinking of the depression–prone person becomes markedly constricted and negative ideas develop about every aspect of his life.
>
> (Beck et al., 1979, p. 16)

By supposing that depressed patients misinterpret events in a negative way, this theory is able to explain the clinical features, like the negative thinking, of depressives.

Martin Seligman sees depression as 'learned helplessness':

> When a traumatic event first occurs, it causes a heightened state of emotionality that can loosely be called fear. This state continues until one of two things happen; if the subject learns that he can control the trauma, fear is reduced and may even disappear altogether; or if the subject finally learns he cannot control the trauma, fear will decrease and be replaced by depression.
>
> (Seligman, 1975, p. 53)

3

When people become depressed, they are in effect learning to be helpless – learning that nothing they do will enable them to avoid the unpleasant events in their lives.

George Brown sees depression as the product of social forces. Adverse social histories and circumstances conspire to engender a state of hopelessness:

> Except in bipolar conditions, I know of little evidence that would support the idea of some basic flaw in bodily or cognitive functions before the onset of the depressive dis-order that is not a direct reflection of the social milieu – past and present. In fact, despite recent progress in biological and cognitive studies in psychology, it is possible, and per-haps useful, to take a radical sociological perspective. . . . The most realistic conclusion, if priorities about aetiological processes were to be given at present, would be that depression is in good part a social phenomenon.
>
> (Brown, 1989, p. 21)

By seeing depression in this way, this sociological theory is able to explain the features of depression, such as its preponderance in the lower social classes.

Still others take an anthropological account of depression. Arthur Kleinman writes:

> Dysthymia would seem to be an instance of the medicaliz-ation of social problems in much of the rest of the world (and perhaps often in the West as well), where severe eco-nomic, political, and health problems create endemic feelings of hopelessness and helplessness, where demoralization and despair are responses to actual conditions of chronic depri-vation and persistent loss, where powerlessness is not a cognitive distortion but an accurate mapping of one's place in an oppressive social system.
>
> (Kleinman, 1988, p. 15)

On this view, depression is an appropriate response to oppressive circumstances.

There are others who see mental illness as a game played to get help when there are problems in living':

> The rules of the medical game define health – which includes such things as a well functioning body and happiness – as

a positive value. Illness thus becomes the opposite – that is, an ill-functioning body and unhappiness or depression. Hysteria, as we have seen, is a dramatized representation of the message: 'My body is not functioning well'. And the mental illness called 'depression' is a dramatization of the proposition: 'I am unhappy'.

(Szasz, 1972, p. 202)

On this view, depression is seen as a game people play to communicate their need for help with 'problems of living'.

This is a confusing array of conflicting theoretical perspectives. Not only are they conflicting stories of the causes of depression, but also of the nature of depression. For one psychiatrist, depression is a disease and the result of abnormal biochemical processes for which the individual has a hereditary disposition. For another, depression is a set of conditioned reflexes caused by a negative schedule of reinforcement. A third sees depression as learned behaviour caused by uncontrollable and aversive events. For a fourth, depression is a cognitive state acquired by faulty cognitive processes, while a fifth sees depression as a social phenomenon caused by adverse social circumstances. A sixth sees depression as the medicalization of chronic demoralization while a seventh sees it as a game people play when they run into problems. There is little consensus and much confusion.

Not only is there a clash of paradigms within psychiatry, but some dispute that psychiatry is even a science at all:

> The criterion of the scientific status of a theory is its falsifiability, or refutability, or testability. . . . Psychoanalytic theories were in a different class. They were simply non-testable, irrefutable. There was no conceivable human behaviour which could contradict them. . . . Those 'clinical observations' which analysts naively believe confirm their theory cannot do this any more than the daily confirmations which astrologers find in their practice. And as for Freud's epic of the Ego, the Super-ego, and the Id, no substantially stronger claim to scientific status can be made for it than for Homer's collected stories from Olympus. These stories describe some facts, but in the manner of myths. They contain most interesting psychological suggestions, but not in a testable form.
>
> (Popper, 1963, p. 38)

Because many of the theories of the human psyche are not falsifiable, the scientific status of psychiatry is challenged.

With its theoretical dimension challenged, psychiatry starts to look more like witchcraft than medicine:

> The techniques used by Western psychiatrists are, with few exceptions, on exactly the same scientific plane as the techniques used by witchdoctors. If one is magic, then so is the other. . . . In order to be scientific, a phenomenon must be explainable by underlying laws. These laws are arrived at by observation, measurement, experimentation, induction, hypothesis formation and testing. The rationale for most therapies used by witchdoctors and psychiatrists is not arrived at in this way – rather the techniques are used on sick clients, the clients get well, and therefore the techniques are thought to work. This is logical, empirical psychiatry and is found among witchdoctors and psychiatrists. And both witchdoctors and psychiatrists make the assumption that their clients get well because of the techniques.
>
> (Torrey, 1986, pp. 11–12)

There are many critics who feel that most of the so-called therapies used by psychiatrists are employed without adequate empirical foundation. While they continue to be used because patients by and large get better, they are worthless if patients get better just as easily without them.

With many paradigms disputing the existence of mental diseases, there are competing views of what psychiatry is doing. If there are no diseases, psychiatry cannot be aimed at treating them. Instead, some argue that psychiatry aims at social control:

> The state has assumed most of the traditional social functions of regulating and controlling human conduct. Because all moral codes are not codified in law, and because the power of the state is limited by rule of law, the state is unable satisfactorily to control and influence individuals. This requires a new social institution that, under the auspices of an acceptable modern authority, can control and guide conduct without conspicuously violating publicly avowed ideals of freedom and respect for the individual. Psychiatry, in medical disguise, has assumed this historical function.
>
> (Leifer, 1969, p. 15)

This clash of paradigms has raised many doubts about the status and aims of psychiatry – alternative paradigms challenge the existence of mental illness and thereby the humanitarian goals of psychiatry. Our task will be to investigate the nature of psychiatric knowledge and practice, and in order to do this, we need first to understand the notion of a paradigm.

THE IDEA OF A PARADIGM

Thomas Kuhn saw science as divided into two different stages – normal science, and revolutionary science (Kuhn, 1970). Normal science occurs when scientists in one domain accept an overall theory of that domain, and proceed to explain everything within that domain with the principles of that theory. Revolutionary science, on the other hand, occurs when that overall theory is overthrown by another such theory. Kuhn calls these overall theories paradigms.

For our purposes, I will define a paradigm as follows:

T is a paradigm for a domain of science D if and only if T is (1) a theory that (2) provides an ontology for D, and (3) provides explanatory laws governing that ontology, such that (4) all the behaviour of the objects in D can potentially be explained, which is (5) accepted by most scientists working in D, and is (6) preserved by them from falsification.

Kuhn uses a broader notion of paradigm such that those accepting a paradigm agree on what counts as needing explanation, on what makes a theory superior, and on experimental procedures (Kuhn, 1970, pp. 181–91). To simplify matters, I will assume the paradigms of psychiatry agree on such matters – e.g. all paradigms agree that it is abnormal behaviour that requires explanation – so that the above definition captures the area of disagreement.

To explain what this all means, let us look at a historical example. Aristotle put forward a theory of motion which held that there were two sorts of objects – earthly bodies and heavenly bodies. Every body had its natural place – earthly bodies on the surface of the earth, heavenly bodies in the heavenly spheres, and it took a force to dislodge and keep any object from its natural place. With this ontology and explanatory law, the theory set out to explain the motions of all objects (Shapere, 1974). Scientists used the theory to explain the puzzling phenomena. Such puzzle-solving Kuhn called normal science. It consists essentially in pre-serving the truth of the explanatory laws of the paradigm and searching for other factors which, together with these laws, can explain the puzzling phenomena. In this way, the paradigm is protected from falsification – any observation not fitting with the theory is seen not as refuting it, but as challenging an auxiliary assumption. For example, Aristotle's theory could not explain why a projectile remained in motion when the force was with-drawn and the projectile released – according to the theory, the projectile should drop vertically to its natural place. But the exist-ence of projectile motion was not taken to refute the theory – it simply undermined the auxiliary hypothesis that there was no force continually acting on the projectile. Aristotelians solved this puzzle by postulating that projectiles displaced the air from in front of them and that this air then rushed in to push the projectile from behind, thereby continuing to keep it from its natural place. According to our definition, then, Aristotle's theory was a para-digm. It postulated the existence of certain sorts of objects, pro-vided explanatory laws governing their behaviour, it was accepted by most scientists working in that domain, was taken as being able to explain all phenomena in that domain, and it was protected from falsification by changes to auxiliary assumptions.

It may sound odd to see normal science as the protection of theories from falsification – testing a theory by checking obser-vational predictions hardly sounds like a genuine test if the theory can always be saved! But we must understand that no theory confronts observations on its own – it does so together with a host of auxiliary assumptions (Duhem, 1962). And so, if the observational predictions are not born out, we cannot know that the theory rather than one of the auxiliary assumptions is false. We cannot infer any observational consequences from the Aristot-elian law that forces are sufficient to displace objects from their natural places without assuming that something exerts a force, that no countervailing force is acting, etc. In order to get any testable consequences out of a theory, we need auxiliary hypo-theses to help generate predictions. But once we require auxiliary hypotheses, then it becomes difficult to know where the fault lies if the observational prediction turns out to be false – all that follows is that either the theory or the auxiliary hypothesis is false. Hence it is not illogical to preserve the theory and postulate that some auxiliary hypothesis is false. When projectiles do not fall vertically, we need only conclude that it is wrong to think there are no other forces acting on it – and not that Aristotle's theory is false.

If normal science preserves the paradigm at the cost of such auxiliary hypotheses, it might be wondered what reasons we can ever have for giving up a paradigm. For it seems possible that paradigms can be saved indefinitely by changes to auxiliary hypotheses. But if a paradigm is false, then it will become more and more burdened with auxiliary hypotheses and auxiliary hypotheses for the auxiliary hypotheses till the point comes that another theory can deal with the puzzle far more simply. Then a revolution in science occurs with a new paradigm supplanting the old. Aristotle's theory has to introduce new forces to explain the motion of projectiles. However, it also has to introduce more forces to explain why we cannot observe the first forces. If there is a wind pushing a projectile from behind, then streamers tied to it ought to be blown forward. But they are not. So, in order to save Aristotle's theory, we not only have to assume that there is some wind, but also that there is some countervailing force that ensures that the streamers are not forced forwards – we are forced to make an infinite regress of auxiliary assumptions making the total theory absurdly cumbersome and implausible.

Kuhn correctly pointed out that it was the presence of an alternative theory that can explain the same phenomena (and more) without the escalation of auxiliary hypotheses that deals the death-blow to any paradigm. It was the emergence of the Galilean paradigm that led to the Aristotelian theory being abandoned. In this new paradigm, forces are not needed to sustain objects in motion – a body continues in its state of rest or uniform motion unless disturbed by a force. And hence no force is needed to keep a projectile in motion (Shapere, 1974). However, an explanation has to be given why objects forced along the ground do not remain perpetually in motion. A counteracting force to retard motion – a frictional force – was invoked. However, unlike Aristotle's theory, there was no necessity for an infinite regress of auxiliary hypotheses because the auxiliary hypothesis itself received observational support – the heat generated supports the existence of such forces. The auxiliary hypothesis did not require further auxiliary hypotheses to protect it from generating false predictions.

Often the protection of paradigms from falsificaton is justified. When the motion of Uranus did not fit the predictions of Newton's theory, Newtonians argued that this anomaly was due to the existence of another planet – i.e. that the auxiliary hypothesis that there are eight planets was wrong. They postulated the existence of another planet, Neptune, which was thankfully later discovered (Putnam, 1975, p. 256)!

For our purposes, there are a number of points about paradigms that need to be understood. First, different paradigms of a given domain are competing, and this means that at some level, they must contradict one another. Newton's theory was a different paradigm from Aristotle's because there was a conflict at the theoretical level – Newton's theory held that an object continued in uniform motion if not acted on by a force, while Aristotle argued that it would return to rest at its natural place. But note that if Aristotle meant by 'natural place' what Newton meant by 'rest or uniform motion in a straight line', the two paradigms would not have been distinct – they would not have contradicted one another, but would have been the same paradigm expressed in different terms. The two paradigms also contradict one another at the observational level, generating conflicting predictions. Aristotle's theory predicts that if we stop applying a force to an object, it will stop moving forwards (immediately), while Newton's theory predicts that it will continue moving.

Second, within any paradigm there can be competing theories explaining any given phenomenon. Thus, within the Aristotelian paradigm, there can be more than one theory explaining why projectiles continue to move when released. What makes them fall within the same paradigm (while still competing) is that they both accept the ontology and explanatory laws of the paradigm – namely, that there are heavenly and earthly bodies, and that an earthly body not acted upon by a force will return to its natural place. These competing theories are conflicting accounts of the additional factors necessary to preserve the truth of the laws of the paradigm. The mere fact that two theories are in conflict does not mean that they constitute distinct paradigms.

Finally, while Kuhn claimed that paradigms were incommensurable – unable to be compared – he was mistaken. We are asked to believe that two theories are opposing theories *and* that they cannot be compared. But this is incoherent. If two theories are opposing, they must first be theories about the same objects, and second, they must have different views of the properties and/or behaviour of those objects. But this implies that they can be compared, at either the theoretical or observational level. And even if observational predictions are couched in theory-laden terms, we can compare them in theory-neutral terms. Aristotle's theory predicts a released arrow falls to the ground (natural place) while Newton's theory predicts it flies through the air (continuing its state of uniform motion) – a contradiction.

PSYCHIATRY IS NOT A NORMAL SCIENCE

Psychiatry appears to be in constant revolution. Far from there being a single paradigm that sets scientists puzzles to solve, numerous paradigms are constantly in conflict. Psychiatry seems far from a normal science! However, to confirm this picture, we must first see whether the theoretical perspectives hinted at above are indeed distinct paradigms. What I hope to show is that the different theoretical perspectives do not constitute distinct paradigms – that the crisis is in appearances only, and that only one paradigm reigns supreme. At most, the other so-called paradigms are competing theories within a single paradigm. This view then opens the way to seeing psychiatry as much more unified than it appears, and I will argue that a single paradigm of abnormal behaviour – the medical paradigm – can be defended.

The diagnosis for this mistaken view of psychiatry comes from a number of sources. First, it comes from a mistaken view of the nature of mental illness. Second, it comes from a mistaken view of the relationship between the mind and the body. Third, it comes from a mistaken view of the relationship between reason and cause. Fourth, it comes from a mistaken view of reductionism. Fifth, it comes from a mistaken view of semantics. And sixth, it comes from a mistaken view of science. It is the failure to understand the nature of mental illness, to understand the relationship between the mind and the body and between reason and cause, and to understand the relationship between different theories, that generates the view that there are many competing paradigms in psychiatry. It is the failure to understand the nature of mental illness that leads to the claim that it does not exist and that psychiatry is aimed at social control. And it is the failure to understand the nature of science that leads to the view that psychiatry is unscientific. If these mistakes are eliminated, a more coherent and humane view of psychiatry can be generated, and it is with this that this book is concerned.

11

T1   The *Causal Thesis*: A sub-class of abnormal behaviour is caused by disease.

T2   The *Conceptual Thesis*: A disease is a process causing a biological malfunction.

T3   The *Demarcation Thesis*: A mental illness is a process causing a malfunction predominantly of some higher mental function.

T4   The *Universality Thesis*: Diseases are not culture- or time-bound.

T5   The *Identification Thesis*: Scientific methodology enables us to identify diseases.

T6   The *Epistemological Thesis*: Scientific methodology enables us to discover the causes and cures for these diseases.

T7   The *Teleological Thesis*: Psychiatry's goal is the prevention and treatment of mental disease.

T8   The *Entitlement Thesis*: Having a disease entitles a patient to enter the sick role.

T9   The *Neutrality Thesis*: Besides the values implicit in the goal of preventing and treating disease, psychiatry is neutral between any ethical or political position.

T10   The *Responsibility Thesis*: Having one's behaviour caused by a mental illness in a certain way excuses one from responsibility.

T11   The *Guardianship Thesis*: Having a serious mental illness entitles the psychiatrist to act against the patient's will.

1

THE MEDICAL PARADIGM

As a branch of medicine, psychiatry is committed to the medical paradigm which assumes that there are such things as mental illnesses. In this chapter I will define the medical paradigm, identify its virtues, and highlight the areas where it comes under fire – it will be with these challenges and the defence of the medical paradigm that the rest of the book is concerned. As will become clear, both the medical paradigm and its challengers make philosophical assumptions, and only when we identify and clarify these will we solve the difficulties generated. Thereby, a philosophic foundation for psychiatry will be provided.

THE MEDICAL PARADIGM EXPLAINED

Psychiatry has three dimensions – theoretical, methodological, and practical. The first consists of the body of theories and laws invoked to explain abnormal behaviour, the second of those methods used to test and evaluate such theories and laws, and the third of the use of such knowledge to prevent and treat the abnormal behaviour.

The medical paradigm of psychiatry consists of eleven theses (see opposite), the first four of which constitute its theoretical dimension. The first of these is the *Causal Thesis* (T1) which assumes that a sub-class of statistically abnormal behaviour is caused by mental disease. The question is left open what sorts of abnormal behaviour are symptoms of mental illness – whether, for example, criminality is a mental illness. Thereby T1 leaves psychiatry with a problem. How do we decide what abnormalities of behaviour are caused by disease? How do we decide that criminal behaviour is not due to a disease, while schizophrenic behaviour is? The answer to this problem is provided by the second thesis.

The *Conceptual Thesis* (T2) defines a disease as a process causing a biological malfunction. A person has a physical disease of his heart if he has some process – e.g. inflammation – that causes the heart to fail to pump blood properly. Similarly, a person has a mental disease if he has some process – e.g. spirochaetal infection – that causes his brain to misperceive the world and his memory to fail. T2 solves the problem generated by T1 – only abnormal behaviour due to a biological malfunction is a mental illness (Lewis, 1955). Criminals are not mentally ill because their behaviour is not due to a biological malfunction, while schizophrenics are because their brains are malfunctioning. Thus we have a criterion for deciding when abnormal behaviour is simply a normal variant rather than symptomatic of a disease. But T2 leaves psychiatry with another problem. How do we decide what are biological malfunctions? How do we identify the functions of the brain, and when they count as failing? How do we know that the adoption of a criminal career does not constitute a *failure* of adjustment to social living? The answer is provided by T5.

The *Demarcation Thesis* (T3) assumes that what constitutes a *mental* disease rather than a *physical* one is that the process interferes predominantly with some higher mental faculty rather than solely with bodily functions. Gout is a physical disease because the inflammatory process affects the functioning of joints, while schizophrenia is a mental illness because the disease process affects the functioning of perception and rational belief formation. In this way, the medical paradigm is able to mark out the legitimate domain for psychiatry.

The *Universality Thesis* (T4) assumes that diseases are not time- or culture-bound entities. An entity is time-bound if it can only exist at a particular time, and is culture-bound if it can only exist in a particular culture. A disease would be time-bound if its identification was theory-laden – e.g. if a condition is only (Hippocratic) melancholia if it is due to an excess of black bile, then melancholia does not exist today. The medical paradigm argues that diseases can exist independently of theories about them, and hence that melancholia and other diseases are not time-bound. This does not imply that disease entities actually exist at all times, but only that they *can* exist at any time. Diseases can come and go – in 1918 encephalitis lethargica swept Europe but has not occurred since. But this does not violate the assumption that it *could* occur now, the disease is not time-bound. Similarly, we all accept that smallpox has been eradicated, but this does not mean that it cannot occur in our time (should the virus escape from our research laboratories).

The medical paradigm also assumes that diseases are not culture-bound. For example, Windigo might be regarded as culture-bound to North American Indian tribes. This mental illness is characterized by withdrawal, the delusion that one has become a cannibalistic monster, and suicidal and homicidal behaviour (Leff, 1988, p. 15). Windigo appears to be culture-bound because only certain cultures believe in cannibalistic monsters, and hence it is only in these cultures that a mental illness can exist with such a delusion. However, the medical paradigm argues that the culture-bound character of Windigo and other mental illnesses is illusory. This does not imply that certain mental illnesses do not only occur in one culture. Cultures not exposed to syphilis will not acquire general paresis of the insane. Similarly, schizophrenia might not occur in certain cultures because the virus supposedly causing it has not infected them (Crow, 1985). The medical paradigm argues that mental disorders could occur in all cultures if the relevant causal agents are present.

The methodological dimension consists of two theses. The *Identification Thesis* (T5) assumes that scientific methodology enables us to decide what is a biological malfunction and hence what is a disease. No biological part comes with a label on it indicating its function, and the medical paradigm needs some means of identifying functions. Every biological part produces a number of effects – e.g. the heart pumps blood as well as producing heart sounds. How do we decide that it is the former and not the latter that is the function of the heart? Similarly, the brain enables us to perceive the world accurately, and enables us to have religious experiences when it is starved of oxygen. How do we decide that it is the former that is the function of the brain and not the latter? The answer is provided by the fact that biological functions are acquired by natural selection – it is the function of the heart to pump blood and not make a noise because only pumping blood was responsible for the natural selection of the heart (Reznek, 1987). Similarly, it is because enabling us to have religious experiences under certain circumstances was not responsible for the natural selection of the brain while its ability to accurately perceive the world was (in part) responsible, that it is only the latter that is the function of the brain. By investigating the evolution of such organs, science can discover the functions.

The *Epistemological Thesis* (T6) assumes that scientific methodology also enables us to discover the causes and cures of mental illnesses. Physical medicine and psychiatry alike use the method of hypothesis formation and empirical testing to yield information about the causes of and cures for diseases, physical or mental. The medical paradigm takes psychiatry to be a science, assuming that there are facts in the world that are open to discovery with the use of scientific methodology.

The practical dimension consists of the remaining theses. The *Teleological Thesis* (T7) assumes that the aim or *telos* of psychiatry is the prevention and cure of mental disease. If psychiatry and medicine are taken to embody any values, it is the value of being free of disease that they enshrine. Psychiatry, like medicine, presupposes that it is better to be free of disease than to be diseased, and consequently sets out to pursue this aim by preventing and treating mental illness wherever it can. In this sense the practice of psychiatry is value-laden.

The *Entitlement Thesis* (T8) assumes that if someone is ill, he is entitled to adopt the sick role. Talcott Parsons argued that the sick role exempts the patient from his normal social duties, it excuses him from responsibility for his illness or considers that he is unable to get well by an act of will, and it requires him to want to get well, to seek help for his recovery, and to co-operate with this help towards the end of getting well (Parsons, 1951). As a branch of medicine, the medical paradigm allows mentally ill patients to assume the sick role.

The *Neutrality Thesis* (T9) assumes that, apart from the value adopted in the aim of psychiatry that it is better to be free of disease than ill, psychiatry (and medicine) does not defend any specific values of what sort of people we ought to be, how we ought to behave, and what sort of society we ought to live in. In other words, psychiatry is neutral between various ethical and political positions. It does not embody one ethical or political standard rather than another, and therefore cannot be used to further one set of values rather than another.

The *Responsibility Thesis* (T10) assumes that severe mental illness excuses a patient from responsibility for actions performed as a result of that mental illness. Mental illness provides an excuse from blame, and is a sound reason for exempting the patient from punishment.

The last thesis is the *Guardianship Thesis* (T11) which assumes that severe mental illness can undermine a patient's competence to make rational decisions, thereby entitling psychiatrists to become his guardian and to make those decisions for him, even it they are against the patient's will.

THE VIRTUES OF THE MEDICAL PARADIGM

The medical paradigm of psychiatry has many strengths. In many ways, it is both an account of the foundations of psychiatry as well as an answer to various problems. In this section we will examine those problems successfully solved.

In society, we are frequently faced with what I will call the *Problem of Deviants*. For example, ever since schools were invented there have been children that have not concentrated on their work, have disrupted their lessons, and have had too much energy for their teachers to contain. In 1957, Maurice Laufer 'discovered' the disease of hyperkinetic impulse disorder which was characterized by over-activity, poor concentration and impulsivity. Such a mental illness has many advantages. First, it enables us to treat such deviant behaviour with drugs – millions of children have been sedated with methylphenidate. Second, the classroom disruption is cured – teachers can now devote their time to more rewarding pupils. Third, the parents can avoid the guilt associated with producing an inferior child or with failing to raise their child correctly. They can explain away his or her poor school performance by reference to a disease that needs treatment. Fourth, the other children are able to benefit from the decrease in classroom disruption. Last and not least, there are many valuable spin-offs. Drug companies benefit, making and selling their drugs to exhausted parents. And as drug companies benefit, so society benefits – jobs are created by the drug companies, and this means more members of society have salaries to spend, and so society as a whole prospers. What started off as being a problem for parents, teachers, and other children, ends up benefiting everyone except those who end up being sedated and depressed on the drugs. By 'discovering' the disease of hyperactivity, the many problems generated by deviant children are solved (Schrag and Divoky, 1975).

The second problem that the medical paradigm solves is the *Problem of Value Relativity*. Many psychiatrists give different definitions of mental health:

> The crucial consideration in determining human normality is whether the individual is an asset or a burden to society and whether he is or is not contributing to the progressive development of man.
>
> (Adler, quoted in Boorse, 1976, p. 69)

> Mental health in the humanistic sense, is characterized by the ability to love and to create, by the emergence from the incestuous ties to family and nature, by a sense of identity based on one's experience of self as the subject and agent of one's powers, by the grasp of reality inside and outside of ourselves, that is by the development of objectivity and reason. . . . The mentally healthy person is the person who lives by love, reason, and faith, who respects life, his own and that of his fellow man.
>
> (Fromm, 1955, pp. 180–1)

> True sanity entails in one way or another the dissolution of the normal ego, that false self competently adjusted to our alienated social reality; the emergence of the 'inner' archetypal mediators of divine power, and through this death a new kind of ego-functioning, the ego now being the servant of the divine, no longer its betrayer.
>
> (Laing, 1967, p. 102)

The influence of the psychiatrist's values is clearly evident. Laing does not value the suppression of our true selves or adjustment to social norms. He therefore incorporates the absence of these traits in his definition of mental health. Fromm is a humanist and defines mental health in terms of humanist values such as love, creativity, altruism and individuality. Adler, because he sees man's value consisting in contributions to society, only regards socially useful traits as healthy.

If mental illness is defined in terms of the departure from some ideal of mental health, disagreement over values will lead to relativity – one psychiatrist's disease will be another's adaptation. This unsatisfactory state of affairs is solved in principle by T2 – by defining mental illness in terms of biological malfunctioning, a mental illness will not depend on the values of the diagnosing psychiatrist. Instead, whether something is a disease will depend on the value-free facts of the matter, and hence any conflict due to competing values can be avoided.

The third problem that the medical paradigm solves is the *Problem of Domain*. Some critics have argued that psychiatry has no legitimate domain, and will ultimately disappear:

> The 'death of psychiatry' movement proposes that, because the major disease categories will likely prove to have brain pathology, the care of patients with such illnesses will devolve to neurologists. And because a medical degree is not required to provide psychotherapy, patients with symptoms not caused by disease will be treated by psychologists, social workers, nurses, and lay therapists. There will be nothing left for psychiatry to call its own and it will therefore wither away.
>
> (McHugh and Slavney, 1986, p. 145)

The medical paradigm can solve this problem with T3. By defining mental illnesses in terms of processes that disrupt higher mental functioning, conditions that disrupt higher mental functions will remain mental illnesses whether they turn out to be brain diseases or not. Hence psychiatry has a proper domain.

The fourth problem that the medical paradigm solves is the *Problem of Disease Status*. There are many psychiatric conditions whose disease status is controversial – e.g. there is a question-mark over the disease status of homosexuality. This issue has been hotly debated in recent years, with no neutral means at hand of settling the issue (Bayer, 1987). The medical paradigm is able in principle to settle such debates with T5 – if there is a fact of the matter as to whether some condition is a disease, a scientific investigation to ascertain whether it is due to a biological malfunction can settle the issue.

The fifth problem that the medical paradigm solves is the *Problem of Credibility*. There are many who are gravely concerned about the status of the claims made by psychiatrists, and who question the reliability and validity of their diagnostic systems, the efficacy of their therapies, and the explanatory power of their theories – i.e. they question whether psychiatry is a science. In 1973 Professor David Rosenhan of the psychology department at Stanford University and seven colleagues presented themselves to twelve different psychiatric hospitals complaining that they were hearing voices saying the single words 'empty', 'hollow', and 'thud'. Beyond this complaint and the falsification of their names, the researchers did not alter any of their personal details. They all managed to get themselves committed, and most received the diagnosis of schizophrenia. In spite of the fact that they ceased to simulate any psychiatric symptoms whatever once admitted, they were confined for periods up to fifty-two days, their normal behaviour being described and interpreted as pathological. Finally, they were released with the diagnosis of schizophrenia in remission.

This study seems to cast doubt on the validity of diagnostic labels. A diagnosis is valid if it is able to pick out a homogeneous group of patients that share important properties besides the ones used to make the diagnosis. For example, we might wish to argue that schizophrenia is a valid diagnostic entity because those patients diagnosed on the basis of their symptoms all share a similar prognosis. But the Rosenhan study appears to undermine the idea that psychiatry has valid diagnostic labels. If normal people can get diagnosed as schizophrenic, then what is this label possibly picking out? It appears that the psychiatric diagnostic system is so insensitive as not to differentiate the sane from the insane!

In 1968 Maurice Temerlin challenged the reliability of diagnostic labels. He played a tape of an interview with an actor trained to provide a convincing performance of normality to groups of psychiatrists and psychologists. The psychiatrists and psychologists were divided into different groups depending on the different cues they were given. The first group was given a cue that the individual interviewed was psychotic, the second that he was healthy, and the last no cue at all. Over 90 per cent of the first group diagnosed the individual as psychotic, while 100 per cent of the second group diagnosed him as normal. 60 per cent of the last group diagnosed him as normal. While this study shows how prejudiced clinical judgement can be, it also demonstrates how unreliable it is. A diagnostic label is unreliable if users cannot agree when to apply it. There was wide disagreement as to the normality of the subject interviewed, and this means that psychiatric diagnoses, even if restricted to the most basic judgement of all – that between normality and abnormality – are unreliable.

Hans Eysenck has criticized psychiatry for not testing the effectiveness of its therapy by using control groups in clinical trials –

one can only prove the effectiveness of any treatment if one demonstrates that treated patients improve more than untreated ones. In an influential study in 1952, he challenged the claim that psychoanalysis was an effective treatment for neurosis. While two-thirds improved with treatment, Eysenck found that two-thirds of a matched group without treatment also improved! The improvement simply demonstrated the short-lived nature of the illness. Reviewing psychiatric treatment in general, he writes:

> How do the methods of treatment in psychiatry stand up to these criteria? The answer is a melancholic one. Physical methods, such as electroshock and leucotomy, lack proper support in well-controlled clinical investigations; this is a major scandal which fully justifies the criticisms made by the anti-psychiatry school of psychiatrists. . . . The position is no better as far as psychotherapy is concerned.
>
> (Eysenck, 1978, p. 175)

Finally, others have questioned psychiatry's claim to constitute an explanatory science. They have claimed that psychiatry can only produce tautologous explanations. A tautologous explanation is one where the explanans (the proposition doing the explaining) does not say any more than the explanandum (the proposition requiring explanation). For example, Molière ridiculed the medical profession's explanation that opium puts people to sleep because it has dormitive power – i.e. opium induces sleep because it induces sleep! Psychiatric explanations sometimes do no better. For example, anti-social acts are explained by the existence of a personality disorder recognized only by those acts it purports to explain:

> In the case of an anti-social act that is said to be due to mental illness, the existence of the illness cannot, without circular argument, be inferred solely from the fact that the act was committed.
>
> (Wootton, 1959, p. 233)

The explanation amounts to the claim that people indulge in anti-social and violent behaviour because they are people who indulge in anti-social and violent behaviour!

The medical paradigm avoids this objection by T5 – with the adoption of scientific methodology, psychiatry can show that the diagnostic terms are valid, are reliable, that her treatments are effective, and that substantive explanations are provided for abnormal behaviour. It also points out that fooling psychiatrists does not show that diagnostic labels are not valid – patients swallowing blood and regurgitating it could fool surgeons that they had bleeding peptic ulcers, but this would not mean that peptic ulcer was not a valid diagnosis! And it points out that Eysenck is simply mistaken to argue that psychiatric treatments, like electroshock, have not been scientifically evaluated.

The sixth problem that the medical paradigm solves is the *Problem of Political Abuse*. Psychiatry has been accused of medical imperialism, of broadening the boundaries of its legitimate domain, thereby enabling itself to be used by the state as an instrument for social control and repression. For example, for twenty years Russian political dissidents have been diagnosed as suffering from sluggish schizophrenia, incarcerated in asylums, and subjected to pharmacological strait-jackets. Thanks to Andrei Sneznevsky and the Moscow school of psychiatry, schizophrenia is divided into three types – the continuous, the periodic, and the mixed. There is also a classification in terms of severity, such that the continuous form can exist in a mild or sluggish form, a moderate or paranoid form, and a severe or malignant form. The interesting thing about this classification is that the sluggish form is recognized by such traits as having self-doubts, rebelliousness against teachers and parents, having reformist ideas, and being self-conscious! As a result of this, numerous political dissidents have been classified as mentally ill and incarcerated in beastly asylums (Reich, 1984). To illustrate how normal traits are interpreted as pathology, let us look at some case notes:

> He expresses with enthusiasm and great feeling reformist ideas concerning the teaching of Marxist classics, revealing in the process a clear over-estimation of himself and an unshakeable conviction of his own rightness. . . . His political thinking is grossly contradictory. He minimizes his actions and does not comprehend their criminal, treacherous nature.
>
> (Bloch and Reddaway, 1977, pp. 251–2)

In this way, psychiatry has been used to further political ends.

It might be argued that the western category of psychopathic personality disorder is one that is designed not to treat those who are ill but to control those who disturb the social order. When a research institute based on psychoanalytic teaching was asked by a western government to discover the causes of strikes in the coal industry, it concluded that the coal miners had developed complexes because they were 'hacking away at mother earth', and that such an activity would naturally give rise to repressed anxiety and re-awaken the Oedipal complex, which would then lead on to irrational behaviour such as strikes! The strike was seen as a symptom of mental illness and not a valid protest (Eysenck, 1975, p. 7). Others argue that common diagnoses like depression serve political ends – by seeing oppressed women as ill, psychiatry avoids challenging the social role that results in such demoralization. By medicalizing the problem, social change is avoided and the status quo preserved (Johnstone, 1989). Psychiatry appears to be used for political ends.

The problem of political abuse cannot be solved by the Neutrality Thesis alone. Because psychiatrists sometimes define politically offensive behaviour as a symptom of mental illness, political ends can be subsumed under the Teleological Thesis – the goal of the treatment of mental illness. But the problem is solved by T2 and T5 – according to them, diseases are malfunctions which are identified by empirical research. This research will hopefully demonstrate that political dissidents and strikers are not malfunctioning and that they should not be treated.

The seventh problem that the medical paradigm solves is the *Problem of Cultural Relativism*. This problem arises from the fact that there appear to be important differences between physical and mental illness. Physical disease is defined in terms of departures (in functioning) from biological norms which can be detected independently of any cultural norms, and hence whether someone is physically ill in any culture or at any time does not depend on the nature of cultural norms obtaining at that time. However, the same does not appear to be true of mental illness. For example, we recognize bizarre behaviour by behaviour that is a radical departure from cultural norms. And we recognize mental illness in part by recognizing bizarre behaviour.

Suppose we find a man on the corner of Oxford and Regent Streets in the 1980s flagellating himself with a whip tipped with iron. He explains that he is trying to atone for the sins of promiscuity that made God send AIDS to plague mankind as a punishment. No doubt we would consider him mentally ill and call in a psychiatrist. However, in the fourteenth century, when the bubonic plague was raging across Europe killing thousands of people, such flagellants were commonplace. They stood in market-places whipping themselves to atone for the sins they presumed had provoked God into sending the Black Death. Such flagellants were regarded with awe and reverence by the people throughout Europe, and were not regarded as mentally ill. Behaviour that would be regarded as bizarre and symptomatic of some mental illness in one culture (or time) would be regarded as commonplace and normal in another culture (or time). What constitutes the symptom of bizarre behaviour is determined by cultural norms, and this implies that whether some behaviour is an illness depends on the culture where we find it.

We also recognize mental illness by identifying delusions. These too cannot be identified independently of cultural norms. If a young man in our culture blames his abdominal pain on black magic inflicted by a former girlfriend, he is likely to be regarded as deluded. However, if the young man is living on a Caribbean island where the belief in black magic is commonplace, his belief would not be a delusion (Rack, 1982, p. 228). Whether some belief or action is symptomatic of a mental illness depends not on norms that are universal, but on local and variable cultural norms. This leads to a disturbing relativity of our attributions of mental illness.

This problem can be solved by T2 – the assumption that mental illnesses are biological malfunctions. Since malfunctions can be identified independently of cultural norms, the medical paradigm is in principle able to avoid this relativity – whether the twentieth-century flagellant or the western believer in black magic are ill does not depend on whether their behaviour or beliefs depart from any cultural norm, but on whether they are due to underlying mental malfunctioning that can be determined independently of any cultural norm.

This concludes the discussion of the virtues of the medical model. It seems to have so many virtues as to be almost unassailable! Nevertheless, it has some serious weaknesses highlighted by competing paradigms. In what follows, we will examine these, and see whether the medical paradigm can survive.

CHALLENGES TO THE MEDICAL PARADIGM

In spite of these virtues, the medical paradigm has not gone unchallenged. First, competing paradigms of abnormal behaviour have been proposed, challenging the causal thesis that abnormal behaviour is caused by disease. Second, in spite of the fact that the definition of disease in terms of malfunctioning solves many of the problems that bedevil psychiatry, the conceptual thesis has been challenged – alternative conceptions of disease have been proposed. The universality thesis has also come into question – in transcultural psychiatry, cultural determinists argue that mental illnesses are culture-bound. Historical studies have also raised doubts as to whether mental illness is not time-bound. The identification thesis has been challenged – its truth depends on the conceptual thesis, and only if a purely factual account can be given of the concept of disease will scientific methodology be able to identify diseases. The epistemological thesis too has been challenged – many doubt whether psychiatry proceeds scientifically. The neutrality thesis has come under attack for the same reason as the identification thesis. It is easy to show that the practice of psychiatry, directed towards preventing and treating mental illness, does not promote any ethical or political ideal as long as disease is defined in terms of biological malfunctioning. But this becomes very much more difficult to show if disease is not defined in descriptive terms. If disease is defined in evaluative terms, the neutrality thesis comes into question. The entitlement thesis has come under attack by those who argue that there are no such things as mental illnesses – there is only voluntary role-playing. It follows from this that those who are playing at being mentally ill are *not* entitled to the benefits of the sick role. For similar reasons, the guardianship and responsibility theses have been challenged. If patients always choose to do what they are doing rather than being forced to do so by mental illness, then psychiatrists have no right to interfere with them, and the patients have no right to expect to be excused from blame and punishment. We will now examine these challenges to see whether the medical paradigm survives.

2

SIGMUND FREUD AND THE PATHOLOGIZING OF NORMALITY

The impact of Sigmund Freud's ideas cannot be overestimated. He created an era where everything from dreams to culture had a psychological meaning, where the present was seen as determined by the past, and where even mistakes were seen as motivated. In this chapter I will concentrate on Freud's attempts to show that we are all mentally ill.

THE ESSENTIALIST FALLACY

Freud adopts a particular conception of mental illness. He argues that neuroses are generated in a specific way:

> *Neurosis is the result of a conflict between the ego and its id.* . . . All our analyses go to show that the transference neuroses [hysteria, phobias, obsessional neurosis] originate from the ego's refusing to accept a powerful instinctual impulse in the id or to help it to find a motor outlet, or from the ego's forbidding that impulse the object at which it is aiming. In such a case the ego defends itself against the instinctual impulse by the mechanism of repression. The repressed material struggles against this fate. It creates for itself, along paths over which the ego has no power, a substitutive representation (which forces itself upon the ego by way of a compromise) – the symptom.
>
> (Freud, 1986, pp. 565–6)

Freud assumes that something is a neurosis if symptoms are caused in a distinct way. A desire (from the id) comes into conflict with the ego (because the satisfaction of the desire comes into

26

conflict with the demands of reality or the demands of the person's conscience or super-ego). The desire is repressed from consciousness, and comes to be satisfied in ways that the ego can no longer recognize. These ways are the neurotic symptoms.

With an understanding of neurosis as the satisfaction of repressed and transformed wishes, Freud sought to understand other phenomena that occur in everyday life. In his popular work, *The Psychopathology of Everyday Life*, he argues that phenomena like slips of the tongue, misreadings, slips of the pen, forgettings, etc., which he calls 'parapraxes', are in fact evidence of psychopathology (hence the title of his book):

> If we compare them [parapraxes] to the products of the psychoneuroses, to neurotic symptoms, two frequently repeated statements – namely, that the borderline between the normal and the abnormal in nervous matters is a fluid one, and that we are all a little neurotic – acquire meaning and support. Without any medical experience we can construct various types of nervous illness of this kind which are merely hinted at – *formes frustes* of the neuroses: cases in which the symptoms are few, or occur rarely or not severely – in other words, cases whose comparative mildness is located in the number, intensity and duration of their pathological manifestations. . . . But there is one thing which the severest and mildest cases all have in common, and which is equally found in parapraxes and chance actions: *the phenomena can be traced back to incompletely suppressed psychical material, which, although pushed away by consciousness, has nevertheless not been robbed of all capacity for expressing itself.*
> (Freud, 1975, pp. 343–4)

The same mechanism that generates neurotic symptoms supposedly generates the parapraxes, and Freud concludes that the parapraxes are therefore instances of psychopathology.

Similar reasoning occurs in Freud's understanding of dreams:

> We will demonstrate the sense of dreams by way of preparing for the study of the neuroses. This reversal is justified, since the study of dreams is not only the best preparation for the study of the neuroses, but dreams are themselves a neurotic symptom, which, moreover, offers us the priceless advantage of occurring in all healthy people.
> (Freud, 1973, p. 111)

Freud explains later why they are neurotic symptoms:

> We must further remember that the same processes belonging to the unconscious play a part in the formation of symptoms as in the formation of dreams – namely, condensation and displacement. A symptom, like a dream, represents something as fulfilled: a satisfaction in the infantile manner.
>
> (Freud, 1973, p. 413)

With these analogies between parapraxes, dreams, and neurotic symptoms, we can reconstruct his first argument. From the conceptual premise that if some behaviour is generated by the repression of some desire and its re-emergence in a disguised form, then that behaviour is a symptom of psychopathology, and the factual premise that normal behaviour such as slips of the tongue is generated by the repression of some desire and its re-emergence in a disguised form, he concludes that such normal behaviour is a symptom of psychopathology. Is this argument sound?

There is little evidence for the factual premise that dreams and errors are unconsciously motivated by repressed wishes – most studies are methodologically unsound (Fisher and Greenberg, 1977; Eysenck, 1985). However, one study of the dreams of Zulu women provides some support for Freud's ideas. In Zulu culture, being fertile is an important determinant of status – barren women are shunned. Thus there is a strong desire to have children, and this desire is probably stronger in those who have had some difficulties conceiving. If Freud is right, we ought to find such women having more dreams about babies, and this is precisely what is found (Lee, 1958). However, while this shows that dreams express wishes, it does not show that they express repressed wishes. In fact, it is hard to believe that the Zulu women were not conscious of the desire for children!

As regards evidence for the causation of errors, most can be explained in ways other than unconscious motivation (Ellis, 1980). I have collected over one hundred errors (including many of my own). The vast majority can be understood in terms of habit, distraction, and poor memory retrieval. For example, having moved recently from Oxford to Edinburgh, I referred to the Royal Infirmary (of Edinburgh) as the Radcliffe Infirmary (in Oxford). This error is best explained as being the result of habit rather than unconscious intentionality. A friend referred to a traditional problem as the 'old nutshell' while clearly intending to say 'old chestnut'. This is best explained in terms of poor retrieval with a similar expression being recalled. When I was typing the sentence 'If it is due to a different process', but thinking of the decision I had to make on the sale of my house, I actually typed 'If it is due to a different house'. The best explanation of this error was that my *conscious* thoughts about houses interfered with the typing of the sentence. In order to sustain the thesis that these errors are unconsciously motivated, Freudian theory has to go to extreme and unnecessary lengths. Therefore the empirical premise is probably false.

The conceptual premise is also false – it commits the *Essentialist Fallacy* (Reznek, 1987, p. 63). This is the fallacy of assuming that because a process is of a particular type – because it has a particular nature or essence – it is a disease. Throughout the history of medicine, grand theories of the nature of disease have been proposed. The Humoral theory was one such theory – according to this, something was regarded as a disease if it consisted of an imbalance in one of the four bodily humours – blood, phlegm, yellow bile, black bile. Melancholia was a disease because it consisted in an excess of black bile, and colds were diseases because they consisted in an excess of phlegm. Later theories developed different ideas of the nature of disease. The Germ theory held that something was a disease if it consisted of an infection, and nutritional disorders like beri-beri were thought to be caused by some unknown germ. From the belief that all diseases share a common nature or essence, the idea developed that something could only be a disease if it had a particular nature. However, this idea is mistaken.

Some diseases have the nature of being infections. But something is not a disease simply because it has this nature. There are some conditions that are infections but not diseases. For example, our gastro-intestinal tracts are 'infected' by bacteria that protect us from developing diarrhoea. If we treated this 'infection' with antibiotics, giving ourselves a permanent low grade diarrhoea, this would not constitute an improvement in our health! Something is a disease not because of its nature or essence, but because of its undesirable consequences (I argue for this in chapter 10). Even if we discovered that all known diseases shared an underlying nature, this would not imply that something was not a disease unless it shared this nature. If a new 'condition' characterized by fever, a green-spotted rash, and progressive muscular weakness plagued the earth, this would be a disease in spite of the fact that it might fail to have the same nature shared by all other diseases. Therefore, being a disease cannot consist in having any particular underlying nature (Reznek, 1987).

Similarly, Freud cannot argue from the fact that parapraxes and dreams are caused by a particular sort of psychological process to the conclusion that they are symptoms of psychopathology. It commits the essentialist fallacy. To see this, let us imagine discovering that all morally good acts are caused by a particular psychological process. A good person first develops a natural desire to harm others which is frustrated by the demands of living together with other men, and he is therefore forced to repress this desire from consciousness. However, because the desire is strong, it re-emerges in a disguised form as the desire to benefit others. Even if this process is identical to the one that generates neurotic symptoms, this does not mean that morally good actions are symptoms of mental illness! Whether or not a process is a mental illness does not depend on its nature, but on the undesirability of its consequences.

Similarly, Freud saw religious behaviour as a neurosis because it was generated in the same way as neurotic symptoms:

> I have never doubted that religious phenomena are to be understood only on the models of the neurotic symptoms of the individual.
>
> (Freud, 1985b, p. 94)

But this is fallacious. Whether some process is a mental illness depends on the undesirability of its consequences, and not on its particular underlying nature.

Freud repeatedly commits the essentialist fallacy:

> I follow Breuer in asserting that every time we come upon a symptom we can infer that there are certain definite unconscious processes in the patient which contain the sense of the symptom. But it is also necessary for that sense to be unconscious in order that the symptom can come about. Symptoms are never constructed from conscious processes; as soon as the unconscious processes concerned have become conscious, the symptom must disappear.
>
> (Freud, 1973, p. 320)

Let us reconstruct this second argument. From the conceptual premise that if some behaviour is motivated by unconscious intentions, then it is a symptom of a neurotic illness, and the factual premise that aspects of normal behaviour are motivated by unconscious intentions, he concludes that aspects of normal behaviour are symptoms of a neurotic illness. Freud's belief that unconscious processes implied illness while conscious processes implied health is captured by the psychoanalytic slogan: Where there was Id, there shall Ego be. But is this argument sound?

For the sake of argument, let us grant the factual premise – much of our behaviour is the result of motives of which we are unaware. In the simplest case, we are all familiar with forgetting why we have sent ourselves somewhere – e.g. to the kitchen in search of something – but nevertheless find our behaviour is still directed by the forgotten (and unconscious) motive (Dilman, 1984, p. 71). The argument then turns on the conceptual premise. But it too commits the essentialist fallacy. Freud assumes that because some behaviour or 'symptom' is generated by unconscious intentions, i.e. has a particular nature, it is due to some disease. But let us suppose that in emergencies our behaviour is unconsciously motivated – i.e. we are not aware of the reasons for which we act. Let us suppose, too, that this way of behaving is in our best interests – if we thought consciously, we would take too long and foul up the whole business of serving our best interests. If this were the case, then we would be better off acting unconsciously, and the processes involved would not be pathological. Therefore, the conceptual premise is false and his argument fails.

THE CONTINUUM FALLACY

There is a third argument contained in the second passage quoted above. From the conceptual premise that if some process differs only in degree from a pathological process, then that process is pathological, and the factual premise that parapraxes and dreams are the results of processes that only differ in degree from a pathological process, he concludes that parapraxes and dreams are the result of pathological processes. Is this argument sound?

For the sake of the argument let us assume that the factual premise is true. In general, we have evidence that many pathological processes differ only in degree from normality. For example, normal fluctuations of mood merge into neurotic depression and into more severe depression without any discontinuity, suggesting that the same processes are going on to varying degrees in all these cases (Goldberg, 1972). Similarly, there is evidence that delusions are the product of the same processes that lead to normal beliefs (Maher, 1988). Finally, the pathological changes occurring in Alzheimer's disease appear to differ only quantitatively from those occurring in normal aging, with symptoms only occurring when a 'threshold' has been crossed (Roth, 1980). The argument then turns on the conceptual premise which makes two assumptions. First, it assumes that processes are classified as pathological because of their natures and not because of their consequences (the essentialist fallacy). And second, it assumes that it is only qualitative differences that make one process pathological and another normal. We have seen that the first assumption is false. The second is also false – it commits the *Continuum Fallacy*.

It is not the case that only qualitative differences count as pathological (Kendell, 1975a). For example, essential hypertension is caused by processes that deviate only quantitatively from the norm (Pickering, 1962). It may be caused, for example, by kidneys that reabsorb more sodium from the filtrate than normal. But if this is so, this does not mean that people with normal kidneys are mildly diseased! Similarly, many cases of mental retardation are caused by quantitative deviations from the norm (Zealley, 1983). It might be that some retarded individuals have neurones that pass signals more slowly than normal individuals. But if this is so, this does not mean that people with neurones that pass signals at an average speed (or an above average speed) are suffering from mild mental retardation! Imagine discovering that all known physical diseases are caused by quantitatively abnormal bodily processes. This would not mean that there are no diseases. Hence, diseases do not have to be qualitatively abnormal bodily processes (Reznek, 1987). Similarly for mental illness. Suppose that we discover that mania is simply an exaggeration of normal high spirits. Perhaps both minor fluctuations in mood and abnormal mood states are caused by varying concentrations of mono-amine neuro-transmitters in a certain part of the brain. But this would not mean that being high-spirited is in fact a mild affective disorder!

Whether some condition is a mental illness depends on whether the consequences of the condition are undesirable and not on whether the condition is a qualitative rather than a quantitative deviation from the norm. It is only where processes or reactions have undesirable consequences that we regard them as pathological. But in the cases discussed above, the normal processes that differ only quantitatively from other pathological processes do not have undesirable consequences. And hence they are not diseases. The continuum fallacy thus makes the same sort of mistake as the essentialist fallacy – it assumes that the disease status of a condition depends on the sort of underlying nature of the condition, rather than on its consequences.

Freud has another similar argument. He sees development as passing through a number of stages, and argues that no one escapes traumatic experiences. As a result of this, the ego is more or less damaged. He writes:

> The ego, if we are to be able to make such a pact with it, must be a normal one. But *a normal ego of this sort is, like normality in general, an ideal fiction.* The abnormal ego, which is unserviceable for our purposes, is unfortunately no fiction. Every normal person, in fact, is only normal on the average. His ego approximates to that of the psychotic in some part or other and to a greater or lesser extent; and the degree of its remoteness from one end of the series and of its proximity to the other will furnish us with a provisional measure of what we have so indefinitely termed an 'alteration of the ego'.
>
> (Freud, 1950, p. 337, my italics)

From these views, we can construct a fourth argument. From the conceptual premise that if some state of mental functioning falls short of the ideal of health, then it is a neurosis, and the factual premise that most people have a state of mental functioning that falls short of the ideal of health, he concludes that most people are neurotic. Is this argument sound?

For the sake of argument, let us grant the factual premise – most people have egos that fall below the ideal in that they have a distorted view of the world. But does this mean we are all mentally ill? The answer is no, and this is because the conceptual premise commits the *Superman Fallacy*. This is the fallacy of assuming that if some individual is not functioning to the best of his abilities or potential, or less well than some paragon, he is ill. This is wrong for both the physical and psychological realms. A person's muscles may work adequately, but he may not be fit. No doubt if he exercised, he could improve their efficiency, power, etc. But the fact that his muscles could be working better does not mean that he now has a muscle *disorder*. He may also be less powerful than Olympic weight-lifters, and slower than Olympic sprinters, but this does not mean he has a muscle *disease*. Hence the assumption that we are diseased because we are not supermen is a fallacy.

Similarly for the psychological realm. Many of us have poor problem-solving skills. But our present skills may be adequate. We could become a lot better at solving problems and thereby more successful if we trained our brains to be better problem solvers. But this does not mean that our brains are malfunctioning – that we are ill – simply because they could work better. We are not suffering from a mental illness simply because brilliant people in MENSA can solve life's problems better than we can. Similarly, we might all have irrational fears. Most of us are frightened of insects while we realize we can't be harmed. But the fact that we could become more rational does not mean that we are mentally ill because of such fears. Hence the conceptual premise is false and the argument fails. If we set health norms too high (the superman fallacy), we all become ill, and the point of the distinction between health and illness is lost.

Freud not only has arguments to show that we are all neurotic, but also that we are all psychotic:

> It is asserted, however, that each one of us behaves in some one respect like a paranoic, corrects some aspect of the world which is unbearable to him by the construction of a wish and introduces this delusion into reality. A special importance attaches to the case in which this attempt to procure a certainty of happiness and a protection against suffering through a delusional remoulding of reality is made by a considerable number of people in common. The religions of mankind must be classed among the mass-delusions of this kind. No one, needless to say, who shares a delusion ever recognizes it as such.
>
> (Freud, 1986, p. 269)

What argument is contained here? From the conceptual premise that if someone's wishes distort his perception of reality, then he is (to a greater or lesser degree) psychotic, and the factual premise that everyone has wishes that distort reality, he concludes that everyone is (to a greater or lesser degree) psychotic. Is this argument sound?

Let us start with the conceptual premise. For the sake of the argument, let us define being psychotic as having a distorted perception of reality which is maintained by internal psychological factors such as wishes rather than external factors such as a lack of education. Then the premise follows by definition. The argument then turns on the factual premise – is this true? I would like to argue that it may well be true. Let us take Freud's example. Many people continue to believe in the existence of God in spite of the amount of evil God fails to prevent. Their behaviour is much like the mother who continues to believe her son is innocent of some charge in spite of the solid evidence against him. The wish to have some order and meaning in their lives distorts their perception of reality. Most non-religious people believe their own lives matter in spite of the fact that they make little difference to the universe in the long run. The wish to be important distorts the perception of reality.

But what does this amount to? That we are all psychotic? That we are all mentally ill? Freud commits the continuum fallacy here. It might be the case that we all distort reality to a greater or lesser extent, but this does not make us all mentally ill. We are only mentally ill if this distortion of reality is undesirable. A good case can be made for that fact that some distortion of reality is necessary to lead happy and productive lives. Two researchers suggest that normal people avoid depression by distorting reality:

> Taken together, these studies suggest that at times depressed people are 'sadder but wiser' than non-depressed people. Non-depressed people succumb to cognitive illusions that enable them to see both themselves and their environment with a rosy glow.
>
> (Alloy and Abramson, 1979, pp. 479–80)

It is plausible to suppose that we are built in such a way to be mild reality-distorters. This makes some evolutionary sense – someone who believed that he was able to control his environment would be more likely to do so – the confidence generated by such a belief becomes a self-fulfilling prophecy. If this is the case, then such a distortion of reality is 'healthy'. It is only when the distortion of reality prevents us from leading worthwhile lives that one might be tempted to call it a mental illness. So while we all might be more or less psychotic (on our definition), we are not all more or less mentally ill.

It can be seen that a major theme in Freud's work is the thesis that normal individuals are more or less mentally ill. Far from being healthy, they suffer from neurotic and psychotic illnesses to varying degrees. Freud attempts to pathologize normality – to construe normal people as diseased. This idea has become incorporated into folk psychology – we all see ourselves as needing psychotherapy to be free of minor ills. But this idea is mistaken. While it might be true that we all distort reality, that we all make unconsciously motivated errors, and that we differ only in degree from neurotic and psychotic patients, this does not mean that we are all ill.

THE NATURALISTIC FALLACY

Freud's work contains another argument in virtue of which he concludes that many of us are mentally ill. He sees man's development as having a distinct goal, and sees alternative goals as departures from health. He writes about sexual maturation:

> For the present you should keep firmly in mind that sexual life (or, as we put it, the libidinal function) does not emerge as something ready-made and does not even develop further in its own likeness, but passes through a series of successive phases which do not resemble one another; its development is thus several times repeated – like that of a caterpillar into a butterfly. The turning-point of this development is the subordination of all the component sexual instincts under the primacy of the genitals and along with this the subjection of sexuality to the reproductive function.
>
> (Freud, 1973, pp. 370–1)

As a result of this natural development, Freud comes to see those who do not achieve the genital ideal as suffering from a developmental disorder he calls a perversion. He writes:

> A disposition to perversions is an original and universal disposition of the human sexual instinct and normal sexual behaviour is developed out of it as a result of organic

36

changes and psychical inhibitions occurring in the course of maturation. . . . We are thus led to regard any established aberration from normal sexuality as an instance of developmental inhibition and infantilism.

(Freud, 1986, p. 365)

From these passages an argument can be reconstructed. From the conceptual premise that if a person's development does not reach the usual end stage, then the person is suffering from a developmental disorder, and the factual claim that the sexual development of homosexuals, fetishists, etc., has not reached the usual end-stage, he concludes that homosexuals etc, are suffering from a developmental disorder. Is this argument valid?

The factual premise is unexceptional – homosexuals etc. end up with an unusual (statistically abnormal) sexual development. But what of the conceptual premise? Here Freud commits the *Naturalistic Fallacy* (Moore, 1903). This is the fallacy of arguing that since development does as a matter of fact generally proceed through various stages to the genital ideal, it is *desirable* for it to proceed through these stages. But to claim that something is part of health is to claim that it is desirable, that it ought to be the case, and this does not follow from any facts. The natural (and common) end of life is death. But if we could take an age-retarding drug and become immortal, thereby avoiding this natural development, nobody would be so silly as to think that we had a disease. On the contrary, we would regard ourselves as healthier. Similarly, many women lead more productive and happy lives on Hormone Replacement Therapy (HRT) for the menopause. But the fact that they avoid the natural (and common) development does not mean that they have an illness. There is a gap between is and ought and hence the conceptual premise is false. The argument fails.

THE PSYCHODYNAMIC PARADIGM

These are but a few of Freud's arguments which purport to show that we are all mentally ill. He also proposes an alternative paradigm of abnormal behaviour – instead of seeing abnormal behaviour as being caused by disease, he sees it as being the result of intrapsychic conflicts, conflicts which occur as a result of early childhood difficulties. In short, he challenges the causal thesis of the medical paradigm.

The psyche is thought to have a certain structure – it consists of the ego, the superego, and the id. The id is governed by the pleasure principle – the sexual and aggressive desires aim at their own satisfaction. The superego is the person's conscience which arises out of resolving early conflicts by identification with the parents. The ego is governed by the reality principle – its job is to satisfy the desires while avoiding the dangers of reality and the wrath of the superego. The psyche is driven by energy or libido from the id. Mental illness is the product of conflict between these entities when the libido has to be satisfied indirectly through the symptoms. For example, Little Hans developed the desire (like all normal boys) to sleep with his mother. However, the satisfaction of this desire came into conflict with the ego's desire for safety – fear of the father prevented the satisfaction of this desire. This conflict between the ego and the id led to the fear of the father being displaced on to a horse, producing a phobia of horses:

> If 'Little Hans', being in love with his mother, had shown fear of his father, we should have no right to say that he had a neurosis or a phobia. His emotional reaction would have been entirely comprehensible. What made it a neurosis was one thing alone: the replacement of his father by a horse. It is this displacement, then, which has a claim to be called a symptom.
>
> (Freud, 1979, p. 256)

The transformation of frustrated libido becomes the symptom. It can be seen that this view of abnormal behaviour makes no reference to disease entities, and therefore constitutes an alternative to the medical paradigm. This conflict will be resolved in chapter 9.

In summary, Freud tries to show that we are all suffering from (neurotic and psychotic) illnesses to varying degrees, but his arguments fail because he makes a number of errors – he assumes that something is a disease because of its essence (the essentialist fallacy), that something is a developmental disorder because it does not proceed in the natural manner (the naturalistic fallacy), that someone is ill because he differs only in degree from those who are ill (the continuum fallacy), and that someone is ill because he falls short of the ideal (the superman fallacy). Freud also challenges the causal thesis of the medical paradigm, arguing that abnormal behaviour is due to psychodynamic forces.

3

HANS EYSENCK AND THE NORMALIZING OF NEUROSIS

Hans Eysenck is a professor of psychology and one of the harshest critics of pschoanalysis and psychiatry. In contrast to Freud, who argued that so-called healthy people are neurotically ill, Eysenck argues that all neurotic patients are in fact healthy – his concern is to normalize neurosis. It will be this theme that runs through the arguments examined below.

LEARNING TO BE NEUROTIC

In *The Future of Psychiatry*, Eysenck argues that there are two sorts of disorders – organic and behavioural:

> Into this category [organic disorders] would presumably fall general paralysis of the insane, epilepsy, and degenerative psychosis of the senium, i.e. mental disorders in old people due to physical processes in the brain. Most if not all this group are also in the field of the neurologists, and it might be tidier to hand them over to practitioners of neurology altogether. . . . Neurotic disorders, personality disorders, and many types of criminal conduct probably come under this heading [behavioural disorders]; these are not to be construed as diseases. . . . The subject which is fundamental to an understanding of behavioural disorders is psychology, not medicine.
>
> (Eysenck, 1975, pp. 4–5)

Eysenck assumes that psychiatry, as a branch of medicine, should treat diseases. He then argues that if disturbed behaviour is due to an organic brain disease, it should fall under neurologists, and if it is not due to organic brain disease, it should fall under psychologists. Hence there is nothing for psychiatrists to do!

But are the behavioural disorders not caused by disease? In explaining them, he writes:

> No such chemical errors are likely to be present in the neurotic, and the causation of his troubles is quite different.
> (Eysenck, 1978, p. 17)

> If neurotic behaviour is acquired through some form of learning or conditioning (and it certainly is not due to physical lesions, which is the only rational alternative) then the knowledge accumulated over the past hundred years by psychologists of the laws concerning learning and conditioning should provide the main, or indeed the only, relevant body of knowledge from which to deduce theories concerning the origins and the treatment of neuroses.
> (Eysenck, 1978, p. 11)

From these accounts we can reconstruct his first argument. From the conceptual premise that something is a disease if a statistically abnormal bodily condition ('lesion') is responsible for the symptoms, and the factual premise that behavioural disorders (such as neuroses) have symptoms that are not due to some statistically abnormal bodily condition, he concludes that behavioural disorders are not diseases (and hence not the province of any branch of medicine). Is this argument sound?

The conceptual premise is false as it stands. There are statistically abnormal bodily conditions (like being excessively muscular) that are not diseases – only statistical abnormalities that have undesirable consequences count as diseases. But since the neurotic conditions Eysenck is referring to *are* undesirable, this point is irrelevant to this argument. With this caveat, let us accept the conceptual premise, and proceed to the factual one. Eysenck claims that behavioural disorders are not due to abnormal bodily conditions (I will use the word 'abnormal' to mean 'statistically abnormal' here). But what reason is there to believe that neurotic disorders have no physical basis? Must we suppose that when someone experiences panic, nothing goes on in his brain? What I hope to show is that first, mental events, even abnormal ones, have physical causes, and second, that abnormal mental events, i.e. mental symptoms, have abnormal physical causes. Because neuroses also have undesirable effects (like anxiety and panic), this means that they *are* diseases.

Mental events are caused by physical events. There have been numerous experiments that have demonstrated this. Walter Penfield stimulated the brains of epileptics on the operating table with electrodes, thereby causing the wakeful subjects to relive many experiences (Penfield, 1975). While this does not prove that *all* mental events are caused by brain events, it provides strong inductive support for this conclusion when combined with the weakness of alternative dualist explanations (see chapter 5). Therefore it is reasonable to conclude that mental events are caused by physical (brain) events. Hence it is likely that abnormal mental events (such as panic) are also caused by brain events.

Can it be possible for someone to have some abnormal mental state without also being in some abnormal physical state? To answer this, we need first to understand how any abnormality in an organism can be explained. Suppose we are looking at our heart rate. The normal rate is between 60 and 80 beats a minute. Let us suppose we are trying to explain a heart rate of 120 beats a minute. To do this we need to understand the many factors that determine the normal rate. First, the thyroid gland secretes a hormone, thyroxine. When this hormone remains within certain (normal) limits, the heart rate too remains within normal limits. Should this hormone be abnormally high, then the heart rate will also become abnormally fast. Second, the blood pressure influences the heart rate via homeostatic reflexes. When the blood pressure drops, the heart rate goes up to compensate. If the blood pressure is abnormally low, these reflexes will ensure that the heart rate is abnormally high. Third, the heart rate is influenced by other hormones in the blood such as adrenalin. When these are within certain (normal) limits, the heart rate is within normal limits. However, when these are abnormally high, such as in states of anxiety, then the heart rate is abnormally high. And so on.

In all cases where the heart rate is abnormally high, it is caused by some *abnormality* in some underlying factor. It is difficult to see how an abnormality at the symptomatic level could be caused by anything else but an abnormality at the explanatory level. It is true that more than one abnormality at the explanatory level can compensate one another so that there is no abnormality at the symptomatic level. A person could have an abnormally low thyroxine level and an abnormally high adrenalin level and his heart rate could remain within normal limits. But it is difficult to find even an imaginary example where an abnormality at the symptomatic level is caused by anything other than an abnormality at the explanatory level. But if all abnormalities at the symptomatic level have underlying abnormalities, then there is something wrong with Eysenck's argument. For he assumes that there can be abnormal psychological phenomena without there being abnormal physical phenomena to explain them. This appears to be impossible.

But it seems untrue that only some abnormality in some underlying variable can explain any abnormality in the heart rate. Suppose a number of factors influencing heart rate are at the upper limit of normality – the thyroxine level is high normal, the adrenalin level is high normal, the blood pressure is low normal, etc., then all these *normal* variables could in combination result in an abnormally high heart rate. Therefore, an abnormality at the symptomatic level need not be explained by an abnormality at the explanatory level. This counter-argument appears to undermine our claim that neurotic disorders, which are defined in terms of symptoms that are abnormal, necessarily have underlying (somatic) abnormalities that are responsible for the clinical manifestations.

However, we can *still* defend the idea that if there is an abnormality at the level of the symptoms, there will be an abnormality at the explanatory level. All the counter-argument shows is that an abnormality at the level of the symptoms need not necessarily be due to a *single* abnormality at the explanatory (physical) level. Thus, while there might not be a single underlying abnormality to explain why someone's heart rate is abnormally fast, there may be a number of factors like the thyroxine level and adrenalin level that are at the upper limit of normal and which together constitute a *combination* that is abnormal. If the combination were not abnormal, most hearts would beat that fast, and that rate would cease to be abnormal. And, therefore, there is an abnormality underlying the abnormal 'symptom', and we have not produced a counter-example to the thesis that if there is an abnormality at the level of a symptom, then there will be an underlying abnormality at the explanatory level.

Thus the factual premise is false and Eysenck's argument fails. It is not true that behavioural disorders lack underlying physical abnormalities. He has therefore failed to show that behavioural disorders are not diseases, and hence do not properly fall under some branch of medicine. This conclusion is further supported by emerging evidence that neurotic disorders like panic (Reiman *et al.*, 1989), obsessive compulsive neurosis (Rapoport, 1989), pathological gambling (Roy *et al.*, 1988), and susceptibility to alcoholism (Begleiter *et al.*, 1984) all have underlying biological abnormalities. It is also supported by the fact that minor disorders such as anxiety disorders, phobias and panic have familial causes (Marks, 1986).

Eysenck assumes that if something is a (brain) disease, it should be treated by neurologists. Thus all we appear to have shown is that the behavioural disorders properly belong in neurology! But this is a mistake. Even if we have shown that the behavioural disorders are organic disorders, this does not mean that they are not psychiatric disorders. And this is because being a psychiatric disorder does not have anything to do with being caused in a particular way. If abnormal behaviour is caused by an organic condition, this does not mean that the disorder is not psychiatric. A condition is a psychiatric one if it disrupts mental functioning (irrespective of cause). And since some organic conditions like general paralysis of the insane disrupt mental functioning, they are (by definition) psychiatric.

Eysenck has other arguments to show that the behavioural disorders are not diseases. He comments on Freud's explanation of neurotic symptoms:

> Medicine distinguishes carefully between an illness, or disease, and the symptoms the patient may complain of. The patient may have a fever, but that is not the illness; we must treat the illness giving rise to the fever not the symptom directly. A disease is something underlying a series of symptoms, or 'syndrome'. . . . Freud very cleverly made use of this medical habit of clearly distinguishing between 'disease' and 'symptom' by declaring that the fears and anxieties the neurotic complained of were but the symptoms of some underlying disease, and that he proposed to treat this underlying disease by means of his new method of psychoanalysis. The symptoms, he declared, were but the outgrowths of an underlying complex; this complex originated in the early years of a child's life, and derived from his

interaction with his parents. . . . Hence Freud produced a proper medical model of neurotic disorder, complete with 'disease' and symptoms, and with a prescription for treatment.

(Eysenck, 1975, pp. 8–9)

But Eysenck goes on to argue that a neurotic's fears and anxieties are not symptoms of some underlying disease:

To put the whole theory in a nutshell, it is now believed that neurotic 'symptoms' are not in fact symptomatic of anything, and that there is no underlying disease, no Freudian 'complex', no medical disorder requiring medical attention. What we are dealing with are learned or conditioned emotional responses, and motor activities initiated and motivated by these emotional conditional responses.

(Eysenck, 1975, p. 10)

Reconstructing the argument, Eysenck argues from the conceptual premise that if thoughts, feelings or beliefs are the product of learning, then they are not symptoms of a disease, and the factual premise that neurotic symptoms are the product of learning, to the conclusion that neurosis is not a disease. If 'symptoms' are the product of learning or conditioning, they cannot be the product of some disease. Is this argument valid?

Let us suppose that the factual premise is true. There is a great deal of evidence that neurotic symptoms are indeed conditioned or learned responses. For example, learning theory can provide a better explanation for the horse phobia of Little Hans than psychoanalysis. The phobia began when Little Hans witnessed a frightening accident involving a horse-drawn cart. Pavlovian conditioning predicts that when a conditioned stimulus (the horse) is associated with an unconditioned stimulus (loud noise), it comes to evoke the unconditioned response (fear). Skinnerian conditioning predicts that when Little Hans avoids horses, this is rewarded by the removal of the aversive stimulus (fear), and becomes a habit – the phobia.

There are some gaps in this explanation. First, not every neurotic has been exposed to repeated pairings of the stimuli assumed to be necessary for acquiring conditioned reflexes. Second, in many cases, no unconditioned stimulus appears to evoke the first episode of anxiety – there is the absence of anything equivalent to the loud noise. Third, not everyone exposed to similar 'learning schedules' becomes neurotic. This seems to imply that the laws of conditioning are not sufficient for becoming neurotic. This conclusion is supported by the finding that there is a familial or genetic element in many neuroses, demonstrating that neurotics are vulnerable to learning neurotic responses. In spite of this, much of the evidence supports the behavioural explanation. Thus let us grant the factual premise.

In the conceptual premise, Eysenck assumes that if the underlying condition producing a neurotic's fears consists in learned responses, then the neurotic does not suffer from a disease. But what reason is there to believe that a learning process cannot be a disease process? Once again we meet the essentialist fallacy, the fallacy of assuming that diseases have particular sorts of natures, like being tumours or infections, and that we can tell from the nature of a condition whether it is a disease. Since being a disease does not consist in having a particular nature, it follows that any nature can count so long as it has undesirable consequences. But if this is so, then being a conditioned reflex can count as the nature of a disease too. And hence it does not follow that learned reactions cannot also be symptoms of a disease.

It is clear that Eysenck does make the essentialist fallacy:

> When is a disease not a disease? Is a person who has an inordinate fear of snakes 'ill' in the medical sense? *There are no lesions anywhere in his nervous system; there is no infection; there is nothing whatever that suggests that he is 'diseased' in a meaningful manner.* Does the golfer suffer from a 'disease' when he habitually slices his drive into the rough? Is the tennis player suffering from a 'disease' when he habitually serves double faults? Is the football player suffering from a 'disease' when he loses his temper, kicks an opponent and is sent off? It is easy to extend the meaning of 'disease' to undue lengths.
>
> (Eysenck, 1975, p. 16, my italics)

Here Eysenck assumes that some behaviour is a symptom of a disease if it is due to something like an infection or some other lesion like a tumour – i.e. he assumes that there is something about the nature of diseases that makes them diseases and that marks them off from the causes of other behaviour, like bad sporting habits, that are not diseases. But this idea is wrong and so cannot be used to identify diseases.

More importantly, we can demonstrate that a disease can be learned. It is well known that autonomic nervous responses can be learned (Miller and DiCara, 1967), and that blood pressure can be brought under voluntary control by bio-feedback techniques (Shapiro, Tursky and Schwartz, 1970). But if it is possible to teach someone to cure hypertension, then it is possible that someone could be conditioned to raise his blood pressure – i.e. someone could be taught to have hypertension, a physical disease. But the fact that someone might have learned to become hypertensive does not imply that hypertension is not a disease. Therefore some diseases can have the nature of being conditioned reflexes. Being caused by a conditioned reflex does not undermine the disease status of the neuroses and Eysenck's argument fails.

There is a second argument contained in the above passages. From the conceptual premise that if thoughts, feelings, or beliefs are symptomatic of some underlying condition, then the person has a disease, and the factual premise that the thoughts, feelings, and beliefs of neurotics are not symptomatic of some underlying condition, Eysenck concludes that neurosis is not a disease. Is this argument sound?

This argument turns on how we should read 'symptomatic'. On a narrow reading, where being a symptom implies being the effect of a disease, it is clear that the conceptual premise is tautologous. Then the burden of the argument rests on the factual premise. But the factual premise commits the essentialist fallacy – it assumes that because the symptoms are a result of a certain type of process, that process is not a disease. Hence on this reading, the argument fails. On a broad reading, where being a symptom just implies being an effect of something else, then the conceptual premise is no longer tautologous but obviously untrue. Many fears and anxieties are caused by the normal operation of the brain. But the mere fact that they are the effects of the brain's functioning does not imply that we are diseased! The factual premise is also false on this reading – a neurotic's problems are caused (in part) by underlying conditioned reflexes. Hence, on this reading too, the argument collapses.

Eysenck has another argument to show that neurotics are normal:

Once we are agreed that learning and conditioning are instrumental in determining the different kinds of reaction we may make to environmental stimulation, we will find it very difficult to deny that neurotic reactions, like all others, are *learned* reactions, and must obey the laws of learning. . . . The fear of the rat thus conditioned is unadaptive (because white rats are not in fact dangerous) and hence is considered to be a neurotic symptom; a similarly conditioned fear of snakes would be regarded as adaptive, and hence not as neurotic. Yet the mechanism of acquisition is identical in both cases. This suggests that chance and environmental hazards are likely to play an important part in the acquisition of neurotic responses. If a rat happens to be present when the child hears a loud noise, a phobia results; when it is a snake that is present, a useful habit is built up.

(Eysenck, 1970, pp. 73–4)

Eysenck appears to reason from a conceptual premise that if the symptoms (manifestations) of a condition are caused by normal processes, then the condition is not a disease, and the empirical premise that neurotic symptoms are caused by normal principles of learning, to the conclusion that neurotic symptoms are not caused by any disease. Is this argument sound?

The conceptual premise is not correct as it stands. Some (statistically) normal conditions can be diseases – whole populations have suffered from malaria, but this does not mean that malaria is not a disease. In addition, we can imagine discovering all mankind currently suffers from a disease – e.g. small traces of copper universally present in our brains might considerably lower IQ (Reznek, 1987). This would be a disease even if we all had it. What of the factual premise? We have seen that laws of conditioning can go a long way to explain why neurotic symptoms occur. But even if a case could be made out for such a theory, we already know that if the behaviour to be explained is abnormal, then there will be an abnormality *somewhere* in the explanation. While it might be true that neurotics acquire their responses by normal processes (laws of learning), they acquire them *to a degree* which *is* abnormal, or in areas which *are* abnormal. And hence it does not follow from the fact that the laws of learning underlying neurotic symptoms are the same laws that underly normal behaviour, that the processes causing neurotic symptoms are normal *in all respects*. They are abnormal to some degree. Hence it is not true that neurotic symptoms are caused by (wholly) normal processes, and the argument collapses. Eysenck thus fails to show that neurosis is not an illness because it is the product of (normal) learning.

RE-EDUCATING AN ILLNESS

Eysenck has other arguments to muster against psychiatry:

> We have seen that psychology provides us with a very well grounded theory, stating in essence that neurotic 'symptoms' are not in fact symptomatic of anything, but are simply learned (conditioned), emotional responses, together with motor responses associated or caused by these emotional reactions. Thus we may quite reasonably say that what is required is not medical treatment, but re-education; behaviour therapy comes into the broad field of education rather than that of medicine.
>
> (Eysenck, 1975, p. 17)

> It was pointed out that objections on the grounds that only doctors are qualified to treat diseases are unjustified because behavioural disorders can only be considered 'diseases' by an undue extension of the meaning of that term for which no rational grounds exist. Behavioural disorders are more in line with an educational model, than with a medical model, requiring medical treatment.
>
> (Eysenck, 1975, p. 25)

From the conceptual premise that something is not a disease if it is correctable by education, and the empirical premise that neurosis is correctable by education, he concludes that neurosis is not a disease. Let us see whether this is valid.

The conceptual premise is false. Robert Kendell points out that there are many diseases that can be treated or prevented by education. Scurvy was (and is) treated by education – learning that the body needs vitamin C is sufficient to produce a change in behaviour and a consequent cure. Educating heart-attack victims about the effects of personality and teaching them to behave differently is sufficient to retard the disease process and reduce the chance of further heart attacks (Thoresen, Telch and Eagleston, 1981). And puerperal sepsis was stopped when doctors were educated about the effects of conducting dissections before proceeding to internal examinations without washing their hands in between! But this does not show that scurvy, ischaemic heart disease and puerperal sepsis are not diseases.

The factual premise breaks down into two claims. First, that neurosis is correctable by behaviour therapy, and second, that behaviour therapy is a form of education. While there is good evidence that behaviour therapy can successfully treat neurotic disorders (Gelder, Marks and Wolff, 1967), it is more difficult to defend the idea that behaviour therapy is a form of education. We usually distinguish between education and indoctrination. If we learned English history by being put into a highly suggestible state with sleep deprivation, would this count as education?

The difference between being educated and being brainwashed lies in the way the new information is acquired. In brainwashing or indoctrination, the person acquires new beliefs when he is in a state unable to rationally evaluate the new information. While in education, the person acquires new beliefs when he can critically evaluate these beliefs. Thus being educated implies that the person has gained the knowledge *in the right sort of way*. He has seen that there are *good reasons* to accept the beliefs, and because his rational or critical faculty remains intact, he is in control, free to accept or reject the new information unlike he would be if he were brainwashed. If education is to be defined in terms of acquiring new beliefs by a process of rational belief formation, then it will follow that behaviour therapy, which uses methods of conditioning rather than reasoning, does not count as education. When a phobia for spiders is treated, the therapist does not provide the patient with good reasons why his fear is irrational – the patient already knows it is. Instead, he provides the patient with a graded exposure to spiders so that his fearful response can be extinguished. Hence the factual premise is false, and the argument collapses.

Of course there are some treatments in psychiatry that could be classified as 'education'. Cognitive therapy aims at removing symptoms by confronting the patient with the lack of evidence for his irrational beliefs and thereby enabling him to become more rational. For example, the cognitive theory of panic disorder assumes that those who experience panic attacks do so because they (irrationally) believe they are having a heart attack, or a stroke, rather than a panic attack. By confronting the patient with the evidence, the patient comes to re-attribute the physical symptoms of anxiety more appropriately (rationally). In this way, education achieves a cure (Clark, Salkovskis and Chalkley, 1985). Similarly, cognitive therapy has been used successfully to treat depression. The cognitive theory of depression assumes that those who become depressed do so because they have developed a (irrational) negative view of themselves, the future, and the world. Treatment proceeds by using evidence from various sources to enable the patient to become less irrationally negative (Beck et al., 1979). But the fact that cognitive therapy can be used to treat panic disorder and depression does not mean that these conditions are not mental illnesses – depression and panic disorder are paradigmatic mental illnesses. Therefore, Eysenck's argument fails.

This illustrates the general point that it is dangerous to define mental illness in terms of the methods that can be used to treat it. This commits the *Treatment Fallacy*. We have seen that it is a mistake to define non-disease in terms of its responsiveness to education. It is also a mistake to define disease in terms of its responsiveness to chemical or physical treatments, and Eysenck makes this mistake too:

> In the first place, we have seen that neurotic disorders are behavioural in nature, not medical. The cure does not consist in tranquillizing pills or other drugs, nor in electroshock or brain surgery of any kind. The former are just palliatives, with the serious habit-forming effects and frequent side effects, and the latter are unproven and unjustifiable interference with the physical substratum of the conscious mind.
>
> (Eysenck, 1978, p. 202)

He appears to assume that if something is treatable with physical or chemical means, it is a disease, and also that if something is not treatable by such means, it is not a disease. But if something is not treatable by physical or chemical means, this might simply mean that it is an incurable disease! And the fact that we can treat some conditions by physical or chemical methods proves nothing. Political dissidence and aggressiveness could be controlled by old-fashioned frontal lobotomies which deprive people of drive, thereby preventing any behaviour whatever! But this does not prove that political dissidence or violence are diseases. Thus Eysenck fails to show that neurotic patients are not ill because they can be cured in a certain way.

THE BEHAVIOURAL PARADIGM

Eysenck challenges the medical paradigm. He does not see abnormal behaviour as being caused by disease. Instead, he sees it as the result of laws of conditioning or, more simply, laws of learning. Where the medical paradigm sees a neurological disorder, and the psychodynamic paradigm sees a conflict of intra-psychic forces, the behavioural paradigm sees learned responses. Eysenck thus contradicts the causal thesis of the medical paradigm.

Instead, he explains symptoms using laws of learning:

> The paradigm of neurotic symptom formation would be Watson's famous experiment with little Albert, an eleven months old boy who was fond of animals. By a simple process of classical Pavlovian conditioning, Watson created a phobia for white rats in this boy by standing behind him and making a very loud noise by banging an iron bar with a hammer whenever Albert reached for the animal. The rat was the conditioned stimulus in the experiment, the loud fear-producing noise was the unconditioned stimulus. As predicted, the unconditioned response (fear) became conditioned to the conditioned stimulus (the rat), and Albert developed a phobia for rats.
>
> (Eysenck, 1973, p. 339)

In this way, symptoms are explained by laws of learning rather than disease entities. We will examine this challenge to the medical paradigm in detail later.

In summary, Eysenck has argued that neurotics are not really ill because their 'symptoms' are the product of conditioning and have no underlying abnormalities, and because we can treat them with education. But these arguments all fail, and Eysenck is unable to show us that neurotics are free of mental disease.

4

RONALD LAING
AND THE
RATIONALIZING OF
MADNESS

Ronald Laing was a British psychiatrist whose radical ideas about schizophrenia challenged the medical paradigm in the sixties. His anti-psychiatry stance led him to argue that madmen are really rational – he argued that if we look carefully enough we will find the hidden desires and beliefs which make their behaviour intelligible. It is this idea that we will concentrate on here.

MADNESS IS METHOD

Laing attacks the disease model of schizophrenia. Instead of seeing the behaviour of schizophrenics as the symptom of some disease, Laing sees it as rational – i.e. as intentional behaviour performed for reasons. Where an orthodox psychiatrist sees a disease causing a symptom like thought disorder, Laing explains the behaviour in terms of the desire to avoid being understood and the belief that by 'talking mad' one will achieve this goal:

> A good deal of schizophrenia is simply nonsense, red-herring speech, prolonged filibustering designed to throw dangerous people off the scent, to create boredom and futility in others. The schizophrenic is often making a fool of himself and the doctor. He is playing at being mad to avoid at all costs the possibility of being held *responsible* for a single coherent idea, or intention.
>
> (Laing, 1965, p. 164)

To regard the gambits of Smith and Jones [schizophrenics] as due *primarily* to some psychological deficit is rather like supposing that a man doing a handstand on a bicycle on a tightrope 100 feet up with no safety net is suffering from an inability to stand on his own two feet. We may well ask why these people have to be, often brilliantly, so devious, elusive, so adept at making themselves unremittingly incomprehensible.

(Laing, 1967, p. 85)

Laing argues that schizophrenic behaviour can be given a *Rational Explanation*. For example, their behaviour can be explained by the desire (to throw people off the scent) and the belief (that such 'nonsense' speech and behaviour will achieve this).

Laing regards such explanations as incompatible with *Causal Explanations*:

If one is listening to another person talking, one may either (a) be studying verbal behaviour in terms of neural processes and the whole apparatus of vocalizing, or (b) be trying to understand what he is saying. . . . Whereas behaviour seen as personal is seen in terms of that person's experience and of his intentions, behaviour seen organismically can only be seen as the contraction or relaxation of certain muscles, etc. . . . In man seen as an organism, therefore, there is no place for his desires, fears, hope or despair as such. The ultimates of our explanations are not his intentions to his world but quanta of energy in an energy system. . . . My thesis is limited to the contention that the theory of man as person loses its way if it falls into an account of man as a machine or man as an organismic system of it-processes.

(Laing, 1965, p. 21–3)

Let us reconstruct Laing's first argument. From the conceptual premise that if behaviour is explicable in terms of reasons (desires and beliefs), then it is not caused by a disease, and the factual premise that the behaviour of schizophrenics is explicable in terms of reasons, he concludes that the behaviour of schizophrenics is not caused by a disease – i.e. the disease schizophrenia does not exist. Laing argues that the so-called signs of schizophrenia such as incoherent speech are not symptoms of disease but are instead motivated by reasons.

What does 'explicable in terms of reasons' mean? On one interpretation, it means providing desires and beliefs which rationalize that action. Suppose we are trying to understand a man who builds a tower of bottle-tops and then proceeds to dance around them, screaming 'Yobbol toddol tu'. We might suppose that he believes that dancing around a tower of bottle-tops screaming 'Yobbol toddol tu', which we translate as 'God is Great', will keep him healthy, and that he wants to be healthy. In this way, his behaviour is explicable in terms of reasons (desires and beliefs). On this interpretation, the empirical premise is trivially true – *any* piece of behaviour is explicable in terms of desires and beliefs. To explain any piece of behaviour B, all we have to do is attribute to the agent any desire D, and the belief that by doing B, he will achieve D.

But on this interpretation, the conceptual premise is clearly false. Let me illustrate this by taking the automatic behaviour that occurs in a temporal lobe epileptic seizure. Someone in such a seizure might smack his lips while walking around. We could invent some beliefs and desires that make such behaviour 'rational'. We could suppose that he believed that Nazis were trying to gas him and that he had to periodically 'taste' the air to see if this was about to happen. This then makes his behaviour explicable in terms of reasons. However, this does not mean that the behaviour is not due to a disease. *Ex hypothesi*, it is caused by temporal lobe epilepsy. Therefore the argument fails.

This interpretation appears to turn Laing's argument into a straw man. However, I include it because Laing invents bizarre reasons that purport to make schizophrenic behaviour rational but produces no evidence that schizophrenics actually possess these (Moore, 1975). If we are allowed to invent reasons, then even the automatic behaviour of a psycho-motor seizure becomes rational which is clearly absurd. Nevertheless, Laing wants to argue that not only can we invent desires and beliefs that rationalize the behaviour of schizophrenics, but also that their behaviour is actually motivated by such reasons. He claims some schizophrenics act strangely because they actually want to remain obscure.

We must then interpret 'explicable in terms of reasons' as 'caused by desires and beliefs actually held by the agent'. The conceptual premise now claims that if behaviour is explained by desires and beliefs, it is not caused by a disease. But this is wrong. In an inherited metabolic disorder called Lesch Nyan syndrome, which causes profound mental retardation, the afflicted individual acquires the desire to mutilate himself. In spite of the fact that the behaviour is caused by a desire, it is also caused by a disease (which causes that desire). So the fact that the behaviour is explained by a desire does not exclude the person having a disease that explains the same behaviour too.

In addition, there are many cases where a disease causes the person to believe something unusual. For example, general paresis of the insane (GPI) causes grandiose delusions – a patient may come to believe that he is the Prime Minister, and as a result demand to be released from hospital. Here we have a disease (GPI) causing a belief (that he is the PM) which in turn causally explains the behaviour (his demand to be released and his consequent protestations). The fact that his behaviour can be explained by desires (to get on with ministerial duties) and beliefs (that he is the PM) does not mean that the behaviour is not caused (at a deeper level) by disease. Therefore, the conceptual premise is false and the argument fails. Even if schizophrenic behaviour is intelligible in terms of a desire (to fool others) and a belief (that by behaving oddly this will be achieved), this does not mean that these desires and beliefs are not themselves the product of some disease process. A rational explanation of the person's behaviour does not mean that the behaviour is not caused (at a deeper level) by a disease.

If we read 'explicable in terms of reasons' as 'caused by desires and beliefs that are themselves not the product of already recognized diseases', this would exclude the above sorts of cases where a disease causes some deviant desire or belief which in turn causes the behaviour. But on this interpretation, the conceptual premise is still false. There is nothing to stop us identifying the acquisition of schizophrenic desires and beliefs as a unique disease process. If a process P1 leads to a schizophrenic acquiring such reasons that motivate his behaviour, while a different process P2 leads to the acquisition of normal desires and beliefs, there is nothing to stop us taking P1 to be a disease process. To assume it cannot be a disease process because the process is one of desire or belief formation is to commit the essentialist fallacy. If schizophrenic behaviour is caused by the desire to appear unintelligible to others and the belief that by adopting schizophrenic behaviour this desire can be satisfied, we can still identify the processes leading to the formation of such desires and beliefs as the disease process of schizophrenia.

It is clear that Laing makes the essentialist fallacy:

In psychiatry, research is directed to *finding* a suitable biological process in the first place to match undesirable states of *mind*, painful or disordered. We are faced with questions that do not arise in physical medicine. In real medicine, we determine a biological process to be a pathological process on *biological* grounds.

(Laing, 1983, p. 42)

Here Laing assumes that in physical medicine, doctors correctly judge that something is a symptom of a disease because it is caused by the right sort of biological process, while in psychiatry, doctors incorrectly judge that something is a disease because it causes things we don't like – symptoms. But what comes first in both physical and psychological medicine are symptoms – i.e. suffering and disability – and whatever causes this is a disease. We do not first judge that some process (of the right biological type) is a disease, and then conclude that whatever it causes must be symptoms! This latter position, adopted by Laing, is the essentialist fallacy. Hence the conceptual premise is false even on this last interpretation.

One of the other mistakes that makes Laing conclude that the schizophrenic strategy is not a disease is the assumption he makes that one sort of explanation rules out another. In a sense, he makes the mistake of many dualists and argues that rational explanations exclude causal ones. He assumes that if the reasons (desires and beliefs) explain some behaviour, then it cannot be explained by some physical process like a disease. And hence he concludes that the behaviour is not the result of a disease. But it is one of the central arguments of this book that dualism is untenable. If a desire or belief is to influence behaviour, it must have a physical basis in the brain and, therefore, if some behaviour is caused by reasons, it will also be caused by physical processes. If we are no longer in the grip of the essentialist fallacy, there is nothing to prevent the physical processes that form the basis of the so-called schizophrenic strategy counting as the *disease* of schizophrenia.

The factual premise consists of the claim that the behaviour of schizophrenics is explained by their desires and beliefs. But in examining whether this is true, we encounter an epistemological problem: how do we gain access to someone's desires and beliefs if all we have access to is their behaviour? The difficulty is generated by the fact that there are two unknowns in the equation.

Suppose we wish to explain why someone jumps off the Firth of Forth bridge. If we know that he wants to kill himself, it is relatively easy to infer his belief that jumping off the bridge will kill him from both his behaviour and his desire. On the other hand, if we know he believes that he can fly, it is relatively easy to infer the desire that he does *not* want to kill himself from both his behaviour and his belief. If we already know one of the unknowns, it is easy to infer the other unknown from the behaviour. The problem is generated by the fact that we have to infer *both* unknowns from the behaviour.

We cannot solve this problem by asking the agent what he believes or wants to do. But this will not help. We can only interpret the noises he makes if we already know what he wants to achieve by making such noises, and what he believes he will achieve – i.e. if we know his desires and beliefs. The difficulty of interpreting speech is especially relevant here because the talk of schizophrenics often seems unintelligible. Laing tries to show that the jumbled speech of schizophrenics is meaningful. For example, one patient called Julie speaks of a 'told bell', 'the occidental sun', and 'Mrs Taylor', and her speech appears to be meaningless (Laing, 1965, p. 192). Laing argues that Julie speaks in a roundabout way that she is a 'told belle' (a girl told what to do and be), that she is an 'accidental son' (because her mother had wanted a boy), and 'tailor-made by her parents' (because she had no identity of her own). If we attribute non-standard meanings to the words being used, we can turn apparently incoherent babble into intelligible talk. But the fact that meaning can be invented for schizophrenic babble does not mean that it actually has this meaning. Our problem is to specify how we can have evidence that the dialogue actually has some meaning and is not simply a Laingian invention.

The epistemological problem is solved by looking for the best explanation of the person's overall behaviour. If we explain the man jumping off the bridge by supposing that he wants to kill himself, and stop him jumping only to find that the next day he slashes his wrists, we have a better explanation of his overall behaviour than if we suppose he wanted to fly. Similarly, if, after stopping him jump off, he says 'I wanted to kill myself', and he later cuts his wrists, the best translation of these words is that they meant he wanted to kill himself (rather than that he wanted to fly). To settle the factual premise we need to ask whether the best explanation of schizophrenic behaviour and talk is provided by the hypothesis that their behaviour is rational and their talk is meaningful.

Donald Davidson argues that we should accept the translation which makes a person's beliefs turn out to be largely true (Davidson, 1984). But this is not helpful especially in the realm of mental disorder. If we accept this principle of charity then no one can ever be translated as having a system of false beliefs – i.e. no one can be grossly deluded. It seems that Davidson's view excludes the very possibility of madness, which cannot be right! And therefore we must reject it.

In some cases (those with paranoid schizophrenia) the individual's behaviour and talk *is* intelligible in terms of his beliefs and desires. A patient might believe that the FBI are after him, that they are monitoring his thoughts, and that they are talking about him. As a result of these beliefs, his behaviour and talk will be eminently reasonable. In such cases, the factual premise looks defensible. However, it still does not provide the best explanation of his overall behaviour because we need an explanation of how he came to such beliefs. It is here that the rational explanation breaks down. The schizophrenic does not rationally infer his beliefs from appropriate evidence. He alludes to experience that is either not evidential or abnormal. To explain his beliefs thus requires *more* than an assumption of his rationality – it must assume that he has an illness disrupting normal reasoning and/or experience.

David Healy argues that schizophrenics (and manic-depressive patients) are as rational as the rest of us – they arrive at different beliefs only because their database (experience) is different (Healy, 1990). If the schizophrenic believes he is being controlled, it is because he has a frontal lobe dysfunction that undermines the planning of actions and which generates the experience of being out of control. He writes:

> No defects of judgement or impairment of the ability to use logic have ever been demonstrated in schizophrenia. Even in subjects who are floridly deluded. Arguably, therefore, the fact that the rest of us do not hold the odd beliefs of a schizophrenic can only be explained in terms of the latter's beliefs arising as a result of the biases of normal rationality operating on abnormal experiences.
>
> (Healy, 1990, p. 158)

However, even if the schizophrenic is as rational as the rest of us, this does not mean schizophrenia is not a disease. A disease process is needed to explain the schizophrenic's abnormal experiences. And second, while it may be the case that no defects in logic have been demonstrated in schizophrenics, when it comes to their delusional beliefs, they are poor inductive logicians. A patient of mine with de Clerambault's syndrome – the delusion that some important person is in love with the patient – inferred support for this conclusion from an entry to a prize draw she had received through the post. With a complex and arbitrary code, she told me that the numbers on her entry meant 'I love you'. She also concluded he loved her because overhead jets left cloud trails as a special message. If this isn't faulty inductive logic, then I don't know what is!

In cases where schizophrenic behaviour and speech are more disordered (as in hebephrenic schizophrenia), hypotheses about rationality have to become more and more outlandish until they cease to have any plausibility – it is more reasonable to conclude that such behaviour and talk is a symptom of some underlying disease rather than the product of intelligible motives. While it is open to Laingians to argue that if the behaviour is extremely odd, the thought incoherent, the emotional responses inappropriate, the beliefs bizarre, the schizophrenic is simply being brilliant in his attempt to make himself incomprehensible, this theory starts to look over-burdened with *ad hoc* hypotheses and thereby implausible. In both extremes of schizophrenia, then, the factual premise looks false. While it might be the case that some of the behaviour is explained by reasons, a reference to a disease process is also needed. And because the argument requires the behaviour to be explained *solely* by reasons, it fails.

The sense of rationality that Laing claims schizophrenics have is a very weak sort of rationality. It does not entail that the behaviour is fully rational (Brown, 1976; Moore, 1975). Behaviour can be motivated by desires and beliefs without those desires and beliefs themselves being rational. While the behaviour of schizophrenics might be intelligible in terms of reasons, this does not mean that the strategy that they adopt is the best way of solving their problems, or that their beliefs are based on evidence, or that their desires are not unintelligible or self-defeating. Being rational in this sense is a very weak form of rationality, but even in these terms Laing fails to show that madmen are rational rather than ill.

THE INSANE SOCIETY

One of the reasons why Laing feels that schizophrenic behaviour is (weakly) rational is that he believes the behaviour arises in social contexts where it would be reasonable to act in this way:

> To the best of my knowledge, *no* schizophrenic has been studied whose behaviour pattern of communication has not been shown to be a reflection of, and a reaction to, the disturbed and disturbing pattern characterizing his or her family of origin. This is matched in our own researches. In over one hundred cases where we have studied the actual circumstances around the social event when one person comes to be regarded as schizophrenic, it seems to us that *without exception* the experience and behaviour that gets labelled schizophrenic is *a special strategy that a person invents in order to live in an unlivable situation.* In his life situation, the person has come to feel he is in an untenable position. He cannot make a move, or make no move, without being beset by contradictory and paradoxical pressures and demands, pushes and pulls, both internally, from himself, and externally, from those around him. He is, as it were, in a position of checkmate.
>
> (Laing, 1967, pp. 94–5)

Laing purports to show that the best explanation of the behaviour of his one hundred cases of schizophrenia is that it is a strategy to cope in an unlivable family situation. He reasons from the conceptual premise that if some behaviour is an intelligible response to some social situation, then it is not caused by a disease, and the empirical premise that schizophrenic behaviour is an intelligible response to untenable family situations, to the conclusion that schizophrenic behaviour is not caused by a disease – i.e. the disease schizophrenia does not exist.

To prove the empirical premise Laing must show not only that schizophrenic behaviour is caused by unlivable family situations, but also that the unlivable family situations result in the formation of a strategy designed to cope in such a situation. But Laing fails to show that the schizophrenic behaviour is caused by unlivable family situations (Sedgwick, 1982). To show this, he needs to show that schizophrenic behaviour occurs more commonly in such families than in others, but he fails to produce any control groups. In addition, he needs a longitudinal study to show that it is the abnormal family set-up that produces the schizophrenic behaviour rather than the reverse. For it is quite possible that it is trying to cope with the abnormal behaviour of the schizophrenic that makes the families abnormal. But he fails to do this.

Current research demonstrates that families that are critical, hostile, and emotionally over-involved do precipitate schizophrenic episodes (Vaughn and Leff, 1976). But Laing needs to show that schizophrenic behaviour is a strategy purposely adopted and not an involuntary reaction to the stress of such families, and he does not do this. But there is some evidence that schizophrenics intentionally put on their symptoms to achieve various ends, and this supports Laing's empirical premise. One such investigation was designed to show that hospitalized patients can manipulate the impressions they make. Acute and chronic patients were given a questionnaire. Some were told that the more items they answered true, the more severely ill they were and the more likely they would remain in hospital for a long time. Others were told that the more items they answered true, the more they knew about themselves, the less severely ill they were and the more likely they were to remain in the hospital for a short time. It was hypothesized that the chronic patients would want to remain in hospital (having made the adjustment), while the reverse would be true of acute patients. It was predicted that the patients would manipulate their answers to give whatever impression they supposed necessary to gain what they wanted. And this was born out exactly by the results. Those chronic patients told that true answers implied illness answered most questions affirmatively, while those chronic patients told that true answers implied health did not. Conversely, those acute patients told that true answers implied illness answered most questions negatively, while those acute patients told that true answers implied health did not (Braginsky, Braginsky and Ring, 1969).

However, the fact that a schizophrenic can manipulate the impression he makes with a questionnaire does not warrant the over-generalization that all the behaviour of schizophrenics is nothing but manipulation of impressions for the sake of various ends, like admission to the safe haven of a hospital. If a patient with a duodenal ulcer knows he will need an unpleasant gastroscope if he owns up to stomach pain, he may manipulate the impression he gives his doctor, making it appear that he is less ill. But this does not mean that he does not have a disease. Similarly, the fact that schizophrenics can create the impression that they are either well or ill does not mean that schizophrenia is not a disease. To demonstrate that all the symptoms of schizophrenia are nothing other than strategies, it will have to be shown that delusions, hallucinations, thought-disorder, poverty of affect, perplexity, inappropriateness of affect, poverty of thought, loss of memory, are all intentional manipulations by the patient to achieve a certain end. And so far, this has not been done.

In addition, Laingians will have to explain the studies that demonstrate that schizophrenia has a genetic cause. Studies of children of schizophrenics who have been adopted by non-schizophrenic families demonstrate that there is a significant genetic component in the cause of schizophrenic behaviour (Kety, Rosenthal and Wender, 1971). Laingians could explain this away by assuming that the genes predispose the individual to adopting the schizophrenic strategy to cope in such a family situation. They will also have to explain the studies that demonstrate that schizophrenics have associated brain abnormalities (Brown *et al.*, 1985). Again they could argue that the anatomical differences predispose to the adoption of the schizophrenic strategy. But if Laingians make all these moves, their theory that the behaviour is due to a strategy differs only in name from the theory that it is due to a disease. It ceases to have distinct consequences, becoming instead a notational variant of the disease theory where the word 'strategy' is simply substituted for 'disease'.

But even if the balance of evidence is in favour of the hypothesis that schizophrenic behaviour is a rational response to certain abnormal family situations, this would not mean that schizophrenia is not a disease because the conceptual thesis is false. Even if the behaviour is a strategy to live in such a situation, and is motivated by a desire (to survive) and a belief (that only such a strategy will enable him to do so), this does not mean that the process whereby such a desire and belief are acquired is not a disease process. Even if we discover that schizophrenic behaviour is caused by certain abnormal family situations, this does not mean that we cannot say that such abnormal family situations cause the *disease* of schizophrenia. To think otherwise is to commit the essentialist fallacy.

To reinforce this argument, suppose someone develops a profound depression following the traumatic loss of his family in an accident for which he was partly responsible. In this sense, the guilt that he feels, the low mood, the loss in interest in daily matters, are all intelligible in terms of the social situation. The response is explicable both in the sense that such loss events have been shown to *cause* depression, and in the sense that such a response is a reasonable or appropriate response in the circumstances. Being an explicable response to a social situation does not mean it is not a depressive illness.

In fact, many psychiatric disorders are understandable reactions to upbringing and/or social circumstances. Anorexia nervosa – the overvaluing of slimness and the consequent loss of weight – is an understandable reaction to a society that places huge importance on the slender feminine figure (Brumberg, 1988). Depression in the elderly is an understandable reaction to their relative poverty, their increased ill-health, their increased isolation, their poor housing, and their alienation (Ratna, 1978). Morton Schatzman has shown that the paranoid illness of Schreber, the nineteenth-century German judge, was an intelligible response to the brutalizing and persecution he received from his father in the name of education (Schatzman, 1971). But the fact that these reactions are understandable in terms of the individual's history or social circumstances does not mean that they are not illnesses. An illness, as I will argue, is a condition that cannot be reversed at will and which causes disability and distress. Illnesses can still be understandable reactions, and hence the conceptual premise is false and the argument fails.

Laing's view that schizophrenia is the product of certain social situations leads to another argument against the existence of the disease of schizophrenia. In *The Politics of Experience*, he writes about the generation of schizophrenic behaviour:

> The behaviour of the diagnosed patient is part of a much larger network of disturbed behaviour. The contradictions and confusions 'internalized' by the individual must be looked at in their larger social contexts. Something is wrong

somewhere, but it can no longer be seen exclusively or even primarily 'in' the diagnosed patient.

(Laing, 1967, pp. 95–6)

From the conceptual premise that if the source of the disturbance is located outside the individual in the social situation, then the individual is not diseased, and the factual premise that in schizophrenia, the source of the disturbance is located outside the individual in the social situation, he concludes that the schizophrenic is not diseased – i.e. the disease schizophrenia does not exist. Is the argument valid?

We have already found the factual premise wanting. The conceptual premise too is false. If we trace the epidemiology of the major infectious disorders that afflict mankind, the interesting thing to note is that they all came under control when standards of living improved and not when antibiotics were introduced (McKeown, 1979). This fact led to the discovery that the major source of these pandemics was poor social circumstances. This is supported by their continued prevalence in communities where there are poor living conditions. For example, TB was well on the wane before the introduction of antibiotics. Nevertheless, it persists in communities where there are poor living conditions – poor sanitation, overcrowding, poor ventilation, malnutrition, etc. Thus it would be reasonable to conclude that the source of the disturbance in TB lies in poor social circumstances. But if we accepted the conceptual premise, we would have to conclude that when an individual acquires TB, he is not diseased. But this is absurd. Although TB is a social disease due largely to poor social circumstances, this does not imply that the individual tuberculotic is not diseased. Therefore the conceptual premise is false and the argument collapses.

Let us look at further of Laing's arguments which stem from his thesis that it is the schizophrenic rather than the normal person that is sane. He writes:

I suggest, therefore, that *sanity or psychosis is tested by the degree of conjunction or disjunction between two persons where the one is sane by common consent.* . . . The 'psychotic' is the name we have for the other person in a disjunctive relationship of a particular kind.

(Laing, 1965, p. 36)

Using the metaphor of planes being in formation (views being in agreement) but off course (out of touch with reality), he writes:

> From an ideal vantage point on the ground, a formation of planes may be observed in the air. One plane may be out of formation. But the whole formation may be off course. The plane that is 'out of formation' may be abnormal, bad or 'mad' from the point of view of the formation. But the formation itself may be bad or mad from the point of view of the ideal observer.
>
> (Laing, 1967, p. 98)

An argument can be reconstructed from these passages. From the two conceptual premises that if someone holds a minority belief (about reality), he is judged to be deluded (mad), and that if someone holds a true belief (about reality), he is 'truly' sane, and from the factual premise that often the beliefs of the majority are false, he concludes that in many cases the person judged to be deluded (mad) is in fact 'truly' sane. Is this argument valid?

The empirical premise is unexceptionable. At many times our culture has held beliefs that were false – e.g. that the earth is flat, and that the sun moves round the earth. And undoubtedly many of our current beliefs are false. The argument, then, turns on the conceptual premises. First, Laing assumes that psychiatrists judge people to be deluded if they do not hold the majority view about reality. But this is false. If the person can produce good evidence for his beliefs, psychiatrists will not judge him to be deluded. To be deluded one must believe something tenaciously in the face of obvious evidence to the contrary. So mere disagreement is not enough. We define delusions in this way because it is irrationality rather than disagreement that we disvalue, and hence it is irrationality rather than disagreement that we wish to make the hallmark of pathology. If we did define delusions thus, we would have to regard Copernicus, Galileo, Darwin, Einstein, etc., as deluded, which is absurd. In addition, if the individual has different beliefs about reality, but belongs to a sub-culture where these beliefs are acceptable, then the individual is not regarded as deluded. The reason why this clause is added to the definition of delusion is that we would have to conclude that whole cultures are and whole epochs were deluded. But if we do this, then the concept of delusion fails to do the work we want it to do. We want it to pick out people who have internal processes that are harmful to them. But simply adopting socially sanctioned facts is not harmful and is unworthy of the title 'pathological'. But once we have accepted this, then culturally sanctioned beliefs that are false are not delusions. Hence Laing's account of how psychiatrists judge delusions is wrong and the first conceptual premise is false.

Second, Laing assumes that 'true' sanity consists in holding true beliefs about reality. But this is also wrong. He thinks our reality consists of 'socially shared hallucinations' and that because our view of the world is false, we are suffering from 'collusive madness' (Laing, 1967, p. 62). But 'true' sanity does not consist in true beliefs just as 'true' madness does not consist in false beliefs. In fact, it is possible for a delusion to be true! Morbid jealousy is a condition where men (usually) become convinced without reason that their wives are unfaithful. Yet it is possible coincidentally that their wives are having undetectable affairs, and that they are right for the wrong reasons. But because they hold their convictions on the basis of the faulty reasons, i.e. without evidence, they are judged to be suffering from a delusion. Holding true beliefs does not imply that one is sane – what is important is not the truth or falsity of one's beliefs, but the way they come to be held.

This means that a schizophrenic might be right to think that society will destroy itself, but if this is irrationally formed, it is a delusion. And it means that if our culture erroneously believes that the Russians are intent on destroying the west, we are not deluded because such a belief arises from social sanctions. Thus it is possible for a culture to hold totally false beliefs about reality and to be sane. Before Copernicus and Galileo came up with a better explanation of the movements of heavenly bodies, the best explanation was the geocentric one. Although the whole culture got it wrong, they were not mad because they got it wrong for the right reasons! They had good evidence for their view.

Laing is not wrong because his argument implies the apparent absurdity that a whole culture can be deluded. This is not absurd. The religious community of around 900 people that committed mass suicide in Jonestown on 18 November 1978 were probably sucked into a 'collusive madness' by their charismatic leader, Jim Jones. Just as someone can be sucked into *folie-à-deux* by living in close proximity and relative isolation with a dominant but psychotic partner, coming to share his delusions, so it seems possible for a whole community to become deluded by falling under the spell of a psychotic but persuasive leader. It is likely that the same process going on in *folie-à-deux* explained the convictions of religious salvation in Jonestown, and therefore that all members were suffering from *folie-à-tout-le-monde*! Since we consider such a process undesirable (unlike the adoption of socially sanctioned beliefs), we would consider it to be a disease and the beliefs to be delusional. Thus Laing is right to think that a whole culture can be mad, but he is right for the wrong reason – only if beliefs are adopted in a particular way are they delusions. They are not delusions simply because they are false. Hence the second conceptual premise is false and the argument collapses.

Because Laing sees society as mad, he develops a completely different view of the nature of schizophrenia. Instead of seeing it as a *disease* process, he sees it as a *healing* process:

> Madness need not be all break-down. It may also be break-through. It is potentially liberation and renewal as well as enslavement and existential death. . . . Can we not see that *this voyage is not what we need to be cured of, but that it is itself a natural way of healing our own appalling state of alienation called normality?*
>
> (Laing, 1967, pp. 110–36)

Laing sees the ego as the instrument of social adaptation, and he believes that it forces us to adapt to a false reality – true reality will only be perceived when the ego is dissolved:

> The 'ego' is the instrument for living in *this* world. If the 'ego' is broken up, or destroyed (by insurmountable contradictions of certain life situations, by toxins, chemical changes, etc.), then the person may be exposed to other worlds, 'real' in different ways from the more familiar territory of dreams, imagination, perception or phantasy.
>
> (Laing, 1967, pp. 114–15)

He thinks like this because he recognizes that disease judgements are value judgements. He writes:

> Lidz calls schizophrenia a failure of human adaptation. In that case, this too is a value-judgement. Or is anyone going to say that this is an objective fact? Very well, let us call

schizophrenia a successful attempt not to adapt to pseudo social realities. Is this also an objective fact?

(Laing, 1967, p. 57)

These passages contain another argument. From the conceptual premise that if the consequences of certain conditions are not valued (on balance), then that condition is judged to be a disease, and the value judgement that schizophrenia has valuable consequences (on balance), he concludes that schizophrenia is not a disease. Is this argument sound?

The conceptual premise is correct and I will argue for it in detail in chapter 10. The argument then turns on the value judgement. Does schizophrenia have valuable consequences (on balance)? Do schizophrenics themselves value being in their disturbed states? While there are undoubtedly a few schizophrenics who prefer being mad to being treated with unpleasant drugs (not quite the same as judging that it is better to be mad than to be sane but free of unpleasant drugs), most patients dislike their psychotic state and are pleased to have it treated (Wing, 1975). In addition, those of us who are not schizophrenic do not value being distressed by delusions and hallucinations, having our thinking become incoherent, our emotional life impoverished, the meaning and colour taken out of our lives, and losing our drive and motivation. It is therefore reasonable to conclude that in spite of Laing's romanticization, schizophrenia is on balance undesirable. And hence the argument fails. In summary, then, Laing has failed to show that schizophrenics are rational and in touch with 'true' reality rather than ill. He has also failed to show that schizophrenia is an intelligible response to intolerable circumstances, or that it is society that is mad.

LAINGIAN PARADIGMS

Laing also challenges the medical paradigm. He does not see the abnormal behaviour of schizophrenics (and other mentally ill patients) as the result of a disease. Instead, he challenges the causal thesis of the medical paradigm. There are a number of different accounts he gives of the causes of abnormal behaviour, and each of these constitutes a distinct paradigm (Siegler and Osmond, 1972). On one conception, which I will call the *Intentional Paradigm*, he sees abnormal behaviour as intentional and the result of reasons. These reasons consist of desires and beliefs which both cause the behaviour and make it intelligible. Abnormal behaviour is simply a strategy to get what one wants.

On another account, he sees abnormal behaviour as the natural healing process of the alienated state into which normal people have been forced. Thus, instead of seeing the behaviour of schizophrenics as being caused by a disease process, he sees it as being caused by a healing process. Far from the schizophrenic having a malfunction, it is the rest of normality that is malfunctioning by adopting a false reality. I will call this the *Transcendent Paradigm*.

Finally, he sees abnormal behaviour as the result of abnormal social situations. Instead of the behaviour being caused by abnormalities inside the individual – i.e. by diseases– Laing sees the behaviour as being caused by abnormalities in the social environment. The abnormal behaviour of the individual is simply an intelligible reaction to the abnormal social environment. As an example of this, he sees schizophrenia as a strategy to cope in a disturbed family. I will call this the *Sociological Paradigm*.

On each of these views, Laing denies that there is such a thing as the disease of schizophrenia. No disease is needed to explain the abnormal behaviour of schizophrenics. And hence in this way Laing challenges the medical paradigm. We will explore this clash in a later chapter.

In summary, then, Laing challenges the medical paradigm by denying the causal thesis. He sees abnormal behaviour as rational and explicable in terms of reasons – it is simply an intelligible reaction to a sick society. However, he fails to show that this means that schizophrenics are not suffering from a disease – even if he is right, the formation of such strategies can be regarded as a disease process. Schizophrenics are not more rational and more in touch with 'true' reality than the rest of us.

5

THOMAS SZASZ AND THE PHYSICALIZING OF DISEASE

The American psychiatrist, Thomas Szasz, has been one of the most vociferous critics of psychiatry. He has challenged its very foundations by arguing that there is no such thing as a mental illness. But we will see that his conclusions only follow from a mistaken view of disease in general.

THE DUALIST FALLACY

Thomas Szasz outlines the medical paradigm of mental illness:

> Mental illnesses are thus regarded as basically similar to other diseases. The only difference, in this view, between mental and bodily disease is that the former, affecting the brain, manifests itself by means of mental symptoms; whereas the latter, affecting other organ systems – e.g., the skin, liver, and so on – manifests itself by means of symptoms referable to those parts of the body.
>
> (Szasz, 1974b, p. 89)

Szasz sees the medical paradigm as assuming that mental illnesses are diseases of the brain that produce mental symptoms rather than physical symptoms. He thinks that this view is mistaken:

> Disease means bodily disease. Gould's Medical Dictionary defines disease as a disturbance of the function or structure of an organ or part of the *body*. The mind (whatever it is) is not an organ or part of the body. Hence, it cannot be diseased in the same sense as the body can. When we speak of mental illness, then, we speak metaphorically. To say that a person's mind is sick is like saying that the economy

71

is sick or that a joke is sick. When a metaphor is mistaken for reality and is used for social purposes, then we have the makings of myth. The concepts of mental health and mental illness are mythological concepts, used strategically to advance some social interests and to retard others, much as national and religious myths have been used in the past.

(Szasz, 1974a, p. 97)

Szasz argues from the conceptual premise that if something has a disease, then it must be a bodily part, and the metaphysical premise that the mind is not a bodily part, to the conclusion that the mind cannot be diseased. Is this argument sound?

The conceptual premise assumes that it is part of the meaning of the term 'disease' that only bodily conditions can be diseases. But no argument is provided for this assumption. In fact, on either of the two most plausible accounts of the concept of disease, not only bodily things can be diseased. The first defines 'disease' in terms of malfunctioning. Some process is a disease, on this definition, if and only if it disrupts some function (Boorse, 1976). TB is a disease because it leads to the lungs malfunctioning, and haemophilia is a disease because it leads to a clotting malfunction. But notice that no assumption is made that the disruption must be of a bodily rather than a mental function. On this definition, there is no reason to exclude mental illnesses. Schizophrenia is a disease because it is a process that causes delusions, hallucinations, and jumbled thinking – i.e. because it disrupts mental functions. Thus it is correct to classify it as a disease, albeit a mental one.

The second defines 'disease' in terms of harm. Something is a disease if and only if it produces discomfort, disability or death – all forms of harm (Culver and Gert, 1982). Trigeminal neuralgia is a disease because it produces discomfort, polio a disease because it produces disability, and lung cancer a disease because it causes death. But on this definition too, there is no reason to exclude mental illnesses. Just as there are processes producing physical disabilities and physical pain, there are processes causing mental disabilities and mental pain. Alzheimer's disease – a condition characterized by progressive intellectual impairment, personality deterioration and memory loss – causes mental disabilities and mental anguish. Thus it is correct to classify it as a disease, albeit of the mind. So on either of the most plausible accounts of the concept of disease, there is no reason to deny that there are diseases of the mind.

Szasz believes that Freud inappropriately extended the concept of illness to include mental problems. But it was not Freud who extended the concept – since Hippocrates, mental problems like depression have been seen as illnesses. Nevertheless an extension of any concept can be justified on the basis of its analogy with a central case. If someone is struck down with a paralysis of his arm, we regard him as suffering from an illness. The discovery that part of his brain has infarcted (died from lack of oxygen) only confirms that he has had a physical illness (a stroke). But if we find no evidence of a stroke, and suspect that this disability has emotional causes, we still have good reason to view it as an illness, albeit a mental one (Margolis, 1966). If Szasz persists in arguing that it is part of the meaning of disease that there can only be bodily diseases, he is operating with a different concept of disease. He is free to do so, but he will not be speaking the same language as the rest of us. All he will be saying is that mental illnesses are not szasziseases, and there is nothing controversial about this! Anybody is free to invent their own language with special meanings for their terms. But if he is using our ordinary concept of disease, then there can be mental diseases. Thus the conceptual premise is false.

The metaphysical premise commits the *Dualist Fallacy* – the fallacy of assuming that the mind is not identical to any physical thing (the brain included). Szasz needs this premise to conclude that if a disorder (like GPI) has a physical basis, it is not a mental illness. I have not sufficient space to argue that (substance) dualism is false. But if the mind is not identical to some physical thing, then it must be made of some completely different substance. Such a theory has at least two serious disadvantages over any non-dualist theory. First, it multiplies entities beyond necessity. Occam's Razor favours the simpler theory – a simpler theory with fewer postulates is less likely to be wrong. Second, if there are two completely different substances in the universe, we need to understand how they can interact, and this turns out to be extremely difficult to explain (Churchland, 1986). If mental events do not interact with physical events, there seems to be even less reason for supposing that they are there. We already know that there is one-way interaction – interfering with the brain (via electrodes, drugs or lesions) affects the mind. But if mental events interact with physical events, then physical laws of nature will be violated, which is also unpalatable. And finally, it is no good being told that they do interact – we also need to be told where and how, and no sensible answer is forthcoming (including Eccles, 1977). For these reasons, substance dualism is probably wrong, and the argument fails.

Szasz has other dualist arguments. He writes:

> If you believe that you are Jesus, or have discovered a cure for cancer (and have not), or the Communists are after you (and they are not) – then your beliefs are likely to be regarded as symptoms of schizophrenia. But if you believe that the Jews are the Chosen People, or that Jesus was the Son of God, or that Communism is the only scientifically and morally correct form of government – then your beliefs are likely to be regarded as reflections of who you are: Jew, Christian, Communist. This is why I think that we will discover the chemical cause of schizophrenia when we will discover the chemical cause of Judaism, Christianity, and Communism. No sooner and no later.
>
> (Szasz, 1974a, pp. 101–2)

Szasz reasons from a conceptual premise that if it is correct to explain undesirable beliefs by reference to causes, then it is correct to explain desirable beliefs by reference to causes, and the metaphysical premise that it is not correct to explain desirable beliefs by reference to causes, to the conclusion that it is not correct to explain undesirable beliefs by reference to causes – i.e. by reference to the disease of schizophrenia. He therefore concludes that 'schizophrenics' are not ill. Is this argument sound?

The conceptual premise is true. It is reasonable to argue that if false or irrational beliefs have causes, then true or rational beliefs will also have causes, albeit perhaps different ones. But the metaphysical premise is false – it presupposes that being the product of reasons and being the product of causes are mutually exclusive – that if a belief is the product of reasoning, it cannot have causes. He writes:

> A disease of the brain, analogous to a disease of the skin or bone, is a neurological defect, not a problem in living. For example, a *defect* in a person's visual field may be explained by correlating it with certain lesions in the nervous system.

74

On the other hand, a person's *belief* – whether it be in Christianity, in Communism, or in the idea that his internal organs are rotting and that his body is already dead – cannot be explained by a defect or disease of the nervous system. Explanations of this sort of occurrence – assuming that one is interested in the belief itself and does not regard it simply as a symptom or expression of something else that is more interesting – must be sought along different lines.

(Szasz, 1974b, p. 13)

Szasz assumes that explaining such beliefs by reasons ('different lines') excludes an explanation in terms of causes. But we have no reason to hold that if some belief is the product of reasoning it has no causes. On the contrary, we expect rational beliefs to have causes – if they did not, they would not be rational.

Being a rational belief consists in being caused (in the right way) by the evidence. If a belief has no cause, and simply springs into existence without any relation to evidence, it would be irrational. If I suddenly come to believe for no good reason that an earthquake will occur in Great Britain in 1999, my belief is irrational even if I am right. On the other hand, if the belief is caused by good evidence, it will be rational. Hence, rational beliefs must be caused. On this notion, irrational beliefs are beliefs that are caused in the wrong sort of way. Someone might believe that there are fairies because of a fairy story. This belief is irrational precisely because it is not caused in the right sort of way – because it is caused by a fairy story rather than empirical evidence. It is causation that is central to the very idea of a rational belief. Thus the metaphysical premise is false – if a belief is caused, this does not mean that we do not believe it for reasons. This means that undesirable beliefs can be explained by causes – i.e. they can be due to underlying disease, and therefore the argument collapses.

Szasz believes that if we conclude that the beliefs of schizophrenics are symptoms (effects) of organic causes, we will have to conclude that our ordinary beliefs are symptoms of some organic cause – i.e. we will have to conclude we are all diseased:

Psychiatrists look for twisted molecules and defective genes as the causes of schizophrenia, because schizophrenia is the name of a disease. If Christianity or Communism were called diseases, would they then look for the chemical and genetic 'causes' of these 'conditions'?

(Szasz, 1974a, p. 102)

His argument here is a *reductio*. From the conceptual premise that if beliefs are caused by some underlying condition of the brain, then those beliefs are caused by some disease, and the factual premise that beliefs in Christianity are caused by some underlying condition of the brain, he infers the absurdity that the belief in Christianity is due to a disease! Christianitis? He argues that once we accept that desirable beliefs have organic causes, we are forced to conclude that we are all diseased!

But the conceptual premise is false. We have seen that rational beliefs must have causes. Rational beliefs about the world must be caused by the world causing our experience. But this does not mean we are suffering from some neurological disease! On the other hand, the factual premise is true – like any belief, the belief in Christianity or Judaism will have organic causes. We might find that one of the causes of 'theism' is prolonged meditation which induces a mystical experience that convinces the meditator there is a God. So we might then be able to say that a particular brain state causes us to believe in God. Of course this does not mean that the belief is false – it might be that judgements in general made in such a state of meditation are more likely to be true. But having a cause does not mean the belief is due to a disease. And hence the *reductio* fails. In summary, then, these arguments all fail because of their implicit dualism.

THE ORGANIC FALLACY

Szasz argues that mental illnesses do not exist because they do not have the same status as organic or physical disease:

> It must be noted, therefore, that Kraepelin and Bleuler discovered no histopathological lesions or pathophysiological processes in their patients. Instead, they acted *as if* they had discovered such lesions or processes; named their 'patients' accordingly; and committed themselves and their followers to the goal of establishing a precise identification of the 'organic' nature and cause of these diseases. In other words,

Kraepelin and Bleuler did not discover the diseases for which they are famous; they invented them.

(Szasz, 1979a, p. 9)

Szasz argues from the conceptual premise that if a condition is classified as a disease prior to the discovery of its organic basis, then the disease is invented, and the factual premise that schizophrenia was classified as a disease prior to the discovery of its organic basis, to the conclusion that schizophrenia is invented. Is this argument sound?

The factual premise is true – the exact organic basis for schizophrenia remains poorly understood. However the conceptual premise is questionable. The problem is that *every disease* currently in our nosology was classified as a disease *prior* to its organic basis being discovered. The organic nature of diseases has only recently, in the last century, been elucidated. Hence, we would have to conclude that every disease was invented. But then it is hardly an objection against mental illness to say that they are mere inventions! And so the argument collapses.

But Szasz has a stronger version of this argument:

Most non-psychiatrists, and even many psychiatrists and laymen, recognize that cadavers can have diabetes and syphilis, but cannot have depression and schizophrenia; in other words, that disagreements and misbehaviours are just that, and not the symptoms of undemonstrated and undemonstrable lesions or processes in the dark recesses of the brain. . . . Instead of discovering new diseases, they [Kraepelin, Bleuler, Freud] extended, through psychiatry, the imagery, vocabulary, jurisdiction, and hence the territory of medicine to what were not, and are not, diseases.

(Szasz, 1979a, pp. 34–5)

Szasz reasons from the conceptual premise that if 'symptoms' are not caused by underlying lesions, then those 'symptoms' are not caused by a disease, and the factual premise that schizophrenic symptoms are not caused by an underlying lesion, to the conclusion that schizophrenia is not a disease. Let us look at this argument.

To judge whether the argument succeeds, we need to understand what 'lesions' are. On one reading, 'lesion' means 'bodily condition causing symptoms'. But if this is what it means, the

77

conceptual premise is trivially true – it amounts to the claim that if symptoms are not caused by conditions that cause symptoms, they are not caused by disease. But if symptoms are not caused by conditions that cause symptoms, they must have no causes. In which case it follows that they are not caused by disease either! But on this reading, the factual premise is false – it amounts to the claim that schizophrenic symptoms are not caused by conditions that cause symptoms – i.e. it amounts to the claim that schizophrenic symptoms have no causes at all! But we have no reason to believe that schizophrenic symptoms are uncaused – there is good evidence that the disorder is caused by genetic (Kety, Rosenthal and Wender, 1971) and social factors (Vaughn and Leff, 1976). Therefore, on this reading, the argument fails.

On another reading, 'lesion' means 'having the nature of a disease'. It is assumed here that all diseases share a similar explanatory nature in virtue of which they are diseases. But this is the essentialist fallacy, and so the conceptual premise is false. Diseases do not share an explanatory nature – some are infections, others cancers, some metabolic disturbances, etc. There is thus no single nature in virtue of which all these conditions are diseases (Reznek, 1987). We decide whether conditions like schizophrenia are diseases not on the basis of the nature of their causes, but on the basis of the undesirability of their effects. It is because schizophrenia has undesirable consequences irrespective of its nature that it is a disease. The factual premise amounts to the claim that schizophrenia has an explanatory nature different from all other diseases. This is a pretty wild claim and is probably false. Thus on this reading too the argument fails.

Finally, we can read 'lesion' as 'statistically abnormal condition'. On this reading, the conceptual premise seems plausible. If we looked beneath observable 'symptoms' and found normal conditions, this would undermine the claim that the 'symptoms' were due to disease. The disease of floating kidney was rejected because patients suffering from alleged symptoms of it were found *not* to have any abnormal underlying anatomy. But this is not the whole story – only if a (statistically) abnormal condition has undesirable consequences will it be pathological – a lesion.

Of course, Szasz wants to say more than that an abnormal condition is necessary for something to count as a disease. He wants to argue that diseases cannot be recognized as such until the underlying abnormality has been discovered. But this is manifestly not true. Most diseases have been so classified before the discovery of any underlying abnormality. For example, Parkinson's disease was accepted as a disease long before the physical basis for that condition was known. Only now do we know that Parkinson's disease is an abnormal process that destroys the brain nuclei known as the *substantia nigra*. Szasz wants to argue that Parkinson's disease was not recognized as a disease until the degeneration of *substantia nigra* was discovered, and that this discovery amounted to the discovery of the disease status of the condition. But this is absurd. It is more reasonable to argue that Parkinson's disease was always recognized as a disease, and that the discovery of the degeneration of the nuclei amounted only to the discovery of the physical basis for the disease (Roth and Kroll, 1986).

While the conceptual premise gives part of the story, the factual premise commits the *Organic Fallacy* – the fallacy of assuming that mental illnesses do not have underlying physical abnormalities. Szasz just assumes that we will not discover any underlying abnormality in schizophrenics' brains. But there is considerable evidence that schizophrenic 'symptoms' are in fact the product of underlying abnormalities. On post-mortem examination, it has been found that schizophrenics have an increased density of dopamine receptors in the meso-limbic part of the brain in comparison to normal controls (Owen *et al.*, 1978). In addition, other postmortem studies have revealed that schizophrenics have enlarged lateral ventricles and cell loss in the dominant para-hippocampal gyrus compared to normal controls (Brown *et al.*, 1986). The factual premise is false and the argument fails.

Szasz produces a more complex argument which purports to show that even if, as he considers unlikely, psychiatrists find a lesion underlying the behaviour of schizophrenics, this will not show that schizophrenia is a disease. He writes:

> The point I want to emphasize here is that each of these terms [like 'schizophrenia'] refers to behaviour, not disease; to disapproved conduct, not histopathological change.
>
> (Szasz, 1979, p. 10)

Depression is the name we give to a particular affective experience. Consider, then, the case of a person who does not feel depressed and whom, because he does not seem to act depressed, no one else considers to be depressed. Comes now the modern psychiatrist who says: 'You are wrong, this man is depressed. I know because I have found that he *has* the clinicopathological correlates of depression.' Without examining the validity or the invalidity of this claim, it seems to me reasonable to ask: When a psychiatrist who writes this way uses the word *depression*, does he mean the same thing people ordinarily mean when they say, for example, about someone who has just suffered a personal loss, that *he is depressed*? I think not. . . . If psychiatric researchers find something wrong with a particular person's brain, then they have demonstrated that the person has a brain disease; but if the person in question is not depressed, then the researchers have, in my opinion, not discovered depression without symptoms of depression – or, as they claim, asymptomatic depression as a discrete brain disease – but have only changed the meaning we usually attach to the word *depression*.

(Szasz, 1987, p. 90)

Szasz reasons from the conceptual premise that if some term refers to behaviour, then it cannot refer to the underlying causes of that behaviour, and the semantic premise that 'schizophrenia' refers to behaviour, to the conclusion that if any underlying cause for the behaviour is found, this will not be schizophrenia. Let us examine this argument.

The conceptual premise is uncontroversial and so I will focus on the semantic one. Here Szasz adopts a mistaken theory of the meaning of our terms. He assumes that disease terms have a meaning given by their clinical features (signs and symptoms) rather than having a meaning fixed by their reference. Gout has been recognized by pain and inflammation in the joints, commonly the first metacarpo-phalangeal joint. If we assume 'gout' means 'having such-and-such symptoms', we are forced to say that 'gout' now has a different meaning. Because of the existence of pseudo-gout – a distinct disease causing a similar clinical picture – we now define gout in terms of its underlying pathophysiology. On the other hand, if we assume that 'gout' refers to whatever process explains the characteristic symptoms, then we can argue that its meaning has not changed. We can then explain why we consider pseudo-gout to be a distinct disease – it is so because it has a different underlying pathophysiology. And we can explain why different signs (tophae) and symptoms (of renal failure) can also be part of gout because they are due to the same underlying pathophysiology.

Disease terms have a meaning fixed by their reference (Putnam, 1976). This has a number of advantages. First, we are not forced to say uncharitably that physicians in the past were talking about different entities. It is more reasonable to say that Sydenham was talking about gout but did not know its cause rather than that he was not talking about gout at all! Second, we can explain the identifications and distinctions we make among diseases. Gonorrhoea and syphilis were at one time thought to be forms of the same disease. This was largely a result of John Hunter's experiment of innoculating himself with pus from a patient with gonorrhoea. Unfortunately for him, the patient also had syphilis and he ended up with both diseases! We now regard them as distinct because each syndrome is due to a distinct underlying process. If disease terms refer to underlying processes, this explains why Hunter thought they were identical and why we now take them to be distinct. Similarly, we can explain why Wernicke's encephalopathy and Korsakoff's psychosis were classified together as cerebral beri-beri when they were found to be caused by the same underlying process.

Therefore, while it is true that schizophrenia has always been *identified* by abnormalities of behaviour, this does not mean that the term 'schizophrenia' *means* 'such-and-such abnormal behaviour'. Like 'gout', it makes sense to see the term as referring to the process explaining the behaviour by which it is identified. This is supported by the intuition that if we discover that some clinically different condition – e.g. autism – shares the identical underlying pathophysiology, we will conclude that it is a form of schizophrenia. This means that when we discover the neurological cause of schizophrenia, we *can* say we have discovered schizophrenia, rather than some different neurological disease. Therefore the semantic premise is false and the argument collapses.

The same point applies to depression. Szasz argues that 'depression' refers to a depressed mood, and that if some term refers to a mood state, it cannot refer to the underlying cause of that mood. From this he concludes that if the underlying cause of depressed mood is discovered, this cannot be the disease of depression. But I would argue that 'depression' does refer to the underlying process explaining low mood, and that if we found the identical process in other clinical conditions, like anxiety neurosis, we would conclude that these conditions are variants of depression.

Szasz has another argument to show that mental illnesses are very different from bodily diseases, and hence not diseases:

> How do we know that a person has an asymptomatic disease? By the signs the disease produces. . . . There are, and can be, only symptomatic mental illnesses; an asymptomatic mental illness is an oxymoron. How could a person who does not gamble suffer from pathological gambling? Or a person who does not drink alcohol suffer from alcoholism? Or a person who is never manic suffer from mania? Ironically, this fundamental conceptual identity between mental illness and mental symptom is tacitly acknowledged by the authors of DSM-III in their characterization of what counts (for them) as a mental disorder: 'In DSM-III each of the mental disorders is conceptualized as a clinically significant behavioural and psychological syndrome or pattern that occurs in an individual and that is typically associated with either a painful symptom (distress) or impairment in one or more important areas of functioning (disability).' Judged by these criteria, there can, in the absence of distress or disability, be no mental illness.
>
> (Szasz, 1987, p. 92)

Reconstructing the argument, Szasz reasons from one conceptual premise that if a condition cannot be asymptomatic, then it is not a disease, and another conceptual premise that mental illnesses cannot be asymptomatic, to the conclusion that mental illnesses are not diseases. This argument too depends on the idea that diseases are identified with organic changes – if they are, it does seem possible for them to be asymptomatic.

The first conceptual premise is true. If diseases are the processes that are responsible for signs and symptoms, then it becomes logically possible for a person to have such processes but for these processes not to have reached a stage where the person suffers from any signs or symptoms, or for other variables to intervene such that no signs or symptoms are manifested. Hence it is logically possible for there to be asymptomatic diseases. Obviously, if a process never causes any signs or symptoms, never causes any disability or distress, then it hardly qualifies as a disease. But this is not what the conceptual premise is claiming. All it claims is that there can be diseases that at some stage are asymptomatic, or in some people never reach the symptomatic level (while of course in others causing symptoms). Some cancers remain asymptomatic for long periods, and some tumours never become symptomatic and are incidental post-mortem findings.

But the second conceptual premise is false – mental illnesses can be asymptomatic. First, diseases like Alzheimer's disease, a mental illness in most people's books, can certainly be asymptomatic in its early stages. The disease is identified by certain changes in the brain, and at the early stages such changes may not produce any symptoms. Even in schizophrenia, the brain abnormalities are present prior to the development of symptoms (I owe this point to Paul Harrison). Hence there can be asymptomatic mental illnesses. In summary, then, these arguments fail because they incorrectly assume mental illnesses lack an organic basis.

THE MALFUNCTION FALLACY

Szasz sees psychiatrists as extending the concept of disease from its proper domain (of physical illness) to mental illnesses. He thinks that this extension is unjustified:

> The adjectives 'mental', 'emotional', and 'neurotic' are semantic strategies to codify – and, at the same time, to conceal – the differences between two classes of disabilities or 'problems' in meeting life: one consists of bodily diseases which, by impairing the functioning of the human body as a machine, create difficulties in social adaptation; the other consists of difficulties in social adaptation not attributable to a malfunctioning machinery but 'caused' rather by the purposes the machine was made to serve by those who 'built' it (e.g. parents, society), or by those who 'use' it (i.e. individuals).
>
> (Szasz, 1972, p. 54)

This contains a further argument. From the conceptual premise that if some disabilities are not caused by a malfunction, then they are not due to diseases, and the factual premise that the disabilities of hysteria are not caused by any malfunction, Szasz concludes that hysteria is not a disease – the disease of hysteria does not exist. Is this argument sound?

The conceptual premise commits the *Malfunction Fallacy* – the fallacy of assuming that a malfunction is a necessary condition for being a disease. It is possible for a bodily part or system to be incorporated into a species not because that part or system has a function, but by accident (Reznek, 1987). It is also possible that, although this part or system does not exert any impact on natural selection, it might have desirable effects for the individual. For example, it is possible that part of the right temporal lobe of our brain has no function, but is there as the accidental by-product of the fact that the opposing part in the left temporal lobe has a function and the fact that the body is symmetrical. Let us suppose that this part of the brain enables us to perceive and enjoy music. If this part of the brain were to be affected by a process (e.g. an infection) in such a way that we were unable to enjoy music, our lives would be severely impoverished, and we would be significantly disabled. In fact, it would be reasonable to conclude that this infection was a disease. But *ex hypothesi*, the infection does not cause a malfunction. Hence the conceptual premise is false.

The factual premise raises questions how we decide what are or are not malfunctions. Suppose a young woman with hysteria is not able to feel any sensation on her arm. This is not caused by any organic lesion, but by intolerable conflict which she resolves by becoming 'ill'. By describing the problem this way, we appear to have assumed that there is a malfunction. For it is reasonable to assume that the function of her sensory system is to enable her to perceive sensations. Thus when she fails to perceive any sensation, we can with good reason claim that her sensory system is malfunctioning. This conclusion seems to be supported by the discovery that sensory signals do not appear to reach the cerebral cortex in hysteria (Hernandez-Pion *et al.*, 1963).

But Szasz might object that by describing the hysterical anaes-thesia as the *inability* to feel, we beg the question that there is a malfunction. He might argue that it is one of the functions of the sensory system to allow itself to be damped down in this way. This would be like saying that it was one of the functions of the pain-perceiving apparatus to allow itself to be damped down by endogenous opiates called endorphins – this has the survival value of enabling the individual to concentrate on life-

and-death matters without distraction. Can the same argument apply to hysterical dissociation? Szasz would have to argue that appearing disabled might have biological advantages – it would inspire help from other members of the community and lead to one's needs being satisfied with little expenditure of energy.

By manipulating the altruism of the community, this 'ability' might have many advantages and might have been naturally selected. But whatever the merits of this debate, the conclusion still does not follow (because the conceptual premise is false). Even if the process of acquiring hysterical symptoms has a biological function, this does not mean that it is not a disease. Suppose we have evolved a system with a biological function that lowers our immunity in overcrowded conditions, thereby enabling us to become ill, to die, and thereby to reduce the overcrowding. Even though this system might have a function, we would view the process that lowered our immunity as a disease – having a function does not preclude a process from being a disease. Therefore, we cannot conclude that hysteria is not a disease. It might be the case that the 'ability' to acquire hysterical symptoms has biological advantages, but we judge that we are better off without such symptoms (just as we consider we are better off not lowering our immune systems). And hence we judge that the acquisition of hysterical symptoms is a disease. Thus the argument fails because it assumes that diseases are malfunctions.

THE COMPUTER FALLACY

Szasz has an interesting argument which purports to show that bodily disease and mental illness are so radically different that the disease status of mental illnesses is undermined:

> We may be dissatisfied with television for two quite different reasons: because our set does not work, or because we dislike the program we are receiving. Similarly, we may be dissatisfied with ourselves for two quite different reasons: because our body does not work (organic illness), or because we dislike our conduct (mental illness). How silly, wasteful, and destructive it would be if we would try to eliminate cigarette commercials from television by having TV repairmen work on our sets. How much more silly, wasteful, and destructive to try to eliminate phobias, and obsessions,

and delusions, and what not by having psychiatrists work on our brains (with drugs, electroshock, and lobotomy).

(Szasz, 1974a, p. 99)

Reconstructing this argument, Szasz reasons from the conceptual premise that if behaviour is due to a software/programming error, it is not due to a disease, and the factual premise that the behavioural manifestations of 'mental illnesses' are due to software/programming errors, to the conclusion that mental illnesses are not diseases.

Szasz tries to persuade us that there are two different sorts of causes for abnormal behaviour and suffering – hardware errors (organic disease) and software errors (so called 'mental illness'). The idea is that hardware errors are physical abnormalities of the nerves, while software errors occur when the nerves are intact (i.e. there is no disease) but simply programmed badly. The argument depends on the computer analogy. If a robot starts behaving in a self-destructive way, there are two different sorts of faults that might explain it. First, there might be something wrong with the machine (a fused wire), and second, the robot might have been programmed incorrectly. Only in the first case is the machine *malfunctioning*. There is no malfunctioning of the actual machine where the programme has been incorrectly written. And to use the analogy, only in the first case is the robot diseased. But is the argument valid?

The conceptual premise begs the question. It simply asserts that software errors are not diseases, while hardware ones are. But why should we arbitrarily restrict the term 'disease' to only *one* sort of fault in a system? Why should we decide that only *one* source of distress and disability counts as a disease and another not? As I have argued above, it does seem possible to 'programme' someone to have a disease. Because the autonomic nervous system can be conditioned, it is possible to train it to produce asthmatic attacks by contraction of bronchiolar muscles, or to train it to produce sustained high blood pressure by contracting arteriolar muscles, or to train it to produce excessive gastrointestinal motility leading to diarrhoea, etc. These conditions are diseases, but they are 'programme' errors. There is thus no reason to think that our concept of disease is conceptually tied to only 'hardware' faults.

The factual premise raises difficulties in applying the computer analogy to an organism. Here Szasz commits the *Computer Fallacy* – the fallacy of assuming the computer analogy applies to organisms. The problem in the case of organisms is that there is no way for us to make the distinction between the hard- and software, and if there is no way for us to make the distinction, any argument based on it must fail. To see why, let us return to the self-destructing robot. Suppose the robot is from Mars and we know nothing of its blue-print. We discover that a single wire connection is responsible for its self-destructive behaviour when in certain situations. Does this wire connection represent a hardware fault, or a software one (or, of course, no fault at all)? Since any programme will have to be realized by some physical state of the robot, there is no reason why the one wire connection cannot represent a certain programme. Without the blue-print, there is no way to tell which of these alternatives obtains.

In the case of the organism, the blue-print is precisely the thing that is missing. And hence, I would argue, the distinction collapses. Let me show why in principle it is impossible to decide whether something is a hardware or a software error. Suppose we discover that paranoid individuals have a certain genetic abnormality that produces an abnormal neuronal connection (wire connection). This unusual neuronal circuitry is responsible for making the paranoid more suspicious and more sensitive, and eventually leads the paranoiac to believe that others are persecuting him. Now is the abnormal circuitry a fault in the hardware, or a fault in the software? I do not think that we can decide. To 'programme' the human brain with this tendency and these beliefs, we would have to 'write' this abnormal circuitry into the brain. For there to be a fault in the hardware, there would also have to be this abnormal circuitry. In either case, there is the same state. In other words, it is impossible to decide what sort of fault there is. And if this is the case, then the distinction cannot apply to organisms, and the argument cannot even get off the ground. The argument fails, then, because the computer analogy fails.

THE OBJECTIVE FALLACY

Szasz has another argument against mental illness based on the putative difference between the norms of physical and mental health:

The concept of illness, whether bodily or mental, implies deviation from some clearly defined norm. In the case of physical illness, the norm is the structural and functional integrity of the human body. Thus, although the desirability of physical health, as such, is an ethical value, what health is can be stated in anatomical and physiological terms. What is the norm, deviation from which is regarded as mental illness? This question cannot be easily answered. But whatever this norm may be, we can be certain of only one thing: namely, that it must be stated in terms of psycho-social, ethical, and legal concepts.

(Szasz, 1974b, p. 15)

Szasz argues from the conceptual premise that if some condition is a genuine disease, then it must be defined in terms of departures from objective norms, and a semantic premise that mental illnesses are not defined in terms of departures from objective norms, to the conclusion that mental illnesses are not genuine diseases. Is this argument sound?

The argument turns on the interpretaion of 'objective norms'. On one interpretation, objective norms are statistically generated. Thus a blood pressure of 180/120 for a man of 21 departs from an objective norm because this blood pressure falls outside two standard deviations from the mean blood pressure for males of his age and species. Thus interpreted, the first premise is obviously true. However, on this reading, there is no reason to think that mental illnesses cannot be defined in terms of such norms. For example, we can objectively determine the average ability to remember things. If a group of people score below two standard deviations from this mean, we conclude they are probably demented. The mental illness of dementia can be defined with reference to these objective norms – and hence we cannot conclude that mental illnesses are not genuine illnesses.

On another interpretation, something is an objective norm if and only if it is entirely descriptive and value-free. On this reading, the semantic premise is true. The norms of mental health are not value-free. For example, chronic schizophrenia is a disease not only because the apathy it produces is statistically unusual, but because it is undesirable – being highly motivated is unusual but is not a disease because it is desirable. Norms of mental health are not entirely descriptive – they embody *value judgements*

(Engelhardt, 1975). But the second conceptual premise commits the *Objective Fallacy* – the fallacy of assuming that norms of physical health are value-free. Something is a disease only if it is an *undesirable* departure from a statistical norm. People who are abnormally fast, abnormally strong, abnormally good at excreting waste products, etc., all fall outside two standard deviations from some mean. But they are not diseased because the deviations are not *undesirable* departures from a statistical norm. The norms of physical health are also value-laden and not entirely descriptive, and thus the conceptual premise is false and the argument fails.

On a final interpretation, objective norms are culture-neutral – i.e. one can judge whether someone has deviated from some objective norm by reference to biology alone independent of any cultural norms or expectations. On this reading, the first premise is true. If we defined disease in terms of cultural norms, then it would turn out that epilepsy was not a disease in some cultures (because it was taken to give spiritual powers), or that intestinal infestation with worms was not a disease in other cultures (because it is so common). Since these conclusions seem absurd, it is necessary to regard genuine diseases as departures from objective or culture-neutral norms.

Szasz believes that the semantic premise is true because mental illness must in part be defined in terms of bizarre or inappropriate behaviour and delusions, both of which can only be defined in cultural terms. Someone has a delusion only if his belief is not culturally sanctioned. Some behaviour is bizarre only if it departs radically from culturally expected behaviour. Some emotional responses are inappropriate if they do not conform to cultural expectations. The belief that an ancestral spirit has placed a snake in one's abdomen which is eating one away is not a delusion in Zulu culture whereas it would be in ours. Going into a trance, talking in tongues, and thrashing wildly about is not bizarre behaviour in some third-world cultures, but it would be in ours. Public wailing and self-flagellation would not be an inappropriate emotional response to bereavement in Iranian culture, but it would in ours. Thus it appears that norms of mental health cannot be defined without reference to culture.

However, while we might *recognize* mental illness by reference to cultural norms, this does not mean that the mental illness itself can only be defined as a departure from culture-laden norms. While the delusions and bizarre behaviour of schizophrenics are recognized by deviations from culturally accepted beliefs and norms, this does not mean that the disease of schizophrenia is not a deviation from culture-free norms. We know already that the disorder, irrespective of culture, has underlying biological abnormalities that are culture-neutral. And we can explain why it looks like the disorder is not culture-neutral. If schizophrenia disrupts a person's ability to follow rules – whether rules of reasoning, language or cultural norms – we would expect to recognize it by culturally unsanctioned beliefs and culturally inappropriate behaviour. And we would expect the form that it takes to vary from one culture to the next. Thus we expect culturally neutral mental illness to appear in culture-laden forms. In any event, standard diagnostic schedules have been devised that enable us to recognize schizophrenia in any culture – its presentation is less culture-bound than this argument supposes (WHO, 1973). Therefore the semantic premise is false and the argument collapses.

Szasz uses another argument which also depends on the idea that mental illnesses are not objective and therefore mythical:

> When a person does something bad, like shoot the President, it is immediately assumed that he might be mad – madness being thought of as a 'disease' that might somehow 'explain' why he did it. When a person does something good, like discover a cure for a hitherto incurable disease, no similar assumption is made. I submit that no further evidence is needed to show that 'mental illness' is not the name of a biological condition whose nature awaits to be elucidated, but is the name of a concept whose purpose is to obscure the obvious.
>
> (Szasz, 1974a, p. 91)

Let us reconstruct this argument. From the conceptual premise that if a condition is classified as a disease only because it causes undesirable behaviour, then it is not a disease, and the factual premise that schizophrenia is classified as a disease only because it causes undesirable behaviour, Szasz draws the conclusion that schizophrenia is not a disease.

The factual premise is false. It is also because schizophrenia causes undesirable experiences, undesirable emotional changes, and undesirable disruption of our reasoning that we consider it to be a disease. The conceptual premise is also false and I will be arguing against it later. The distinction between disease and normality reflects precisely the important feature of the undesirability of disease. But if this is what the distinction consists in, then classifying one cause of behaviour as a disease because the resulting behaviour is undesirable and another as healthy because its consequent behaviour is desirable is perfectly legitimate. To take a non-behavioural example, the post-mortem examination of Einstein's brain revealed a proliferation of glial cells. Let us suppose that this was responsible for his genius. It is precisely because we consider genius desirable that we would not consider this abnormality to be a disease. Conversely, it is because we consider that mental retardation is undesirable that we classify phenylketonuria as a disease. Thus the argument collapses – mental illnesses are just as 'objective' as physical disease.

THE VOLUNTARY ARGUMENT

Szasz puts forward an alternative paradigm of mental illness:

> Physicochemical disorders of the body. . . are happenings or occurrences; developing carcinoma of the colon is an example. In contrast, so-called mental symptoms are doings or actions; for example, a hand-washing compulsion. Such 'mental symptoms' do not happen to one, but are (unconsciously) willed.
>
> (Szasz, 1972, pp. 155–6)

> I would state that so-called mental illnesses share only a single significant characteristic with bodily diseases: the sufferer or 'sick person' is more or less disabled from performing certain activities. The two differ in that mental illnesses can be understood only if they are viewed as occurrences that do not merely happen to a person but rather are brought about by him (perhaps unconsciously), and hence are of some value to him. This assumption is not necessary – indeed, it is unsupportable – in the typical cases of bodily illness.
>
> (Szasz, 1972, p. 72)

Let us reconstruct this argument. From the conceptual premise that if some behaviour is willed, it is not caused by disease, and the factual premise that hysterical behaviour is willed, Szasz concludes that hysteria is not a disease. Is this argument sound?

The conceptual premise requires some clarification. If it is claiming that some condition is not a disease if it can be acquired at will, then it is false. For one can give oneself lung cancer by smoking, or more obviously, one can give oneself gonorrhoea by sleeping with the wrong woman, and these are still diseases. If it is claiming that some condition is not a disease if it can be cured at will, then it is false. One can cure a urinary tract infection by a single act of consuming some antibiotics, but it remains a disease. To avoid these sorts of cases, we have to introduce the notion of direct acts of the will. It is clear that we can voluntarily give ourselves diseases and cure them, but these actions are achieved indirectly with the use of viruses and antibiotics – without these aids, the disease could not be voluntarily induced. States are under the direct control of the will if they can be induced without the mediation of any artificial devices. If conditions can be acquired and removed by direct acts of will, they will not be diseases. Suppose we could acquire a myopathy (muscle disorder causing weakness) by thinking of Fermat's last theorem, and remove it by thinking of Godel's theorem. It would be more like an action than a disease. It would be much like going red in the face from straining – this is not a symptom of a disease because it is under voluntary control. This is the *Voluntary Argument* and it supports the conceptual premise.

Is there any evidence that hysterical behaviour is intended? The fact that the patient's beliefs influence the nature of his symptoms supports the conclusion that the behaviour is intentional. If behaviour is the result of beliefs and desires, it qualifies as intentional, and in hysteria the patient's conception of illness *does* influence his behaviour. For example, cases of hysterical anaesthesia do not follow anatomically based patterns – no possible neurological damage can produce such a pattern. Rather, it is the patient's *conception* of how his body works that influences the pattern of anaesthesia – i.e. the patient's beliefs about what symptoms he would have if ill influences his actual symptoms. But this does not show that the behaviour of hysterical patients is intentional. Although a person's conception of illness influences the pattern of symptoms, this does not mean that the symptoms are the product of a belief *and* a desire – i.e. intentional. For it might be the case that there is no desire to use the illness in this way. It could be that anxiety about becoming ill in a suggestible person might cause the person to become ill (in a way compatible with the person's conception of the illness). In this way, the person's beliefs would influence what sort of symptoms he would acquire *without* it being the case that he desires (and therefore intends) to have those symptoms. Thus the discovery that the symptoms are in part a product of the patient's beliefs about illness does not show that hysterical symptoms are intentional.

However, there is considerable anecdotal evidence that hysterical symptoms are the product both of the patient's beliefs about illness *and* his desire to become ill. In all cases of hysteria, there is what Freud called 'secondary gain' – i.e. the situation is such that the patient has a good reason for wanting to be ill. For example, in the cases of hysterical disorders amongst soldiers at war, the gains of being ill are too obvious to mention. In fact, if there is no evidence of such gains from being ill – if there is no evidence that the patient has a good reason for wanting to be ill, the diagnosis is thrown into doubt (Gelder, Gath and Mayou, 1984, p. 98). This means that the behaviour of hysterics is probably intentional.

But it does not follow that hysteria is not a disease because the symptoms are not under voluntary control. While they are intended, they are not consciously intended and therefore are not voluntary. The best explanation appears to be that the experience of distress leads to development of the unconscious intention to communicate the need for help which then produces the hysterical disabilities. But there is nothing in this description that precludes us calling this process a disease process. Since it occurs outside the individual's awareness, he cannot reverse it by a simple act of will. And therefore the voluntary argument cannot be used to show it is not a disease. Nevertheless, Szasz has produced a powerful argument against the medical paradigm. If it can be shown that some 'mental illness' consists entirely in voluntary behaviour, and can be removed at will, then we will have shown that it is not a disease.

THE GAME-PLAYING PARADIGM

Szasz challenges many of the theses of the medical paradigm. For example, he challenges the teleological thesis – according to him, the goal of psychiatry is to control the behaviour of social deviants and not to cure so-called mental illness. He thereby disputes the neutrality thesis too – psychiatry is not neutral between ethical and political positions. In fact psychiatry is nothing but the disguised attempt by society to impose some moral and political order on deviant individuals. By inventing mental illness and treating deviants, psychiatry is able to impose these values on its population. In addition, he challenges the guardianship thesis – because so-called mental illness consists of the agent's free acts of will, there are no grounds for depriving him of his liberty. For the same reason, he rejects the responsibility thesis and regards all mentally ill patients as responsible for their actions. Finally, the universality thesis is also challenged. Because mental illnesses are invented, they will vary from culture to culture and from era to era depending on the needs of that culture or era to suppress dissent.

But most importantly, he challenges the causal thesis – he does not see the abnormal behaviour of so-called mentally ill patients as being caused by disease. Instead, he sees it as the voluntary and intentional communication of the request for help. In this way, mentally ill patients play a game that is governed by certain rules. Choosing the example of hysteria, he writes:

> 'Hysteria' refers to the expression and communication – chiefly by means of non-verbal, bodily signs – of a state of disability or 'illness'. The implicit aim of the communication is to secure help. If the problem of hysteria is framed in this way, it becomes logical to ask: Where did the idea originate that the rules of the game of life ought to be so defined that those who are weak, disabled, or ill should be helped? The first answer is that this is the game usually played in childhood. . . . The second general answer to this question is that the rules prescribing a help-giving attitude towards the weak derive from the dominant religious traditions of Western man. . . . In short, *men learn how to be 'mentally ill' by following (mainly) the rules of these two games.*
> (Szasz, 1972, p. 169)

Mental illness, then, is nothing other than rule-following and strategic behaviour. In this sense, the game-playing paradigm is identical to Laing's intentional paradigm. We will examine the challenge of this paradigm in a later chapter.

In summary, Szasz challenges the causal thesis of the medical paradigm – he argues that the symptoms of mental illness are really voluntary actions. But he fails to show that mental illnesses do not exist. His assumptions that they lack organic changes, that they are not objective, that they are not disturbances of some bodily part, that they cannot be asymptomatic, are all suspect. And his arguments that they are not malfunctions, or that they are merely software errors, are irrelevant. Because Szasz fails to understand physical disease, he makes errors about mental illness. However, he does show that if some behaviour is wholly voluntary, it is *ipso facto* not due to disease.

6

PETER SEDGWICK AND THE SOCIAL CONSTRUCTION OF ILLNESS

Peter Sedgwick was a psychologist, a tutor in psychiatry, and a politics lecturer. This range of interests led him to see psychiatry in its social and political context, and formulate arguments that strike at the heart of psychiatry.

INVENTING DISEASE

Sedgwick argues that disease is a social construction:

> If we examine the logical structure of our judgements of illness (whether 'physical' or 'mental') it may prove possible to reduce the distance between psychiatry and other streams of medicine by working in the reverse direction to Wootton: not by annexing psychopathology to the technical instrumentation of the natural sciences but by revealing the character, of illness and disease, health and treatment, as social constructions. For social constructions they most certainly are. All departments of nature below the level of mankind are exempt both from disease and from treatment – until man intervenes with his own human classifications of disease and treatment. The blight that strikes at corn or at potatoes is a *human invention*, for if man wished to cultivate parasites (rather than potatoes or corn) there would be no 'blight', but simply the necessary foddering of the parasite crop. Animals do not have diseases either, prior to the presence of man in a meaningful relation with them. . . . Outside the significances that man voluntarily attaches to certain conditions, *there are no illnesses or diseases in nature* . . . .The

fracture of the septuagenarian's femur has, within the world of nature, no more significance than the snapping of an autumn leaf from its twig: and the invasion of a human organism by cholera-germs carries with it no more the stamp of 'illness' than does the souring of milk by other forms of bacteria.

(Sedgwick, 1973, pp. 30–1)

From the conceptual premise that if something is a social construction, it does not exist independently of the construction, and the factual premise that disease is a social construction, Sedgwick draws the conclusion that no disease exists independently of the social construction. The threatening aspect of this argument is that if there are no diseases in nature (independently of the social construction), then it is up to every culture to draw the line between health and disease where it likes. Since the distinction is invented, there is no factual matter as to who is correct. And this seems to open up the way to the sort of psychiatric abuse that has occurred in Russia. But is this argument sound?

It turns on the notion of a 'social construction'. On one reading, something is a social construction if the concept denoting it is something constructed by society. The factual premise is true but trivial. Every concept occurs in a social language, and every language is constructed by society, and so diseases are no worse off than cows and people – if diseases are invented, then so are cows and people. However, the conceptual premise is false. It might be the case that all our concepts are the products of society, but this does not mean that the entities denoted by those concepts do not exist independently of the concepts. To suppose that objects for which we have no concept do not exist until we develop a category for them, thereby enabling them to spring into existence, is absurd. I do not have all the concepts of the different sorts of cloud that exist, but this does not mean that there are not many different sorts of cloud. We have not dreamed of the fundamental particles we will yet discover. But this does not mean that these particles do not now exist. Therefore, on this reading, the argument fails.

On another reading, a distinction is a social construction if it does not rest on any natural division between the objects discriminated. Thus the distinction between disease and health is a social construction if there is no natural division among conditions into those that are diseases and those that are not – i.e. if diseases do not constitute a natural kind. Being a natural kind consists in having an underlying nature that marks it off from other kinds (Reznek, 1987). Gold is a natural kind because all gold has the underlying nature of a particular atomic structure (containing 78 protons in the nucleus). Humans constitute a natural kind because all possess the underlying nature consisting of having 46 particular chromosomes. On the other hand, weeds do not constitute a natural kind because there is no underlying nature possessed by all weeds that marks them off from other plants and in virtue of which they are weeds. Similarly, precious stones do not constitute a kind because there is no underlying nature possessed by all precious stones which mark them off from semi-precious and worthless stones in virtue of which they are precious stones.

On this reading, the factual premise is true. Diseases do not as a matter of fact share a common nature that mark them off from normality. We have seen that while some have the nature of infections, there are some normal conditions like the colonization of our bowels that are also infections. We have also seen that there is often no sharp line between normality and illness – many diseases like essential hypertension differ only in degree from normality. But the point is still trivial, for *most* things are social constructions because they are not natural kinds. Cloud types are not natural kinds – there is no natural division between cumulus clouds and stratus clouds – the one shades imperceptibly into the other. Similarly, lakes do not constitute a natural kind – where a pond ends and a lake begins is an arbitrary matter. Similarly for mountains – where a hill ends and a mountain begins is a matter of convention. Diseases are in good company, and if they are invented, then so are mountains, lakes, clouds, and most other things besides. In any event, on this reading the conceptual premise is false. There is something absurd about the picture of the world where everything is as it is, but there are no clouds, lakes, mountains, etc., simply because concepts referring to these entities do not exist in the language! Thus the argument fails.

On another reading, something is a social construction if it is a distinction that is relative to human interest. Sedgwick believes that the disease status of a condition is relative to human interest – blight would be classified differently if we had an interest in culturing fungae rather than cultivating potatoes:

Plant-diseases may strike at tulips, turnips, or such prized features of the landscape as elm trees: but if some plant-species in which man had no interest (a desert grass, let us say) were to be attacked by a fungus or parasite, we should speak not of a disease, but merely of the competition between two species.

(Sedgwick, 1973, p. 31)

On this reading, the factual premise is true – diseases are social constructions because they reflect our interests (in avoiding discomfort, disability and death). But again the point is trivial. There are many distinctions that reflect our interests. Western culture does not distinguish different sorts of snow, or different sorts of rice, but Eskimos and Chinese make such distinctions because it is of importance to them. Virtually all of our concepts reflect some human interest or other – if we did not have such interest, we would not draw such distinctions. We do not have concepts of trees with 63 branches, or people with 143 freckles, or a river that makes 29 turns in its course, because we have no interest in such things. However, if we held certain religious beliefs in terms of which such things *were* of significance, then we *would* have such concepts in our language. On the other hand, it is because we have an interest in scoring a one hundred runs in cricket that we have the concept of a century, and it is because we have an interest in nourishing ourselves that we distinguish food from poison. Since a case can be made that all concepts reflect our interests, the factual premise makes a trivial point.

In any event, the conceptual premise is false. It is absurd to think that by developing an interest in something, we can create it! If I become interested in different sorts of snow, surely I do not bring into existence all those different types? If I become interested in species of beetle, surely I do not suddenly create thousands of different species of beetle? The conceptual premise is implausible. But more importantly, it is not the case that the disease status of conditions for all organisms is relative to *human* interest. Man has no interest in (the survival of) desert grass, but this does not imply that desert grass cannot be diseased. It is not true that organisms in which we take no interest or for which we have a positive dislike, cannot be diseased. For example, when there was a population explosion of the rabbits introduced to Australia, they became a pest. The problem was solved by introducing the myxoma virus into the population to decimate the rabbits (Dubos, 1965, p. 186). No one spoke of this as finding some 'foodstuff' for the myxoma virus! Instead it was spoken of as introducing the disease myxomatosis into the pestilent rabbit population. This manner of speaking would not be possible if human interest determined what was a disease. The rabbits were still diseased in spite of the fact that we had no interest in their survival. Desert grass and pestilent rabbits can have infectious diseases (even though we have no interest in their survival) because the infection does *them* harm.

Perhaps the concept of being a social construction has something to do with values. Sedgwick writes:

> A careful examination of the concept of illness in the human species will reveal the same value-impregnation, the same dependency of apparently descriptive, natural-scientific notions upon our norms of what is desirable. To complain of illness, or to ascribe illness to another person, is not to make a descriptive statement about physiology or anatomy.
>
> (Sedgwick, 1982, p. 31)

On a final reading, something is a social construction if the concept cannot be defined in descriptive terms alone. The factual premise is then true – disease is a social construction because it is not a descriptive notion. This idea will be defended later.

Is the conceptual premise true on this reading? If something is an expression of an evaluation, does it fail to exist independently of that evaluation? If there were no gardeners – no one to pass value judgements on the desirability or otherwise of certain plants, would there be no weeds? Yes. It is only because of the values of the gardener that there are such things as weeds. If he did not express any values about the different plants in his garden, then there would be more or less successful wild plants, but no weeds. Similarly for diseases. If there was no one to make value judgements on bodily conditions, there would be no diseases. Just as the weed-status of a plant varies with the values of the gardener, so the disease-status of a condition varies with the physician. We do not regard masturbation as an illness, but the puritanical sexual mores of the Victorians led them to classify it as a mental illness (Skultans, 1979). Small deformed feet were not considered pathological by the ancient Chinese, but we disagree.

Therefore the conceptual premise is true, and the argument succeeds.

This is a powerful argument against the medical paradigm of psychiatry. Whether something is a disease does not depend on factual matters like whether it is a malfunction, but on our values – the conceptual thesis is false. And if the concept of disease is not a purely descriptive concept, then diseases cannot be discovered by any scientific methodology – they are in a fundamental way the product of our values, and the identification thesis is false. Sedgwick thereby resurrects a whole host of problems that the medical paradigm had ostensibly solved.

THE SPECTRE OF CULTURAL RELATIVISM

Sedgwick's argument reopens the threat of cultural relativism:

> Social and cultural norms also plainly govern the varying perception, either as essentially 'normal', or as essentially 'pathological', of such characteristics as baldness, obesity, infestation by lice, venereal infection, and the presence of tonsils and foreskins among children. Once again it can be argued that these cultural variations apply only to marginal cases of sickness and health, that there are some physical or psychological conditions which are *ipso facto* symptomatic of illness, whether among Bushmen or Brobdignagians, duchesses or dockworkers. But there is no reason to believe that the 'standardized' varieties of human pathology operate according to a different logic from the 'culturally dependent' varieties. The existence of common or even universal illnesses testifies, not to the absence of a normative framework for judging pathology, but to the presence of very widespread norms.
>
> (Sedgwick, 1982, p. 33)

From the conceptual premise that if conditions taken to be diseases vary with cultural expectations as to what is normal, then disease judgements express cultural norms, and the empirical premise that the conditions taken to be diseases vary with cultural expectations as to what is normal, Sedgwick concludes that disease judgements express cultural norms. He then argues from the conceptual premise that if disease judgements express cultural norms, then what is a disease in one culture will not be a disease

in another culture, and the previous conclusion that disease judgements express cultural norms, to the conclusion that what is a
disease in one culture (with one set of norms) will not be a disease
in a another culture (with a different set of norms). Sedgwick's
argument appears to commit us to cultural relativism – a disease
in one culture is not a disease in another – which seems untenable.
Let us see whether the argument is sound.

The first conceptual premise is tautological and therefore true.
If judgements did not vary with cultural expectations of what
was normal, then those judgements would not express cultural
norms. The empirical premise is also true. For example, most of
a South American tribe have dyschromic spirochaetosis. This is
not only responsible for considerable morbidity and mortality,
but also for a rash of attractive rose-coloured spots. The disorder
is taken to be normal by the tribe, so much so that those without
it are excluded from marriage (Dubos, 1965, p. 54). Given their
cultural norms, the condition is not taken to be a disease.
Amongst some African tribes, infestation with worms is so
common as to be considered normal. Axillary odour, which is
uncommon among Japanese (but common among Caucasians)
was taken by the Japanese to be a disease they called 'osmidrosis
axillae' – a disease that warranted hospitalization and exemption
from the army (Wing, 1978, p. 16). What is normal in one culture
with one set of expectations of normality is taken to be a disease
in another culture with a different set of norms. Therefore the
argument succeeds.

But while the conclusion follows, we are not committed to
cultural relativism because the second conceptual premise is false.
While the conclusion entails that what is *judged* to be a disease in
one culture might not be *judged* to be a disease in another, this
does not mean that we have to accept the idea that one and the
same condition is both a disease (in one culture) and not a disease
(in another culture). There is a world of difference between the
claim that what is judged to be a disease in one culture is not
judged to be a disease in another culture with different norms,
and the claim that what is a disease in one culture is a disease in
another culture with different norms. The conceptual truth that
disease judgements express cultural norms only entails the former,
and not the latter. Let me explain.

It is one thing to accept that disease classifications vary from
culture to culture, but another thing to accept that disease status

varies from culture to culture. I might accept that other cultures have judged that various conditions, like dyschromic spirochaetosis, infestations, epilepsy, etc., are not diseases, while still accepting that they are diseases. Conversely, I might accept that other cultures have judged that various conditions, like axillary odour, masturbation, etc., are diseases, while still accepting that they are not. In other words, by accepting that disease *judgements* express cultural norms, I do not have to accept relativism – the thesis that what is a disease in one culture is not a disease in another. The second conceptual premise is false and the argument fails.

This is true even if the concept of disease is evaluative. When I judge that some condition is a disease, I *express* the value judgement that the condition is not desirable. If I observe that other cultures (with different cultural norms) judge normal conditions like masturbation to be diseases, I *describe* them as judging normal conditions to be diseases. If I were to say that in this culture, normal conditions *are* diseases, I would be committing myself to the claim that normal conditions are undesirable in this culture. But this is not something that I am doing. Similarly, I am not saying that dyschromic spirochaetosis is normal in the South American tribe – I believe that it is undesirable even there. If disease judgements express values in this way, I am not committed to cultural relativism. Disease judgements might express cultural norms, but this does not entail relativism.

In summary, Sedgwick has challenged the medical paradigm. He challenges the conceptual thesis, arguing that disease must be defined in value-laden terms. He thereby undermines the identification thesis, showing that scientific methodology can play no role in identifying diseases because they are invented rather than discovered. He reopens many of the problems ostensibly solved by the medical paradigm. If disease cannot be defined in value-free terms, we can no longer easily solve the problem of political abuse, the problem of value relativity, and the problem of disease status. We have seen, however, that we are not thereby committed to cultural relativism.

7

THOMAS SCHEFF
AND THE
LABELLING OF DEVIANCE

Labelling theory presents a powerful challenge to the medical paradigm by arguing that mental illnesses are only labels. Thomas Scheff, a professor of sociology, is the most eloquent of the labelling theorists, and we will examine his ideas here.

STRONG LABELLING THEORY

Scheff summarizes his labelling theory as follows:

> The theory of mental illness outlined. . . . is that the symptoms of mental illness can be considered to be violations of residual social norms, and that the careers of residual deviants can most effectively be considered as dependent on the societal reaction and the processes of role-playing.
>
> (Scheff, 1966, p. 169)

Every society has implicit rules ('residual norms') that govern 'normal' conduct. Each culture has a different set of rules which govern such conduct. In our culture, it is not appropriate to look at someone's left ear while conversing, while in other cultures it is not appropriate to look others in the eye. Frequently such rules will be broken for any number of reasons which are unimportant. But what is important is that sometimes such rule-breakers, usually coming from powerless sectors of society, are labelled with a 'mental illness' label and treated by society as mad. This societal reaction ensures that the rule-breaking does not spontaneously subside as it would if it went unlabelled. By being treated as mad, the labelled person is induced to act out the social stereotype of madness – he does not become ill, but simply plays at being mad:

104

When societal agents and persons around the deviant react to him uniformly in terms of the traditional stereotypes of insanity, his amorphous and unstructured rule-breaking tends to crystallize in conformity to these expectations, thus becoming similar to the behaviour of other deviants classified as mentally ill, and stable over time.

(Scheff, 1966, p. 82)

Scheff thinks that mad roles are much like sick roles whose content is determined by cultural stereotypes. In our culture, we tend to retire to bed and talk in a plaintive voice to signal that we are ill. In New Guinea, the sufferer retires from the community into his hut, strips himself naked, smears himself with ash, and talks in a quavering falsetto.

Such people are not merely suffering illness: they are performing it, thereby announcing both to themselves and to the community that they are sick and in need of care and attention. In New Guinea this is such a well-recognized form of behaviour that one is tempted to regard it as a formal ritual.

(Miller, 1978, p. 50)

The theory Scheff defends, which I call *Strong Labelling Theory* (SLT), challenges the medical paradigm. It contradicts the causal thesis, denying that mental illnesses exist, and denying that the form of mental illness is determined by the underlying disorder. Instead, abnormal behaviour is caused by labelling, and the content of the resultant behaviour is determined by the social stereotype to which the labelled individual is expected to conform.

Behind the challenge of the causal thesis lies an important argument. From the conceptual premise that if some behaviour is the expression of a social role, it is not a symptom of any mental illness, and the factual premise that the behaviour taken to characterize 'mental illness' is the enactment of a social role, Scheff concludes that the behaviour taken to characterize 'mental illness' is not a symptom of any mental illness. This is Scheff's argument against the causal thesis. It is similar to Szasz's argument that hysteria is not a mental illness but a role in a game. But Scheff's position is different:

Although Szasz states that role-playing by mental patients may not be completely or even mostly voluntary, the implication is that mental disorder be viewed as a strategy chosen

105

by the individual as a way of obtaining help from others. . . . The present discussion also uses the role-playing model to analyse mental disorder, but places more emphasis on the involuntary aspects of role-playing than Szasz.

(Scheff, 1966, p. 56)

Scheff differs from Szasz in seeing the adoption of the role as involuntary. But is his argument sound?

The conceptual premise sounds correct. It is part of the concept of disease that a disease is not something that is voluntarily performed, and if social roles are things that are voluntarily performed, then they cannot be diseases. I have argued that although we have some control over disease, we do not have the direct control that we have over moving our limbs. If we did have this sort of control over disease, this would itself undermine the disease status of the condition. If a mother found that her son was turning on a temperature and a rash at will when he had to go to school, and turning it off when he had holidays, she would probably think that he was being naughty rather than ill. She would see that he was not so much suffering from a disease but performing some clever trick.

This means that symptoms and voluntary actions are incompatible. Robert Kendell objects that the symptoms of many mental illnesses consist in voluntary actions. For example, one of the features of anorexia nervosa consists in behaviour such as dieting, over-exercising, and laxative abuse designed to lose weight. Here we have voluntary actions that are also symptoms of a disease (anorexia nervosa). But I think that this objection is ill-founded. The anorectic is either able to control her dieting behaviour or she is not. If she is not, then the behaviour is not fully voluntary, and can be a symptom. If she is, then the behaviour is not a symptom of the disorder – it is more like an adjustment to a symptom as in closing one's eyes if one has photophobia from migraine – i.e. a voluntary accommodation to symptoms of a disorder. In either case, the dietary behaviour is not simultaneously fully voluntary and a symptom of disease. (Anorexia is a disease because the anorectic attitude to weight cannot be voluntarily reversed, and because this leads to suffering and disability.) Therefore, if adopting a social role is a voluntary action, then the conceptual premise is correct – playing a role cannot be the symptom of a disease.

However, social roles can be adopted under different circumstances. At the one extreme, someone may wish to adopt the social role of a doctor and voluntarily assume that role. At the other extreme, we may subject someone to hypnotism and get him to play out a social role as a post-hypnotic suggestion. In the first case, the social role is something that the person voluntarily *does*, and so cannot be a symptom of an illness. In the second case, the person is induced into adopting the social role, and the social role is not something that he voluntarily does. Instead, his behaviour is more like a symptom than a voluntary action. Scheff argues that the adoption of the mentally ill role is something that happens to one rather than something one does. The adoption of the mad role happens 'involuntarily' without one having control of what is going on – and in this it is more like a symptom than an action. We can no longer use the argument that voluntary actions are not symptoms to argue that the adoption of a social role is not a mental illness. If the role is much like a symptom, then the process of adopting it is much like a disease process. To think otherwise is to be a victim once more of the essentialist fallacy. If this is so, then as far as mad roles are concerned, the conceptual premise is false.

The factual premise claims that the behaviour taken to characterize 'mental illness' is simply healthy agents who are playing social roles of madness. Scheff sees SLT as an empirical theory which stands and falls on the basis of evidence:

> The actual usefulness of a theory of mental disorder based on the societal reaction is largely an empirical question: to what extent is entry to and exit from the status of mental patient independent of behaviour or 'condition' of the patient?
>
> (Scheff, 1966, pp. 128–9)

Let us see what the evidence tells us.

First, SLT entails that behaviour does not become markedly deviant until the individual is labelled. This entails that we should find that people become more disturbed once they have been classified as mentally ill, and that before this occurs their behaviour should only be mildly disturbed. But this is clearly not born out by the facts (Yarrow *et al.*, 1955). Patients who eventually get labelled as mentally ill and admitted to psychiatric hospital have usually already been significantly disturbed. This undermines the idea that labelling *causes* such deviant behaviour and hence that mental illness is a social role. Instead, it looks more like such deviant behaviour is the consequence of an illness already well established by the time that the labelling doctors arrive on the scene.

Second, SLT entails that behaviour does not become chronically deviant until the individual is labelled. This means that mentally ill patients should not have been disturbed for long periods prior to being officially labelled. However, this is clearly false. Frequently, patients with major psychotic illnesses have been chronically disturbed but tolerated for up to years prior to being officially labelled (Johnstone *et al.*, 1986). This undermines the idea that it is the labelling that turns the usually transient deviant behaviour into the chronic career of the mentally ill patient.

Third, if labelling consolidates and enhances minor deviations from social roles, we would expect people admitted to hospital to become worse and to seldom warrant discharge. However, this is clearly false (Karmel, 1969). Patients do get better after spells in hospital, and are discharged with *fewer* symptoms or *less* deviant behaviour than they had when they were first admitted. But this would not occur if labelling reinforced and cemented the social role of mental illness. Therefore it is unlikely that mental illness is a social role. Rather, it looks like hospitals are places where mental illness gets treated.

Fourth, if labelling is the cause of 'mental illness', we should not find any other causes for such deviant behaviour apart from the induction into the social role. However, this is clearly not the case. For psychotic mental illnesses, genes play a major causal role. Adopted children of schizophrenic and manic-depressive parents are much more likely than adoptive controls to suffer from schizophrenia and manic-depression respectively (Kety, Rosenthal and Wender, 1971; Mendelwicz and Rainer, 1977). In addition, life stresses have been implicated in the causation of these disorders (Brown and Birley, 1968; Paykel, Myers and Dienelt, 1969). But this is not what the labelling theory predicts. These facts are more in keeping with an explanation in terms of mental illness.

Fifth, SLT entails that it is people in a powerless position in society that get labelled. This entails that more people from the lower social classes become mentally ill. Whether this is true depends on the mental illness in question. There is more depression in the lower social classes (Brown, Bhrolchaim and Harris, 1975). But while most schizophrenics come from the lower social classes, this is because of social drift – they start out being evenly spread throughout the social classes until the mental illness forces a social decline (Goldberg and Morrison, 1963). Even if we concede that mental illness is more common in the lower social classes, does this prove that mental illness is nothing else but a social role? No. For we could equally argue that the stresses attendant with living in the lower social classes cause there to be more mental illness there. And hence this fact does not prove the case that mental illness is merely a social role.

Sixth, SLT entails that mad people are simply playing a role. But if schizophrenia is simply a matter of role-playing, it is difficult to explain why the role has such a poor prognosis – why labelled individuals continue to play the role for life and are unable to function intellectually, occupationally, and socially at premorbid levels. To explain the long performance SLT might argue that the role itself is somehow addictive just like many maladaptive behaviours can be self-reinforcing. Many mental disorders can be seen as maladaptive behaviour that is self-reinforcing. For example, the compulsive hand-washing in obsessional neurosis reduces anxiety and so reinforces itself. The avoidance of supermarkets in agoraphobia reduces panic and so reinforces itself. The self-reinforcing properties of the behaviour ensure that the neurotic becomes stuck. But if this is what playing a role is like, then as I have argued above, it looks more like a disease than it does a performance. To explain the poor prognosis, SLT might argue that the role has certain harmful properties to the individual, undermining his intellect and social skills. But then the role is both harmful and something that the individual is unable to shake off – i.e. it counts as a disease. And then SLT ceases to count as a competitor to the medical paradigm!

Seventh, SLT entails that the manifestations of a mental illness are determined by social stereotypes (rather than by different mental illnesses). But if the manifestations are determined by social stereotypes, it is reasonable to expect that, in diverse cultures, the manifestations will be radically different. Just as the manifestations of other social roles vary, so we would expect the roles of mental illness to vary across cultures. As Scheff argues:

The idea that cultural stereotypes may stabilize residual rule-breaking and tend to produce uniformity in symptoms, is supported by cross-cultural studies of mental disorder. Although some observers insist there are underlying similarities, many agree that there are enormous differences in the manifest symptoms of stable mental disorder *between* societies, and great similarity *within* societies.

(Scheff, 1966, p. 83)

But is this true?

The major mental illnesses do not appear to vary like this from culture to culture. The International Pilot Study of Schizophrenia showed that by using a standardized diagnostic schedule, schizophrenia can be detected with a similar incidence in cultures as diverse as Russia, USA, Nigeria, Taiwan, Colombia and India (WHO, 1973). Schizophrenia can be recognized in all cultures and takes a remarkably similar form in all of them. The Eskimo of north-west Alaska recognize an illness called *nuthkavihak* which is manifested by such behaviour as talking to oneself, talking to people who patently do not exist, believing that others have been murdered when no one else believes it, believing oneself to be an animal, not eating, refusing to talk, drinking one's own urine, making strange grimaces, and becoming violent. The Yoruba of rural Nigeria also recognize a similar disorder called *were* which manifests itself by such phenomena as hearing voices and trying to get others to hear them, laughing inappropriately, talking either all the time or not at all, unprovoked violence, believing that there is an odour being continuously emitted from one's body, picking up sticks and leaves for no purpose apart from putting them in a pile, defecating in public and refusing to eat (Murphy, 1976). While clearly there are differences between these two forms of behaviour, they can clearly be recognized as schizophrenia – individuals suffer from auditory hallucinations (they hear voices which they take to be coming from reality), they develop delusions (odd fixed beliefs not in keeping with the rest of the culture and which appear to be unfounded in the culture's own terms), and their behaviour becomes bizarre and inappropriate. These similarities are not what one would expect if the content of mental illness is determined by cultural stereotypes. Instead, the evidence is more compatible with the idea that there is some mental illness that occurs in all cultures.

Of course we expect there to be *some* variations from culture to culture. We expect British schizophrenic patients to express their delusions in English, and French schizophrenic patients to express theirs in French. At a less trivial level, we expect that schizophrenics from cultures which believe in demons and spirits to express their delusions in terms of such agents, and schizophrenics in our culture to express their delusions in terms of the FBI, Martians, and laser beams. And this is what we find:

> A number of researchers in the field of cross-cultural psychiatry take the position that the underlying processes of insanity are the same everywhere but that their specific content varies between cultural groups. A psychotic person, it is thought, could not make use of the imagery of Christ if he had not been exposed to the Christian tradition and he could not elaborate ideas about the *wittiko* cannibalistic monster if not exposed to Cree and Ojibwa Indian traditions.
>
> (Murphy, 1976, p. 1023)

But this variation does not support SLT.

SLT entails that there will not be *any* similarity in mental disorder across cultures. Psychiatry makes a distinction between the *form* and the *content* of a symptom. For example, the form of a symptom might be that it is a delusion, and the content would be the actual belief held. If SLT were true, we would expect both the form and the content of any symptom to be determined by the varying cultural stereotypes of mental illness. But all we find is that the content varies. This is better explained by the medical paradigm. If a disorder like schizophrenia causes alien feelings and a sense of being out of control, then we expect the affected individual to understand this using concepts with which he is familiar. Hence we expect someone from a traditional Christian culture to express his delusions of control in terms of the Devil, someone from a modern culture to express his delusions of control in terms of mind waves and laser beams, and someone from a rural Indian culture to express his delusions of control in terms of possession by spirits. If a disease like schizophrenia causes disruption of normal belief formation, we expect people to develop delusions and for these to be expressed in concepts familiar to them. In fact, it would be inexplicable if a disease caused beliefs using concepts unknown to the individual. Any plausible disease theory would not see the disease process causing a specific belief like 'I am Jesus Christ'. It would assume the disturbance was at some deeper level, such as in belief formation, and we would therefore expect the beliefs to be expressed in culturally familiar terms. Hence the cross-cultural data support the medical paradigm over SLT.

It is open to SLT to argue that the reason why schizophrenia does occur in so many divergent cultures is because the stereotype of insanity is the same. Just as most cultures share the taboo against incest, so they share the same stereotype of madness. But we need an explanation for the sharing of any stereotype. In the case of the incest taboo, it has been argued that it is so widespread because it probably has a genetic basis. Some evidence for this comes from the fact that unrelated children growing up together in kibbutzim rarely intermarry. This suggests that they mistakenly think they are siblings and are genetically predisposed not to see each other as potential mates (Barash, 1981, p. 95). We have seen that schizophrenia has a genetic basis too, and so SLT gets the explanation the wrong way round. Schizophrenia is not the same across cultures because the same stereotype of madness occurs in all cultures. The stereotype of madness is the same across cultures because schizophrenia occurs in all cultures. On balance, therefore, the empirical evidence does not support the factual premise that the behaviour of so-called mentally ill patients is simply the expression of a social role. Therefore the argument collapses, and with it, SLT.

WEAK LABELLING THEORY

In spite of these arguments, a weaker version of labelling theory appears defensible for three reasons. First, some psychiatric disorders do seem to be bound to specific cultures. Second, it does appear that certain psychiatric disorders are transmitted in a way most compatible with the view that they are social roles. And third, it does appear that culture influences the course of psychiatric disorder. As a result of these facts, *Weak Labelling Theory* (WLT) becomes a plausible paradigm. WLT does not deny the causal thesis of the medical paradigm – it admits that there are such things as mental illnesses. However, it adds this causal ingredient – it argues that the form of mental illness is determined by cultural stereotypes. A distressed person will select a stereotype available to him from his culture in order to express his distress and call for help. In addition, this stereotype will influence the course of the illness. Let us examine these sources of support for WLT.

First, some psychiatric conditions are not universal. For example, anorexia nervosa is found almost entirely in western cultures (Brumberg, 1988). On the other hand, possession states – characterized by altered behaviour and speech and the accompanying belief that one is possessed by a spirit – are rarely found in western culture, but are common in third-world cultures (Varma, Srivastava and Sahay, 1970). Does this mean that adolescents in one culture adopt one stereotype while adolescents in a different culture adopt another? Or is it that one culture predisposes to getting one disorder rather than another?

If anorexia nervosa were a stereotype of illness that was adopted, then the adolescent in question would have to *know* that such a disorder exists before she 'became ill'. However, there are many cases where this is manifestly not the case – there is surprise and relief when an anorectic discovers she is not alone. Hence it seems more reasonable to see anorexia nervosa as a mental illness whose form is determined by the underlying disorder and not imposed by the adopting of the stereotype. In addition, WLT leaves certain facts unexplained – if a disorder is a matter of following some cultural stereotype, it is difficult to see how the disorder ever gets started!

The second support for WLT lies in the transmission of some disorders which appears to follow a pattern that would be inexplicable unless the disorder were a stereotype adopted to express distress. For example, the rapid rise of parasuicides over the last twenty years has reached epidemic proportions. It is difficult to explain this unless we assume some sort of 'copy-cat' or 'modelling' hypothesis – i.e. unless we assume that adolescents see others attempting suicide and come to do it too *because* of the stereotype. This is supported by the observation that parasuicides come from a subculture where such behaviour is common (Kreitman, Smith and Eng-Seong, 1970). It is also supported by evidence that an increase of parasuicides can follow the suicidal behaviour of soap opera characters (Phillips, 1982), and that more parasuicides than controls report recent contact with suicidal behaviour (Platt, 1990). Similarly, epidemic hysteria is probably trasmitted in this way (Wessely, 1987). Usually abnormal illness behaviour occurs in key individuals in a suggestible group. As a result of the perception of disturbance in the one individual, the suggestible individuals are struck down by a hysterical illness that takes the same form. Here the spread of disorder is best explained by the successive adoption of a stereotype of illness – the shape of the disorder is imposed by the stereotype.

Other disorders have had epidemic proportions. There was a rapid rise of shell shock in the First World War. This was in fact conversion hysteria – psychological distress manifesting itself as physical symptoms taking the form the patient believes they should. Shell shock had obvious advantages – it enabled the soldier to avoid almost certain death in the trenches, and its rise might be explained by the fact that it became a stereotype of illness which excused the soldier from duty. However, shell shock might more charitably be seen as having increased rapidly because of the sudden increase in massive amounts of stress at the time of war. Therefore, it may not have been transmitted by the adoption of stereotypes.

Perhaps the rise of myalgic encephalomyelitis (ME) in recent years is the consequence of the spread of a stereotype. ME is a condition that is presumed to follow viral infections and is characterized by fatigue and emotional disturbance (Behan *et al.*, 1985). One of the first epidemics of ME was at the Royal Free Hospital in 1955, and two psychiatrists comparing one hundred cases with one hundred matched controls concluded the disorder was hysterical (McEvedy and Beard, 1970). Some argue that the existence of sporadic cases undermines this diagnosis, but the sporadic cases could also have been influenced by the existence of the ME stereotype now available to our culture. Even today, people feel stigmatized by being diagnosed psychiatrically ill, and there is an incentive to have a more 'genuine' physical disorder like ME. This pressure comes from some medical quarters too which see psychiatric illnesses as 'feigned'. Perhaps people with affective disorders adopt the ME stereotype rather than admit they are depressed. This hypothesis is supported by the fact that depression leads to identical physical symptoms (Mathew, Weinnman and Mirabi, 1981), and that ME responds to anti-depressants (Taerk *et al.*, 1987). Of course, this hypothesis does not mean that ME is not a 'genuine' illness, or even that it is not a physical illness.

Not only can WLT explain how a disorder becomes widespread, but also why a disorder declines. Conversion hysteria has virtually disappeared from western cultures (Leff, 1988). WLT explains this by arguing that the disorder no longer brings a sympathetic response from the social environment because it is suspect not only among physicians but also among sophisticated persons generally (Veith, 1965). The fact that the stereotype has lost its popularity and appeal might be the best explanation why hysteria has virtually disappeared in the west.

The third support for WLT comes from the fact that the prognosis of a mental illness does appear to be influenced by the stereotype the culture has of that illness. The most convincing evidence for this comes from a study of a number of long-stay wards in different psychiatric hospitals (Wing and Brown, 1970). This found that negative symptoms of schizophrenia – social withdrawal, blunting of affect, poverty of speech, and amotivation – were correlated with poor social milieu as measured by the absence of personal possessions, the lack of day-time activities or occupational therapy, and the absence of hope for progress held out by the staff. In wards where there was an impoverished social milieu, patients were most likely to exhibit such features of schizophrenia – i.e. in wards which embodied the idea that schizophrenia is a chronic and hopeless condition, the illness was more severe. In wards that were more optimistic, operating with a less hopeless concept of the disorder, there were fewer negative features. As a result of their study, those hospitals with poor social milieus improved the ward conditions, and this led to an improvement in the negative symptoms. In addition, schizophrenia appears to have a different prognosis in different cultures (Sartorius *et al.*, 1986). In third-world countries, the prognosis is much better than in western industrialized nations. This might be related to the fact that in our culture, schizophrenia is seen as a hopeless disorder, while third-world cultures might have less negative conceptions.

There are two interpretations here. According to WLT, the prognosis of the disorder is influenced by the culture's concept of the disorder. If they conceive of it as having a poor prognosis, then this expectation will become a self-fulfilling prophecy, and conversely (Eisenberg, 1988). According to the medical paradigm, the prognosis of the disorder is influenced by such factors as rehabilitation practices – if schizophrenics are given structured daily activity, they will become less blunted and socially withdrawn. It is not so much the concept of the disorder but the way the disorder is treated that influences prognosis. But these two interpretations are not truly distinct. The concept of the disorder can hardly exert its effect on prognosis magically and unmediated by such factors as the way the disorder is treated. But if this is so, WLT is none other than the medical paradigm!

A sophisticated medical paradigm of mental illness accepts that social factors influence the course of schizophrenia. In fact, there are many such studies showing that the way a family behaves towards a schizophrenic influences his relapse rate (Vaughn and Leff, 1976). If they are overly critical, taking his illness to be an expression of his personality, and blaming him for it, then he is likely to relapse more often. If this social environment can be changed, then the relapse rate is thereby reduced (Leff *et al.*, 1982). But this does not prove that the medical paradigm is false. All it shows is that social factors influence the outcome of mental disease. In showing prognosis depends on social factors, one is not undermining the medical paradigm – one is just enriching it:

> Course and outcome are determined by the meaning which the culture ascribes to the disease, by the treatments to which the patient has access, and by the pathology of the disease process, itself an outcome of the interaction between the noxious agent(s) and host resistance.
>
> (Eisenberg, 1988, p. 5)

WLT might be correct, but it does not constitute a challenge to the medical paradigm.

VALUES AND RELATIVITY

There are other arguments that Scheff advances in an attempt to undermine the medical paradigm. As a sociologist, he sees values influencing classification, and argues that what is or is not a mental illness does not depend on any fact, but on our values:

> It appears that mental health is not a physical fact, but a value choice about what kind of men we *should* be and what kinds of values we should encourage in our society. Whether one selects a notion such as aggressive mastery of the environment, traditionally a western ideal, or the more inward-turning goal of self-actualization, which is more akin to traditional ideals in the Orient, is not dictated by the

natural order of stably reoccurring regularities in nature, but by human choice. Just as mental health may be seen as a value choice about how men should behave, so the symptoms of mental illness can be seen as value choices about how men should not behave.

(Scheff, 1975, p. 15)

It may be argued that the evaluation of conventional sanity as desirable and of 'mental disease', such as schizophrenia, as undesirable should be reversed. According to the conventional picture of schizophrenics, they would not have the competence or the motivation to napalm civilians, defoliate forests and rice crops, and to push the button that would destroy much of the world that we know. These activities are carried out by persons sane by conventional definition. . . . Current definitions of insanity mobilize society to locate, segregate, and 'treat' schizophrenics and other persons who are 'out of touch with reality'. Perhaps the time has come to consider the possibility that the reality that the so-called schizophrenics are out of touch with is so appalling that their view of the world may be more supportive to life than conventional reality.

(Scheff, 1975, pp. 18–19)

Scheff argues from one conceptual premise that if the disease status of a condition depends on our values and not on the facts, then the status of schizophrenia as an illness depends on our values, and another conceptual premise that the disease status of a condition depends on our values, to the conclusion that the status of schizophrenia as an illness depends on our values. The alarming aspect of this argument is that Scheff makes out a case for valuing schizophrenic behaviour over normal and ultimately much more self-destructive behaviour.

The first conceptual premise is a tautology and raises no objections. The second conceptual premise is also true and will be defended in detail later. Suppose there were a condition which we called geniitis. Like schizophrenia, it is a condition that runs in families, and which appears to be precipitated by important life events, but in this case, usually pleasant ones like getting married, or having children. The condition is characterized by increased energy, increased creativity, and increased productivity. There is a reduced need to sleep, and an increased pleasure in

117

living. These 'symptoms' cluster together to form a syndrome. The condition has a natural history too, and usually lasts for a few months before a return to more normal levels of functioning. However, once the individual has had one episode, he remains liable to suffer from further episodes.

Is geniitis a disease? It is characterized by a cluster of signs and symptoms, it has a determinate cause, and has its own natural history. But clearly it would never enter our heads to classify the 'syndrome' as a disease. And this because having such a condition is desirable. We value being able to be creative, productive, and enjoy life. And if some people, in virtue of their genetic constitutions, are capable of this, they are indeed fortunate. It is because of our *values* that we consider that geniitis is not a disease, while schizophrenia is. It is because we value being in touch with reality, being able to experience the full range of emotions, being able to think logically, and so on, that schizophrenia is judged to be a disease. Disease status depends on our values. Where Scheff goes wrong is to think that because we do not value war-mongering, we must also value dreadful diseases that make their sufferer unable to accomplish anything, including warfare. Valuation is not a transitive matter – one can value something without valuing all its causes.

Scheff has another argument that undermines the medical paradigm:

> It is suggested that there are culture-bound rules about thought and about reality. To illustrate rules about reality, consider the effort western parents go through to convince their children that dreams and nightmares are not real, but that disease germs are real. The child has seen and experienced nightmares but has never seen germs. After some struggle, the parents convince him. But in some traditional societies the scheme is reversed: the dreams are real, and the germs are not.
>
> (Scheff, 1975, p. 18)

Here Scheff reasons from a conceptual premise that if mental illness is attributed when there has been a deviation from social norms, e.g. of reality, then what counts as mental illness will vary from culture to culture, and the factual premise that mental illness is attributed when there has been a deviation from social norms, e.g. of reality, to the conclusion that what counts as

118

mental illness varies from culture to culture. We are pushed into relativism once we have granted the premises.

We have met this argument before. Mental illness is attributed on the basis of bizarre behaviour and bizarre beliefs, and what is bizarre will vary from culture to culture. If a man believes that his penis is disappearing, this will be considered a bizarre belief in our culture, but not in south-east Asia (Leff, 1988, p. 12). Similarly, the self-flagellation described at the beginning of the book is bizarre in our culture, but not in medieval culture. But relativism does not follow. There are two readings of the conclusion. On the first interpretation, the claim is that one and the same belief will count as evidence of mental illness in one culture but not in another. But this is perfectly innocent. If mental illness is something that interferes with normal belief acquisition, then it is reasonable to expect mentally ill individuals to acquire abnormal beliefs. What the illness causes is the deviation from the norm, and not a particular abnormal belief. Because cultures often do not share beliefs, then it is quite possible for a particular belief to be a sign of mental illness in one culture (because it is a deviation) but not a sign in another (because it is not a deviation).

On the second interpretation, the claim is that one and the same condition will be a mental illness in one culture but not in another. This claim is not trivial, but it does not follow from the premises. The sort of mental illness under discussion is not something that causes a particular belief, like the belief in spirit possession. It is far more likely that the mental illness disrupts normal belief acquisition, and causes a *deviation* from normal cultural beliefs. Thus, if one and the same *condition* were to occur in a different culture, we would not expect the condition to cause the same belief as it appears to do in the original culture, but instead we would expect it to cause a deviation from the different cultural beliefs. It is not the case that one and the same condition will be differently regarded in the two cultures – both cultures will regard it as a mental illness because in both cultures (because of the disruption of normal belief acquisition) there will be a *deviation* from cultural norms. Thus, on the first interpretation, the conclusion follows but is trivial. On the second interpretation, the conclusion is non-trivial, entailing a pernicious relativism that undermines the universality thesis of the medical paradigm. But on this interpretation, the conclusion does not follow. Hence the medical paradigm remains unthreatened.

In summary, Scheff has argued that the behaviour of so-called mentally ill patients is nothing more than the enactment of a social role. However, he fails to show mental illness does not exist. But he does show that cultural stereotypes of mental illness may shape its form, and influence its prognosis. This enriches rather than undermines the medical paradigm – stereotypes simply modify the expression and course of underlying psychopathology. This does not deny the existence of mental illness, and thus the medical paradigm remains unchallenged.

8

MICHEL FOUCAULT
AND THE
CIVILIZING OF MADNESS

Michel Foucault is an influential French thinker whose ideas span the fields of anthropology, psychiatry, history, philosophy, and psychoanalysis. His account of the history of psychiatry challenges the orthodox view and deserves to be examined.

STANDARD PSYCHIATRIC HISTORY

There is what one might call a standard account of the history of psychiatry, and it makes a number of assumptions: first, the *Universality Thesis* assumes that the mental illnesses now in existence were (by and large) always in existence – they are not the sort of things invented by psychiatrists in each era. Second, the *Semantic Identity Thesis* assumes that psychiatrists throughout the history of medicine are talking about the same things when they talk about mental illness in general, and specific diseases like hysteria and melancholia in particular. Third, the *Empiricist Thesis* assumes that knowledge is gained about the nature, causes, and effects of mental illnesses principally by observation – we observe a mental illness, and then go on to observe its underlying nature, its causes, and its effects. No theory is needed to assist us in this process. With these theses, the standard view purports to show that the history of psychiatry consists in the steady growth of knowledge. From the universality thesis, it follows that psychiatrists in all eras deal with the same things. From the semantic identity thesis, it follows that psychiatrists in all eras talk about the same things. From the empiricist thesis, it follows that psychiatrists in successive eras are able to observe more and more about those same mental illnesses, and formulate such observations in a common language so that all can see the progress made over time.

For example, standard psychiatric history argues that the same mental illness of hysteria has existed from Greek times to the present day. It also argues that the term 'hysteria' has the same meaning over time. And finally, that observations have increased our knowledge of hysteria. For example, we have discovered that hysteria is not due to a wandering womb. With these theses, the history of psychiatry can be seen as the steady growth of knowledge. Similarly, the standard view argues that manic-depression was first recognized by the Greeks – according to Hippocrates, the syndrome of depression, known as melan-cholia, was due to an excess of black bile. Thus while they were able to recognize part of manic-depression, and referred to it, they held false beliefs about it. The Hippocratic theory held sway for over a century. Willis, in the seventeenth century, first recognized that melancholia alternated with mania. While still referring to the same condition – manic-depression – he learned more about it, recognizing its biphasic nature. Finally, in this century, we have observed that manic-depression has a genetic cause, and can be treated with Lithium salts. This steady growth of knowledge follows from the assumptions that manic-depression has always existed, that successive generations have referred to it, and that observations have led to more and more knowledge about it.

According to this view of history, the central motivating force of psychiatrists is first and foremost the desire to help the mentally ill, and serving this aim is the quest for knowledge – the best guarantee of serving the patient is knowing the illness. Thus the standard history of psychiatry is at a stroke humane, liberal, and progressive. It is humane because the aim of psychiatry has always been the treatment of the mentally ill, it is liberal because it has not aimed at controlling and repressing those who are different, and it is progressive because knowledge is gradually acquired.

FOUCAULDIAN HISTORY

This view of history has not gone unchallenged. In *Madness and Civilization*, Foucault describes the history of attitudes towards mental illness from the Middle Ages till the birth of the Asylum in the late eighteenth century. On his account, the first significant event in this story is the emptying of the leprosaria at the end of the Middle Ages. This, according to Foucault, left society without someone to fill the role that lepers had played:

> What doubtless remained longer than leprosy, and would persist when the lazar-houses had been empty for years, were the values and images attached to the figure of the leper as well as the meaning of exclusion, the social importance of that insistent and fearful figure which was not driven off without first being inscribed within a sacred circle. . . . Poor vagabonds, criminals, and 'deranged minds' would take the part played by the leper, and we shall see what salvation was expected from this exclusion, for them and for those who excluded them as well.
>
> (Foucault, 1971, pp. 6–7)

Foucault argues that lepers were excluded not because of fear of contagion but because they fulfilled the roles for society as objects of fear and hatred and as a model of how not to behave.

The next important event in this story is the Great Confinement, starting with the foundation of *l'Hôpital Général* of Paris in 1656, largely in response to economic forces:

> The classical age used confinement in an equivocal manner, making it play a double role: to absorb unemployment, or at least eliminate its more visible social effects, and to control costs when they seemed likely to become too high; to act alternately on the manpower market and on the cost of production.
>
> (Foucault, 1971, p. 54)

Instead of being ferried from port to port in 'ships of fools', madmen came to be classified along with the idle, the libertines, the vagabonds, and incarcerated together with them.

Foucault is at pains to argue that this implies that madmen were not classified as distinct from the other people confined:

> To inhabit the reaches long since abandoned by the lepers, they chose a group that to our eyes is strangely mixed and confused. But what is for us merely an undifferentiated

sensibility must have been, for those living in the classical age, a clearly articulated perception.

(Foucault, 1971, p. 45)

This 'clearly articulated perception' saw madness as a species of disordered mores and conduct – of unreason. Housing madmen along with criminals supposedly laid the foundation for classifying any deviant behaviour as due to mental illness. We are led to believe that the origins of the repressive psychiatric role of procuring social control begins here.

The next significant event in the history of psychiatry is the 'liberation' of the insane at the end of the eighteenth century by a Quaker reformer, William Tuke, who built an asylum specially for them outside York, and by a medical reformer, Phillippe Pinel in France, who unchained the 'ferocious madmen'. But far from this being a humanitarian gesture, Foucault argues that it was motivated by the desire to spare the other internees the trauma of being confined along with madmen:

> The great reform movement that developed in the second half of the eighteenth century originated in the effort to reduce contamination by destroying impurities and vapors, abating fermentations, preventing evil and disease from tainting the air and spreading their contagion in the atmosphere of the cities. . . . The ideal was an asylum which, while preserving its essential functions, would be so organized that the evil could vegetate there without ever spreading; an asylum where unreason would be entirely contained and offered as a spectacle, without threatening the spectators; where it would have all the powers of example and none of the risks of contagion.
>
> (Foucault, 1971, pp. 206–7)

It was this act that cast psychiatrists into the role of protectors of society, and the suggestion is that psychiatry is committed to securing the status quo.

It was in the asylum that mental illness was first recognized. Whereas before, madness had been conceived of as a physical disturbance, now it was seen as a psychological one requiring moral treatment:

> In the classical period, it is futile to try to distinguish physical therapeutics from psychological medications, for the

simple reason that psychology did not exist. When the consumption of bitters was prescribed, for example, it was not a question of physical treatment, since it was the soul as well as the body that was to be scoured; when the simple life of a laborer was prescribed for a melancholic, when the comedy of his delirium was acted out before him, this was not a psychological intervention, since the movement of the spirits in the nerves, the density of the humors were principally involved.

(Foucault, 1971, p. 197)

In other words, Foucault identifies the birth of psychiatry exclusively with the beginnings of a psychological or moral approach to treatment. Far from liberating the mentally ill, the new reformers had embarked on a new form of social control:

We must therefore re-evaluate the meanings assigned to Tuke's work: liberation of the insane, abolition of constraint, constitution of a human milieu – these are only justifications. The real operations were different. In fact Tuke created an asylum where he substituted for the free terror of madness the shifting anguish of responsibility; fear no longer reigned on the other side of the prison gates – it now raged under the seals of conscience.

(Foucault, 1971, p. 247)

In short, Foucault claims that 'the absence of constraint in nineteenth century asylum is not unreason liberated, but madness long since mastered'. He argues that the moral managers are not doing what they claim to be doing.

While I concede that my account is an over-simplification, Foucault sets out to demonstrate a number of theses: first, that the aims of those dealing with madness throughout history have not always been humanitarian – frequently, the goal has been social control. Second, that madness has not occupied centre stage in the story – instead, it has been society and its protection that has been central. Third, that conditions spoken about by each era are constituted by the conceptual framework through which those conditions are perceived, and hence that it is not the case that when one era talks about madness, it is talking about the same thing as another era with a different conceptual framework. And fourth, that psychiatry was born only when it was recognized

125

that madness was a mental rather than a physical illness – when it was seen as amenable to moral or psychological treatment rather than physical cures.

I have not the space to explore the history of psychiatry in full, but a number of replies must be made. First, as a historical account, it is sadly wanting. For example, we are given no evidence that there ever existed such 'ships of fools':

> There is no evidence that any actual ships of fools put to sea with groups of the mentally ill in their indefinite custody. It seems probable that individual lunatics were sometimes transported away from towns into which they had wandered by a variety of means and that these occasionally included ships. There is some evidence that in the fourteenth and fifteenth centuries, such burdensome persons were returned to the town or parish from whence they had come and which was responsible for their care.
>
> (Maher and Maher, 1982, p. 760)

In addition, Foucault argues that the mental asylum was created at the end of the eighteenth century. But this gets the history of psychiatric institutions wrong. As William Parry-Jones has shown, institutional care for the insane was provided on a wide scale throughout the eighteenth century. There were many private madhouses for both private patients and pauper lunatics. Thus the nineteenth century did not usher in the beginning of institutional care for the insane – it was already there a century before (Parry-Jones, 1972). As a piece of history, Foucault's work is highly suspect.

Second, Foucault places no weight on the professed intentions and explanations of the historical figures themselves. Instead, he imposes his own motives. For example, Foucault sees industrial therapy as an attempt to bring the price of labour down, and Pinel's own view in 1806 is ignored:

> I am very sure that few lunatics, even in their most furious state, ought to be without some active occupation.
>
> (Pinel, 1962, p. 216)

As we have rediscovered, the single most important rehabilitating factor in chronic schizophrenia is structured daily activity (Wing and Brown, 1970). It is reasonable to infer that Pinel thought the same. Foucault imposes his own motives on Pinel and we are given no reason not to take Pinel at his word.

Third, Foucault assumes that the history of the development of the psychiatric institution is identical to the evolution of psychiatric intervention in madness. But the history of a medical approach to madness is much older. Ever since Hippocrates, abnormal behaviour has been seen as a medical or psychiatric illness and treated in a medical way. Hippocrates saw all disease as the consequence of imbalances in bodily humours, and low mood was seen as the consequence of an excess of black bile. Such a condition was treated by agents thought to reduce black bile. In addition, even in medieval times, physicians like Paul of Aegina saw depression as a disease of the brain and recommended medical treatment such as purgings (Jackson, 1986, p. 59). Thus it would be false to identify the beginning of psychiatric treatment with the birth of the psychiatric institution.

Fourth, Foucault sees the aims of psychiatry as being far less humanitarian, thereby challenging standard psychiatric history. While it must be conceded that the insane were first incarcerated (with criminals and paupers) as a measure of achieving social control, this does not mean that psychiatric treatment is synonymous with measures of social control. While there have been many cases throughout the history of psychiatry where psychiatric diagnosis has been used to achieve social control, this again does not prove Foucault's point. We have seen that Soviet psychiatry diagnosed political dissidents as suffering from sluggish schizophrenia because of their 'manic reformism' and 'conviction of rightness'. And in the slave-owning society of the Southern States of America, Dr Samuel Cartwright discovered a number of diseases afflicting slaves. There was drapetomania, the disease making slaves run away, and dysaesthesia aethiopis, the disease making them destroy their master's property (Cartwright, 1851). As a result of these illnesses, slaves were treated by being anointed with oil and by having this 'slapped' into their skins with leather straps! But these few examples do not prove that all psychiatric diagnosis aims at achieving social control.

Most psychiatric illnesses cause more suffering to the affected person than a challenge to the stability of society. Those suffering with depression or schizophrenia are hardly going to rock the foundations of society. On the contrary, it is more likely that mental health is needed to constitute a threat to society. And hence it is difficult to sustain this thesis about psychiatric diagnosis.

Fifth, Foucault erroneously assumes that psychiatry is committed to seeing abnormal behaviour in psychological terms, and to psychological rather than physical treatments. But psychiatry has never been committed to such a dualism. For example, when Alois Alzheimer discovered at the turn of the twentieth century that dementia has a physical basis in the brain, he did not declare that he had discovered that dementia was no longer a psychiatric disorder. In spite of its neurological basis, dementia remains a psychiatric disturbance treated by psychiatrists. Even Freud, who discovered that physical symptoms like hysterical paralyses had psychological causes, did not deny that these psychological processes were in reality physical ones: 'For the psychical field, the biological field does in fact play the part of the underlying bedrock' (Freud, 1950, p. 342). And psychiatry has never been committed only to psychological treatments. Melancholia has been treated by physical means such as purging and blood-letting since the days of Hippocrates (Jackson, 1986, p. 31), and continues to be treated today by such physical treatments as ECT and psychosurgery.

Finally, Foucault undermines the orthodox conception of psychiatric history by undermining the empiricist thesis:

> Certainly Willis's methods are of great interest, chiefly in this particular: the transition from one affection to the other is seen not as a phenomenon of observation for which it was then a matter of discovering the explanation, but rather as the consequence of a profound natural affinity which was of the order of their secret nature. Willis does not cite a single case of alternation which he had occasion to observe; what he first discovered was an internal relation which engendered strange metamorphoses.
>
> (Foucault, 1971, p. 131)

Often it is not observation that leads to progress in our knowledge – it is advances in theory. What appears to come first in the history of psychiatry is theory – the alternation of mania and depression followed from theory rather than observation. Only after theory does observation appear to play a role, contrary to the empiricist thesis (Popper, 1963).

And because theory comes first, he argues that particular disease entities like melancholia are defined not in terms of their observable symptoms, but in terms of their theoretical basis:

> Now this clear and coherent syndrome was designated by a word that implied an entire causal system, that of melancholia: 'I beg you to regard closely the thoughts of melancholics, their words, visions, actions, and you will discover how all their senses are depraved by a melancholic humor spread through their brain'.
>
> (Foucault, 1971, p. 118)

In other words, Foucault argues that something is not melancholia because it consists of certain observable symptoms, but because it has a particular theoretical pathology – the excess of black bile. This means that on one theoretical definition of melancholia, seizures can become symptoms because these are seen as the consequence of an excess of black bile. While on another definition, mania can become symptoms because this is seen as the consequence of the dynamics of animal spirits. But if mental illnesses are defined and identified in terms of the different theories that explain them, then two different theories cannot be talking about the same thing when they talk about some mental illness. And this means that we cannot say that different eras (with different theories) *are* referring to the same thing and learning more about it. Foucault's argument purports to undermine the semantic identity thesis and with it standard psychiatric history.

Foucault is right to argue that empiricism is dead. Psychiatry cannot make any progress without first elaborating theories and exposing them to empirical test – observation without theory is blind. When psychiatry tries to be theory-free, it leads to absurd results. According to the American diagnostic system (DSM III-R), schizophrenia is defined in terms of hallucinations, delusions, thought disorder and disturbance of affect of at least six months duration, while schizophreniform disorder is defined in terms of the same symptoms but of less than six months duration. So one night a patient goes to sleep with schizophreniform disorder and wakes up with schizophrenia!

But even if empiricism is dead, this does not mean that no two theories can talk about the same thing. We need to make a distinction between meaning and reference. It might be argued that Hippocrates meant something different by 'melancholia' than is meant by the term as used by DSM III-R today, simply because

Hippocrates would not have regarded something as melancholia unless it was due to an excess of black bile, while DSM III-R does! But this does not mean that they are not referring to the same thing. They are both referring to patients who complain of being miserable, of loss of appetite, weight, energy, and libido, of poor sleep, of agitation, of suicidal ideas, and who are slowed up mentally and physically. While it might be conceded that no description is theory-free, and hence that this description is itself theory-laden, what seems important is that it is a description that is *neutral* between both the Hippocratic theory and current psychiatric theory. And if it is neutral between them, then both can agree that this is what they are talking about and that they are indeed talking about the same thing (but formulating different theories about its underlying nature). Thus while it is true that psychiatry, like other sciences, does not proceed in an empiricist manner, this does not mean that the history of psychiatry cannot be seen as the progressive, albeit frequently unsteady, accumulation of knowledge about the same things.

In summary, while Foucault has provided an alternative history of psychiatry, it is one with many flaws. He is often inaccurate, and all too commonly imposes his own interpretation on events to fit with his own view of psychiatry as an instrument for social control. He makes unwarranted assumptions about the nature of psychiatry, namely, that it is concerned with conditions amenable to psychological treatment, and he erroneously assumes that the history of psychiatry is to be identified with the history of its institutions. While he does show that standard psychiatric history is wrong, this is not as pernicious as it first seems. His demonstration that empiricism is dead and that theory precedes observation does not mean that different theories cannot be about the same thing, and does not mean that successive theories cannot accumulate knowledge about the same thing. It simply means that we have to give a more sophisticated account of the growth of psychiatric knowledge.

9

PARADIGMS OF MENTAL ILLNESS

It is time to look at alternative paradigms of mental illness as no paradigm can be properly evaluated in isolation from its competitors. I will concentrate on three questions. First, whether any competing theory is a paradigm. Second, whether that theory constitutes a distinct paradigm. And third, whether the balance of evidence supports that paradigm. This is relevant to understanding psychiatry which, as a branch of medicine, appears committed to the medical paradigm.

A TAXONOMY OF PARADIGMS

The medical paradigm argues that abnormal behaviour is caused by disease. It also assumes that disease consists of a malfunction, and that having a disease entitles one to enter the sick role. There are other assumptions of course, but these are central.

The *Psychodynamic Paradigm* challenges the medical paradigm by arguing that there are no mental illnesses:

> Most mental disorder, according to the psychodynamic model, involves disturbed functioning even though all parts of the body are in working order. The disturbed functioning is not an illness, but more a conflict between different levels of functioning.
>
> (Tyrer and Steinberg, 1987, p. 33)

Each psychodynamic theory postulates that the psyche has a certain structure, with each part having its own function, and with conflict between these parts producing the 'symptoms'. Such theories usually share a number of assumptions: first, that symptoms have their origin in past experiences. Second, that these past experiences generate intrapsychic conflict. And third, that this conflict leads to the symptoms being unconsciously motivated. Let us briefly examine this paradigm.

The psychodynamic paradigm *cannot* deny that there are mental illnesses. It is self-contradictory to argue that there is no malfunction when the functioning of one part interferes with the functioning of another. In Freud's theory, the function of the Id is to satisfy its desires, the function of the Ego is to adapt to external reality, and the function of the Superego is to obey social norms. When these mental subsystems are in conflict, one of them will inevitably malfunction. If the Superego clashes with the Id, the satisfaction of desires will have to be accomplished without the Ego knowing what is going on – i.e. with the Ego being out of touch with reality or malfunctioning. If the Id clashes with the Ego, the desires will have to be satisfied in a form that the Ego cannot recognize. But if this is achieved, the Ego will be out of touch with what is going on and malfunctioning. Thus there is very little difference between the psychodynamic paradigm and the medical paradigm – both assume that symptoms are generated by a malfunction. Because the psychodynamic paradigm accepts there are processes producing malfunctions – i.e. diseases – it does not conflict with the medical paradigm. It is in fact a disease theory within the medical paradigm.

We cannot argue that the two paradigms are distinct because the medical paradigm postulates that symptoms are generated by certain physiological (neurobiological) processes while the psychodynamic paradigm postulates that symptoms are caused by psychological processes. This difference is simply a difference of the level with which the process is described. One can describe the way a car works in terms of systems – one system will deliver the fuel, another the air, one will deliver a spark, etc. Or one can describe how the car works in terms of describing the actual physical bits of the engine, not as different functional units, but as bits of metal, wires, etc. These two descriptions look superficially like they have nothing in common. But as soon as we identify the system that delivers the sparks with the spark plugs, etc., we see that the two descriptions are of the same thing but at different levels. If the Ego were identified with the dominant cerebral hemisphere, the Id with the non-dominant hemisphere, etc., this would show that the psychodynamic paradigm is not a distinct theory from the medical paradigm.

Let me give a more fine-grained illustration. Let us suppose we are trying to explain why a man who has been bereaved has become manic – i.e. euphoric, over-active, and grandiose. The medical paradigm argues that the stress of the bereavement causes over-activity of the nor-adrenergic neurones of the limbic system. On the other hand, the psychodynamic explanation argues that this loss awakes the memory of an early abandonment, that this is too painful for the person to acknowledge, and that he evades it by forming grand plans, convincing himself he is fine, and embarking upon ceaseless activity – i.e. adopting the 'manic defence'. The discovery that the nor-adrenergic neurones of the limbic system *are* over-active in mania would not show the psychodynamic paradigm is false. If the symptoms are due to a 'manic defence', there will be a neurological mechanism for this which will consist in some abnormal – because the manic defence is unusual – process in the brain. The psychodynamic paradigm can argue that the over-activity of the nor-adrenergic neurones is none other than the operation of this manic defence mechanism. But this means that the psychodynamic paradigm entails that those who have the manic defence have some abnormal process producing some malfunction (of the ego) – i.e. have a disease. The psychodynamic paradigm is a disease theory, and far from contradicting the medical paradigm, it *entails* it!

The two paradigms still appear to conflict. In the example above, the psychodynamic paradigm entails that there should be more traumatic early experiences in those with mania as compared to normal controls, while the medical paradigm assumes that there are likely to be biological causes for mania such as genetic factors. If we discover that mania does run in families, and that traumatic early experiences are not more common in such individuals as compared to normal individuals, this will be evidence that the medical paradigm is true and the psychodynamic paradigm is false. But this only means that one species of disease theory is false. Because the psychodynamic paradigm is a disease theory, its truth does not undermine the medical paradigm – it is simply one theory *within* the medical paradigm.

I have argued that the medical paradigm entails that those who are diseased are entitled to enter the sick role – they are exempted from responsibility for their illness and their normal duties, and expected to want to get well and to seek help. In addition, if the illness undermines their competence to consent, psychiatrists are entitled to treat the person against his will. In contrast, the psychodynamic paradigm allows those who are disturbed to enter the 'psych' role. Someone in the 'psych' role is not usually exempt from his normal duties, is sometimes held responsible for not getting better, may not be expected to want to get well, and is seldom treated against his will (Siegler and Osmond, 1980, p. 46).

However, we must guard against seeing the medical paradigm committed to an unsophisticated entitlement thesis. First, not all diseases entitle one to all the benefits of the sick role. Athlete's foot does not exempt one from social responsibilities and duties. Second, the patient is frequently regarded as (partially) responsible for his illness – a man with ischaemic heart disease or lung cancer is frequently to blame for his illness because of his refusal to give up smoking. He may also be partly responsible for his failure to get better – e.g. by failing to comply with medication. And third, it is acknowledged that being sick has such advantages that many might not find the sick role undesirable. There are thus fewer differences between these two roles than is first apparent.

The psychodynamic paradigm is ostensibly committed to the scientific method, and on this score, does not conflict with the medical paradigm:

> The bare fact is that truth cannot be tolerant and cannot admit compromises or limitations, that scientific research looks on the whole field of human activity as its own, and must adopt an uncompromisingly critical attitude towards any other power that seeks to usurp any part of its province.
> (Freud quoted in Eysenck, 1985, p. 9)

Freud thought scientific method should determine the fate of psychoanalysis.

The *Behavioural Paradigm* also assumes that there are no mental illnesses. Instead, abnormal behaviour is explained by processes of learning or conditioning.

> The most basic assumption of behaviourism – the assump-tion that most behaviour is conditioned behaviour and that maladaptive behaviour is simply the result of less successful conditioning – constitutes a rejection of the medical model, since it denies that any clear line can be drawn between normal and abnormal. According to the behaviourists, all human beings have different conditioning histories, which

mold their responses into different forms. None of these responses can be called either sick or healthy. Some simply work better than others within the context of society. And those that don't work can be remolded so that they do work.

(Calhoun, 1977, p. 73)

There are a number of behavioural theories, but most make the following assumptions. First, that 'symptoms' can be acquired by respondent (Pavlovian) conditioning and operant (Skinnerian) conditioning. And second, that 'symptoms' can be acquired by faulty cognitive inferences. In so far as the behavioural paradigm offers an alternative explanation of abnormal behaviour to the psychodynamic paradigm, it is ostensibly in conflict with it too. It does not see symptoms as being secondary phenomena caused by either disease processes or unconscious forces:

The behavioural model looks no further than the symptoms, which, together with the behaviour that follows from them, *are* the disorder. The symptoms develop through a process of learning, or conditioning, and because they are unhelpful they are described as maladaptive learned responses.

(Tyrer and Steinberg, 1987, p. 49)

Let us briefly examine this paradigm.

Two reasons are given above why the behavioural paradigm is in conflict with the medical paradigm, and both reasons are suspect. First, the behavioural paradigm supposedly contradicts a premise of the medical paradigm which holds that a clear line can be drawn between normal and abnormal. For the purposes of clarity, let us distinguish two medical paradigms. The first (with the *Entity Thesis*) assumes that diseases are entities – i.e. are qualitatively distinct from the norm. The second (with the *Continuum Thesis*) assumes that diseases can also deviate quantitatively from the norm. The behavioural paradigm is only in conflict with the first sort of medical paradigm. In fact some diseases, like essential hypertension, only differ in degree from normality. Therefore, the most plausible medical paradigm makes the continuum assumption which is compatible with the behavioural paradigm.

Second, the behavioural paradigm supposedly contradicts a premise of the medical paradigm which assumes that there are underlying causes for any symptom. But I have argued above that if some behaviour is learned, there will be some underlying neurological state that encodes such learned behaviour. It would be miraculous indeed if a person acquired some maladaptive behaviour without there being some change in his brain responsible for this behaviour. But if this is the case, then the behavioural paradigm also assumes that symptoms have underlying causes. And therefore the behavioural paradigm is not in conflict with the medical paradigm on this matter.

But most importantly, the behavioural paradigm *cannot* deny that there are mental illnesses. We can argue that abnormal behaviour has underlying causes which are abnormal – if the neuronal states causing the unusual behaviour are common, then the behaviour should be common. But, *ex hypothesi*, it is not common. Therefore, the neuronal states causing the behaviour must be unusual too. And if the behaviour is maladaptive, then it is reasonable to infer that it fails to achieve the desired result, producing frustration and suffering. But a disease is none other than an abnormal process producing suffering. The behavioural paradigm entails that a behavioural disorder is a disease – it is simply another disease theory and therefore it does not conflict with the medical paradigm!

Let me give an example. The behavioural paradigm explains depression in terms of learned helplessness – i.e. a person who has become depressed has simply learned that whatever he does, he cannot remove the aversive stimuli – he is helpless. The medical paradigm explains depression in terms of stresses that induce a lowering of nor-adrenalin in the limbic areas of the brain. Let us suppose that we discover that depressed patients do indeed have low limbic nor-adrenalin levels. Does this mean that depression is not learned helplessness? No. One would only be inclined to believe this if one was a dualist. If depression is learned helplessness, this state will have to be realized by some state of the brain. It is open to the behavioural paradigm to argue that the state of lowered nor-adrenalin encodes the lesson of helplessness. Thus the behavioural paradigm is compatible with the medical paradigm.

However, the two paradigms still appear to be in conflict – the medical paradigm entails that biological causes like genes are responsible for depression, whereas the behavioural paradigm entails that a learning schedule is sufficient for depression. But while the different predictions show that the two theories are distinct, it does not show that they are distinct *paradigms*. They are only distinct paradigms if the behavioural theory contradicts the causal thesis. But learned helplessness is a disease theory – it postulates that some (statistically) abnormal neurological state encodes the state of helplessness which causes suffering and distress. But a disease is an abnormal process that causes disability and distress. Learned helplessness is simply one disease theory *within* the medical paradigm.

If the behavioural paradigm saves itself by arguing that genes simply predispose the person to learning the lesson of helplessness from stressful events, and accommodates all the biological facts known about depression, it is clear that it becomes a notational variant of the medical paradigm. The only difference is that the medical paradigm will describe a process in neurobiological terms which the behavioural paradigm will call the 'learning of helplessness'. When the theories converge like this, their distinctness is no longer evident. The only difference lies in the language used – one talks of learned helplessness and the other talks of depletion of nor-adrenalin. But difference in language alone is not sufficient for paradigm distinctness. If it were, I could propose an alternative theory to relativity which was identical in form but used terms such as rezmass, rezvelocity, rezenergy, etc. But such a theory would only be a notational variant.

We cannot argue that the two theories are not identical because one refers to psychological processes and the other to physiological processes. To be convincing, such an argument must presuppose dualism which we have already had reason to reject. The behavioural paradigm must assume that psychological processes have underlying physiological processes – it would be totally mysterious if psychological processes were not realized by physiological processes. If it is to avoid talking about nothing (because a mind substance does not exist), the behavioural paradigm will have to talk about physiological processes when it talks about psychological processes. Giving a psychological description is simply to describe the workings of the brain in terms of systems with in-puts and out-puts, while a neurobiological description is a fine-grained description of these workings. The two theories *are* referring to the same thing.

If the behavioural paradigm is simply one theory within the medical paradigm (because it entails that learning leads to a disease), and the psychodynamic paradigm is another such theory within the medical paradigm, it is reasonable to infer that these two paradigms must be in conflict. Since they are both formulated in psychological terms, we cannot argue that they are simply the same theory describing the causes at different levels. We can see this by looking at the way they both explain phobias. In the case of Little Hans, Freud, using a psychodynamic theory, explained the boy's phobia of horses by postulating that he had Oedipal desires for his mother which had come into conflict with the fear of castration from his father. This led the boy to repress the incestuous desire from consciousness, which required him to redirect the fear of his father on to horses, giving him a phobia of horses. On the other hand, the behavioural paradigm points to the fact that prior to the development of the phobia, the boy witnessed a frightening accident involving a horse-drawn carriage. It argues that the accident (unconditioned stimulus) evoking fear (unconditioned response) was associated with the stimulus of the horse (conditioned stimulus) such that the horse alone came to evoke fear (conditioned response). By a process of Pavlovian conditioning, horses came to evoke fear. These theories clearly conflict – they entail distinct consequences, some of which are testable. The psychodynamic theory entails that the accident need not have been frightening in order for the phobia to emerge, that if the boy had not been frightened of his father, he would not have developed the fear of horses, that if the Oedipal complex were resolved, the phobia would disappear, etc. On the other hand, the behavioural theory entails that the phobia could be resolved by systematic desensitization (habituation of the fearful response by graded exposure to the feared stimulus), that the avoidance of horses is likely to perpetuate the phobia, etc. Both theories cannot be correct.

If the phobia is found to be caused by such and such a physiological process, we can argue that this is either the realization of the conditioned reflex or the transformation of the fear of the father into the fear of the horses. So the correctness of the medical paradigm is not at issue here. But in evaluating the two explanations of phobias, there does appear to be considerably more evidence for the behavioural explanation. First, it is more parsimonious, not invoking such unobservable entities as Oedipal complexes. Second, it is born out by experimental induction of phobias – remember how Little Albert acquired a phobia for white mice by having the mice associated with a frighteningly loud noise (Watson, 1930). And third, the usefulness of systematic desensitization as therapy supports the behavioural explanation (Gelder, Marks and Wolff, 1967).

The behavioural paradigm not only challenges the medical paradigm at the theoretical level, but it also questions whether being mentally ill entitles one to enter the sick role.

> It [the behavioural paradigm] maintains that the sick role is inappropriate for many psychological disorders, and may contribute to handicap. Worse, still, it may create new illness (i.e. is iatrogenic). By adopting a passive role the patient is rewarded by the medical model. . . . What worries the behaviourist is that each time the patient adopts the sick role, whether it is appropriate or not, he is rewarded by attention by the prestigious medical profession. . . . At subsequent consultations and relapses his power to shape his own destiny is gradually whittled away until he no longer thinks or acts independently, reaching its final form in the stereotyped institutional behaviour of the chronic hospitalized patient. This state has been reproduced in animals when they are placed in situations where others decide what happens to them. It is an apathetic, sad condition which has been called learned helplessness. Doctors who follow the disease model unwittingly encourage learned helplessness and thereby promote new 'illness'.
>
> (Tyrer and Steinberg, 1987, pp. 64–5)

While the sick role can cause disability, it is only a caricature of the sick role that does this.

A sophisticated account of the sick role sees the patient as at least partly responsible for getting better. Not only must he want to get well, but he must participate actively in his treatment. He must follow the doctor's instructions, and embark on an active rehabilitation programme. Far from being treated as a passive victim, the patient is expected to improve only if he takes an active role in his treatment. This applies to physical disease, such as heart attacks and strokes as much as it does to mental illness. The sick role, then, does not entitle the patient to sit back passively. Hence, it is not iatrogenic in the way the behavioural paradigm cautions. There is thus little difference from the client role the behavioural paradigm offers the disturbed person and this sophisticated sick role. Both see the person as not having voluntarily produced his symptoms, and both expect him to take an active role in his treatment.

The *Intentional Paradigm* also assumes there are no mental illnesses. Instead, abnormal behaviour is seen as the voluntary adoption of strategies to cope with difficult circumstances.

> Our view of psychosis constitutes more a 'way of life' hypothesis than a 'disease' hypothesis. We assume the patient to have what he regards as good reasons for behaving the way he does – that he has in mind some purpose from which his behaviour logically follows.
>
> (Rakusin and Feiner, 1963, p. 140)

Both Laing, who sees schizophrenic behaviour as a strategy people adopt to live in an unlivable social situation, and Szasz, who sees hysterical behaviour as a game played by a person to get help, subscribe to such a paradigm. It explains the disturbed behaviour with the following assumptions: first, that 'symptoms' are really voluntary actions performed as a result of desires (to cope) and beliefs (that this strategy is the best way to cope). And second, 'symptoms' occur as a result of situations where such strategies are intelligible. Let us examine this paradigm.

The intentional paradigm does not entail that there are no mental illnesses, and therefore fails to achieve distinctness from the medical paradigm. It is in fact yet another disease theory. For example, the intentional paradigm sees schizophrenia as the intentional strategy to cope with a difficult family situation. The schizophrenic adopts behaviour that is obscure in an attempt to be himself in a situation where he is given conflicting demands – double binds (Bateson *et al.*, 1956). Unless the intentional paradigm adopts a dualist assumption, it entails that there is some state of the brain that realizes this strategy. On the other hand, the medical paradigm sees the behaviour as a result of an excess of dopamine receptors in the meso-limbic pathways of the brain. Let us suppose that we discover that schizophrenic behaviour is indeed the immediate result of an excess of dopamine receptors. Does this mean that the intentional paradigm is false? No. The intentional paradigm can argue that this brain state realizes or embodies the intentional adoption of the strategy. And because this strategy leads to suffering, the intentional paradigm is committed to the existence of brain processes producing suffering –

i.e. diseases. Therefore the intentional paradigm is not in fact a distinct paradigm – it is a disease theory *within* the medical paradigm.

We cannot argue that the two paradigms are distinct because the one explains the behaviour in terms of psychological processes while the other explains it in terms of physiological processes. This simply means that the two paradigms use different concepts to refer to the same thing. We cannot argue that the two paradigms are distinct because one is supported by the discovery of biological causes like genes while the other is not. The intentional paradigm can argue that the genes simply predispose the individual to adopt such a strategy. But if the intentional paradigm modifies itself in this way in an attempt to account for all the facts, it ceases to be a distinct theory. It differs only in calling the physiological consequences of the genes and family stresses a strategy instead of a disease, becoming a notational variant of the medical paradigm.

I have argued that there is little evidence that such behaviour is in the voluntary control of the patient and simply a strategy. While we have evidence that patients can control the impression they make for various ends, and while most nurses confirm that patients on chronic wards become more 'disturbed' when psychiatrists are around as this is the 'currency' with which patients get attention, unless this evidence is wildly over-generalized, it does not prove that all such symptoms are in the control of the disturbed patient and are manipulated to achieve various ends. Therefore, this particular disease theory within the medical paradigm is probably false.

The intentional paradigm denies that the disturbed patient is entitled to the sick role. Since he is voluntarily bringing about his disturbed behaviour, he is responsible for it. In fact, on this paradigm, it is often the very existence of the sick role that makes such disturbed behaviour possible. According to the intentional paradigm, people will play at being mad in order to avail themselves of the benefits of the sick role:

> The patient emerges as an individual who, for reasons we shall specify, very often chooses, though not necessarily consciously, institutionalization as either an intermittent or enduring way of life. Once in the institution, the schizophrenic exploits his environment in a wholly effective and

rational manner in order to extract from it personally satisfy-
ing outcomes.

(Braginsky, Braginsky and Ring, 1969, p. 162)

In addition, the intentional paradigm rejects that idea that mental
illness undermines a person's responsibility. This follows by
definition – if the behaviour labelled as mental illness is fully
voluntary, then the person is responsible for his actions.

The *Sociological Paradigm* also contradicts the medical paradigm
in assuming that there are no mental illnesses. Instead, disturbed
behaviour is seen as the consequence of social forces.

> The social model maintains that mental illness is related
> clearly to social factors and there is no difficulty in predict-
> ing that one will follow from the other. For example, it has
> been shown in many studies that people who live in poor
> deprived geographical areas, who are unemployed and in
> unsatisfactory housing and have no special occupational
> skills, are all likely to suffer higher rates of mental illness
> than the rest of the population.
>
> (Tyrer and Steinberg, 1987, p. 77)

Abnormal behaviour is seen as a symptom of a disturbed society,
and for this reason the individual is not considered ill – if anything
is ill, it is society. This paradigm makes a number of assumptions.
First, that abnormal behaviour can be the result of labelling. And
second, that abnormal behaviour can be the result of adverse
social circumstances. In this way, the sociological paradigm seeks
an explanation for the patient's behaviour outside that individual
in a sick social group:

> The basic premise of family theory is that the family is
> the unit of conceptualization. The patient is thereby only
> externalizing through his symptoms an illness which is
> inherent in the family itself. He is a symptomatic organ of
> a diseased organism.
>
> (Meissner, 1964, p. 1)

Let us briefly examine this paradigm.

The sociological paradigm *cannot* deny that the individual is
mentally ill. Discovering that the source of the disturbance lies
outside the individual does not mean that it is not the individual
but the (social) circumstances that are diseased. TB and many

142

other diseases are by and large caused by poor living conditions – overcrowding, poor sanitation, etc. But this does not mean that a tuberculous individual is not suffering or malfunctioning. If TB is to be eradicated, social circumstances will have to be 'treated'. But this does not mean that the individual with TB is not ill.

In order to argue that an entity is diseased, one of two things has to be proven. Either it must be shown that that entity can suffer, or that that entity has parts that have a function. It is clear that society is not an entity that has feelings, that can experience unpleasant mental states, and therefore society is not an entity that can suffer. Neither is it an entity that has parts that have a function. In order for it to have parts that have functions, it must either have been consciously designed by somebody, or it must have been unconsciously designed by forces of natural selection. But neither is the case. Hence society is not an entity with parts that have a function. Therefore, society cannot be diseased.

The sociological paradigm can argue that diagnosis is inextricably tied to treatment, and that by making a diagnosis, one is saying that treatment should be directed here rather than there. By saying that some condition is a renal disease rather than a cardiac disease, one is saying that we must treat the former rather than the latter if we are to restore health. Thus if social factors are responsible for something, we ought to say that the society and not the individual is sick because this is where treatment must be directed. But this is wrong. First, because cardiac disease is often treated by diuretics acting on the kidney. And second, because medicine is not so callous. To imply that we should treat the social conditions rather than the individuals who are already sick is to deny the humanitarian function of medicine.

The sociological paradigm must accept that while society might be disordered, this does not mean that the individual is not ill. Thus the paradigm fails to achieve distinctness from the medical paradigm. Let me illustrate this with a sociological theory of depression:

> The current predeliction in psychiatry is to turn inward in its search for causes – to personality traits, long-term emotional schemata and biologically-based dispositions. But we need also to give more than lip service to an outward perspective – to the possibility that depressive conditions, in no small

number, are the result of complex transactions between the
individual and his or her social environment.

(Brown, 1989, p. 22)

Depression is seen as the result of social factors such as life
stresses, lack of social support, lack of an outside job, having
more than three children under fifteen, etc. (Brown and Harris,
1978). On the other hand, the medical paradigm sees depression
as the depletion of nor-adrenalin. But does the discovery that
these social factors cause depression undermine the claim that
depression is a mental illness? Does the discovery that those who
are depressed have a depletion of nor-adrenalin mean that
depression is not the (remote) consequence of such social factors?
The answer to both questions is no. The demonstration that there
are social causes of depression does not show that these causes
do not result in the depletion of nor-adrenalin. The sociological
paradigm is in no conflict with the medical paradigm. It is thus
not an alternative paradigm at all.

This is supported by our conclusions about the status of labelling theory. This version of the sociological paradigm is not in
conflict with the medical paradigm. Because it concedes that the
adoption of a social role is not a voluntary action and is something
that produces suffering and disability, it accepts there are diseases
– diseases are none other than abnormal involuntary processes
that produce harm. Hence it does not deny the causal thesis of
the medical paradigm and fails to constitute a distinct paradigm.

The sociological paradigm is in fact compatible with all of the
other paradigms. It is compatible with the behavioural paradigm.
The demonstration that depression has social causes does not
undermine the view that it is due to learned helplessness. All it
shows is that social factors are conducive to learning helplessness.
Similarly, it is compatible with the intentional paradigm. The
demonstration that depression has social causes does not undermine the claim that it is an intentionally adopted strategy. All it
shows is what circumstances provoke the adoption of this strategy. And finally, it is compatible with the psychodynamic paradigm. The demonstration that depression has social causes does
not undermine the view that depression is anger turned inwards.
All it shows is that social factors are conducive to such psychological processes.

A UNIFIED VIEW

Let us review our conclusions so far. We have examined a number of supposed paradigms of mental illness. If they are to count as paradigms, they have to satisfy a number of conditions. First, they must purport to explain the domain of abnormal behaviour, and they do. Second, they must be distinct – they must conflict with other paradigms rather than being the identical theory in another dress. Should a proposed paradigm fail to conflict with another, it then ceases to be a paradigm, becoming a theory within the same paradigm instead. We have seen that the psychodynamic, the behavioural, the intentional, and the sociological paradigms do not conflict with the medical paradigm. They do not deny the causal thesis and concede that mental illness is responsible for abnormal behaviour. While it is true that any one psychodynamic, behavioural, intentional, or sociological theory may conflict with some other medical theory, this does not mean that these are not all conflicts between theories *within* a single paradigm. Conflict alone cannot settle the paradigmatic status of a theory – within any paradigm, there can be a conflict between any two theories giving the same sort of explanation. The medical theory explaining schizophrenia in terms of genes and family stresses conflicts with the intentional theory explaining it in terms of a strategy. But because the intentional theory does not entail that the process of adopting the strategy is not a disease process, it does not conflict with the medical paradigm. As long as the different theories accept the causal thesis – i.e. that mental illness causes the behaviour – they fall within the medical paradigm. The intentional theory is thus a disease theory *within* the medical paradigm and not a distinct paradigm at all. What look like competing paradigms:

The Psychodynamic Paradigm:
Disturbed ⟶ Unconscious ⟶ Signs and
upbringing   conflict   symptoms

The Behavioural Paradigm:
Conditioning ⟶ Conditioned ⟶ Signs and
schedules   reflexes   symptoms

The Intentional Paradigm:
Problems of ⟶ Intentional ⟶ Signs and
living   strategies   symptoms

145

The Sociological Paradigm:

Social stresses ⟶ Reaction to stress ⟶ Signs and symptoms

The Medical Paradigm:

Social and physical factors ⟶ Abnormal biological process ⟶ Signs and symptoms

end up looking like this:

The Sophisticated Medical Paradigm:

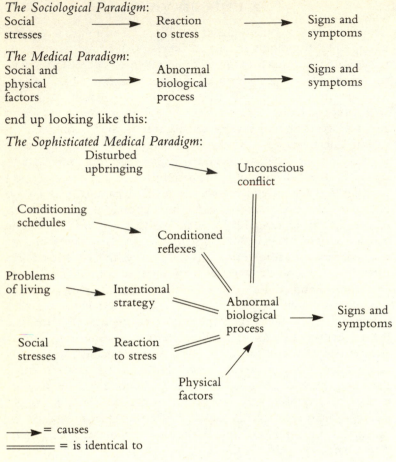

⟶ = causes

═══ = is identical to

There are a number of reasons why these alternative theories have been taken to be paradigms. First, it is assumed that if something is a disease, it must have a particular nature. And hence it is argued that conditioned reflexes, adoption of roles, playing of games, psychological conflicts, etc., cannot be the natures of a disease. And hence it is argued that such explanations of abnormal behaviour must conflict with the medical paradigm. But this is the essentialist fallacy. Something is not a disease because it has a particular underlying nature, but because it has undesirable consequences whatever its nature – hence conditioned reflexes, psychodynamic conflicts, etc., can be diseases. Therefore the conflict with the medical paradigm falls away.

Second, it is assumed that if something is a disease, it must be a discrete condition qualitatively distinct from the norm. Hence it is argued that causes like conditioned reflexes, psychological conflicts, adoption of roles, etc., which operate in the normal population too, cannot be the causes of disease. However, diseases do not have to differ qualitatively from the norm – they can be quantitatively distinct too. And hence this apparent conflict with the medical paradigm evaporates.

Third, a dualist theory of the mind is assumed. If there are two different substances, mind and matter, then a theory about mental causes such as psychological conflicts, learned responses, etc., will be clearly different from a theory about physical causes such as depletion of nor-adrenalin in the brain. However, substance dualism is probably incorrect – it is unlikely that there are two sorts of substance in the world. Therefore a theory about psychological conflicts or conditioned reflexes is not about something completely different from neurobiological processes. And hence this source of conflict does not exist.

Fourth, a descriptive theory of semantics is assumed. If our terms have meanings given them by a descriptive definition, then a theory about conditioned reflexes will clearly be a different theory from one about acquired neuronal connections. Something is a conditioned reflex if it is a new behavioural response to a stimulus. Something is an acquired neuronal connection if it is a new functional connection between one neurone and another. Since one theory is about behaviour, and another about nerves, the two seem different. But if we adopt a referential theory of semantics, our terms will refer to the underlying natures of things. On this account, conditioned reflexes will be about whatever it is in the brain that is responsible for the acquired response. But then it becomes clear that the theories are not talking about different things. And hence the conflict disappears. Similarly, the theory of learned helplessness seems different from the theory of nor-adrenalin depletion. Learned helplessness is defined in terms of the state of having learned that one's behaviour makes no difference, while nor-adrenalin depletion is defined in terms of the relative lack of the substance nor-adrenalin in the brain. Such theories appear to be about different things only if we adopt a descriptive semantics for our terms. If instead they refer to underlying natures, then it is no longer evident that the state of learned helplessness is distinct from the state of nor-adrenalin depletion.

But if they are about the same thing, then the apparent conflict falls away.

And finally, it is assumed that one theory cannot be reduced to another. One theory is reducible to another if it can be shown that the terms in the theories refer to the same things and that the theories postulate the same laws regulating the behaviour of these things. I have argued that theories supposedly constituting alternative paradigms can be reduced to a theory within the medical paradigm. My strategy has not been to select a particular theory and show that it reduces to a medical theory – this would only prove that reductionism works in one case. Instead, it has been to choose purely general theories about unconscious conflicts, strategies, conditioned reflexes, and physical processes, and show that we have a dilemma: the non-medical theories are either true or false. If they are true, then they take into account all the biological facts such as genetic causation etc. But given a plausible definition of disease, such theories entail that a disease causes behaviour – they admit that the biological factors (and psychological and social ones) cause the disease, but refer to the disease *in different terms*. Thus the theories are reducible – identical – to the medical theory. If, on the other hand, the non-medical theories are false, they cannot be identical to any correct medical theory. But they are nevertheless still disease theories within the medical paradigm. Since all competitors to the medical paradigm can be reduced to a disease theory *within* the medical paradigm, no conflict arises.

The above argument assumes that types of psychological process can be identified with types of physical process – e.g. that learned helplessness can be identified with nor-adrenalin depletion. Donald Davidson has a theory of mind called anomalous monism which challenges this assumption (Davidson, 1980). He argues that, while it is the case that individual mental events are identical to individual brain events, types of psychological event are not identical to types of physiological event. This follows from the fact that one type of psychological event might be realized in different individuals by different types of brain event (McGinn, 1978). One pattern of neurone firing might perform the function in my brain of motivating me to go to a movie, but the same desire to go to a movie might be realized by a different pattern of neurone firing in a different individual. Different types of brain events can be the same psychological event because they can play the same role in the working of the psyche (and because a type of psychological event is identified by its role in the working of the brain). Therefore, so the argument goes, the type of psychological event cannot be identified with any one of the types of brain event that underlies it. From this it follows that an explanation of abnormal behaviour in terms of one type of psychological state will not be identical to an explanation in terms of *one* type of physiological state.

But all that follows if anomalous monism is true is that talk about the psychological state is in fact talk about *a number of* physiological states, and not that talk about the psychological state is not talk about physiological states at all. If we group the different physiological states together, the two theories will be identical – the one will reduce to the other. If there is a group of physical abnormalities – i.e. diseases – underlying any psychological state, this only means that the psychological state is not identical to a single disease, and not that it is not identical to a *group* of physical disorders.

But more importantly, anomalous monism is probably false – it is in conflict with known anatomical and physiological facts. We know that for humans to raise their right arm a certain sequence of left pre-frontal cortical neurones must be stimulated – this is how we are 'wired up'. Thus the psychological state of intentionally moving one's right hand is realized by the same physiological state in all of us, and therefore a type of psychological state *is* identical to a type of physiological state. If it were not, then each person's brain would have to be radically different, which it is not. If the psychological state of intentionally moving one's right arm were identical in some humans to a different sequence of neurological events, then given the facts about human anatomy, they would not end up moving their right arm at all! But this would mean, *contra hypothesi*, that this was not the intention to move the right arm. Hence the uniformity of structure and function of the human brain supports an identity between types of (human) psychological states and types of (human) physiological states. This is supported by the fact that researchers *have* found uniform physical abnormalities underlying abnormal psychological states – for example, people with obsessions and compulsions (Rapoport, 1989) and panic attacks (Reiman *et al.*, 1989) have uniform underlying physical abnormalities. Thus this objection to reductionism fails.

This means that we do not have any alternative paradigms as we first supposed. Only the medical paradigm remains within which there are a number of alternative disease theories. Since none of these deny mental illness causes the behaviour, they do not constitute alternative paradigms. While they postulate different causes for abnormal behaviour, this is not sufficient to make them into distinct paradigms. The medical paradigm does not contain any assumptions about the sorts of causes mental illnesses must have, and hence different aetiological theories do not amount to different paradigms. It also does not assume that mental illnesses must be processes of a certain sort, so theories postulating different processes do not amount to different paradigms. The obvious virtue of this is that different causal factors can be combined into a grand theory of the aetiology of any one mental illness. In fact, it is difficult to explain any mental illness without reference to biological, psychodynamic, behavioural and social factors. I will illustrate how this works within a single (sophisticated) medical paradigm. While the specific theory expounded may not be correct, its truth is unnecessary to demonstrate the general point.

THE SOPHISTICATED MEDICAL PARADIGM

The example I will use is agoraphobia. In defining it, we must be careful not to beg the question in favour of some particular paradigm. If we say it is some disorder of the brain, we beg the question in favour of the medical paradigm. We have to identify agoraphobia in neutral terms, using complaints (symptoms) and behaviour (signs). Remembering that not only women suffer from agoraphobia, someone with agoraphobia complains of panic attacks in situations where she feels trapped and cannot easily exit, or cannot exit without attracting too much attention. These situations commonly include queues, cinemas, buses, supermarkets, etc. As a result of the panic attacks, she avoids such situations, becoming progressively house-bound. If she is able to venture into these situations, it is only with her husband. In addition, she gets anticipatory anxiety when she thinks about approaching such situations.

A biological theory might explain the features as follows. There is a nucleus in the hindbrain, the locus coeruleus, that appears to be responsible for producing anxiety. Electrical or pharmacological stimulation of the locus leads to biochemical, physiological, and behavioural effects of fear in animals (Redmond and Huang, 1979). On the other hand, lesions in the locus produce the opposite effect. In humans, the alpha-two nor-adrenergic receptor antagonist, yohimbine, can induce the subjective and physiological consequences of panic in normal subjects (Charney, Heninger and Redmond, 1983). In addition, the alpha-two nor-adrenergic receptor agonist, clonidine, can reduce the subjective and physiological consequences of yohimbine-induced panic. This shows that alpha-two receptors modulate the activity of the locus coeruleus. A biological theory might hypothesize that a deficiency of alpha-two nor-adrenergic receptors in the locus coeruleus is responsible for panic (Redmond, 1977). Such a deficiency would lead to the automatic discharge of the locus and consequent panic. In general, any biological theory supposes that the brain has parts and that there is such a thing as their normal operation. It then supposes that a biological abnormality explains the abnormal features of any condition.

Psychodynamic theory offers a different explanation. A patient's history generates a conflict. This arouses anxiety which in turn is displaced on to the outside world, leading to its avoidance (Nemiah, 1981). For example, a woman might wish to leave a violent husband. This might come into conflict with her need to be looked after – a conflict deepened by her own experience of being abandoned by her mother as a child. This conflict arouses anxiety which is displaced on to the outside world which symbolizes her leaving home, and she consequently stays indoors. In general, the psychodynamic theory supposes that the psyche has a certain structure with parts interacting in certain ways. It then supposes that conflict between such parts arouses anxiety which is repressed and transformed into the symptoms of the condition.

A behavioural theory has a different explanation. A person acquires agoraphobia because she is exposed to stimuli that naturally evoke fear, like unexpected loud noises. If this happens in a supermarket, the stimulus of the supermarket comes to evoke fear (Pavlovian Conditioning). Once the supermarket comes to evoke the fearful response, the individual generalizes and similar situations come to evoke fear. Such situations are avoided and this reduces the fear and reinforces that behaviour (Skinnerian Conditioning). As a result of these two forms of conditioning, the person acquires the symptoms of agoraphobia. In general, the behavioural theory sees behaviour as the consequence of learning. The emotional and behavioural features of any disorder are explained by operant and respondent conditioning.

A cognitive theory explains agoraphobia differently. There is a normal fluctuation of anxiety in all of us, and panic occurs when a person develops a catastrophic misinterpretation of the physiological symptoms of this anxiety (Clark, 1988). For example, he interprets his heart racing as a heart attack. This naturally leads to more anxiety and so a vicious circle is established. Once a panic attack has occurred, it leads to anticipatory anxiety and avoidance. The panic attack is an unpleasant and aversive event, and tends to be feared for its own sake. And so thinking about going into similar situations leads to anticipatory anxiety. The person quickly learns that he can reduce this anxiety by avoiding those situations where he first became panicky, and eventually becomes house-bound. In general, this more sophisticated behavioural theory assumes that behaviour is influenced by cognitive processes such as the interpretation of events, the formation of beliefs, and thoughts about future events. It then supposes that irrational cognitive processes are responsible for the features of agoraphobia.

The intentional theory sees agoraphobia as an intentional strategy. A wife might become fed up with the fact that her husband is leading an independent and interesting life while she is stuck with having to do onerous tasks like shopping all on her own. She might also worry that he is not spending enough time with her and that they are drifting apart. She might then see becoming fearful of the outside as a very useful way to pull her husband back into her life – if he has to accompany her everywhere, they will spend more time together. In general, the intentional theory sees all behaviour as intentional and motivated by reasons. In particular, agoraphobia is a strategy designed to achieve certain ends.

The sociological theory explains agoraphobia by social forces. A variety of social factors, such as social upbringing of women making them dependent on others and encouraging them to remain in the home – 'a woman's place is in the home' – combined with adverse social circumstances, may lead to a woman spending most of her time at home. As a result of her dependence and the unfamiliarity of going out, the outside may become a frightening place, leading to panic and consequent avoidance. In general, a sociological theory assumes that social factors cause distress, and that factors encouraging women to be dependent and remain in the home lead to the features of agoraphobia.

Do these explanations conflict? Or can they be harmonized in a certain way? Before we answer this question, we can see that each theory has its weaknesses. The biological theory can explain how panic occurs, but needs other assumptions to explain why avoidance and anticipatory anxiety occur. The psychodynamic theory has to refer to unobservable processes. The behavioural theory has to resort to single case learning to explain the respondent conditioning, and although it can explain the avoidance, it needs other assumptions to explain the anticipatory anxiety. The cognitive theory has difficulty explaining why physical factors such as genes (Moran and Andrews, 1985) and drugs (Zitrin, Klein and Woerner, 1978) affect the condition. The intentional theory has difficulty explaining the obvious distress and inability to control behaviour that occurs in agoraphobics. And the sociological theory has to refer to intervening processes to explain why social factors lead to such behaviour.

To see how these explanations relate to one another, let us assume that we discover that the biological theory is correct and that agoraphobics have a deficiency of alpha-two nor-adrenergic receptors in the locus coeruleus. Does this mean that the other theories are false? Not necessarily. The behavioural theory could argue that the conditioned reflexes underlying the condition are realized by this physical state. The psychodynamic theory could argue that the repression and transformation of the desire is achieved by this physiological process. The cognitive theory could argue that the abnormal cognition (that the symptoms of anxiety are due to a heart attack) is encoded in this biological state. The intentional theory could argue that the intention to play at being house-bound is identical to this brain state. And the sociological theory can argue that social factors cause agoraphobia via causing this change in the brain.

For these identifications to be coherent, we have to show that the conditioned reflex or cognition or intention is indeed identical to this particular brain state. For this to be so, the brain state must have exactly those sorts of in-puts and out-puts that the psychological state has. If the change in the locus is to be identical to the conditioned reflex, it would have to be caused in the way conditioned reflexes are, and have the same consequences as a conditioned reflex. However, if we find that the change in the locus also leads to panic in other situations, then we cannot identify it only with the conditioned reflex in question. In addition, a conditioned reflex is already partly an anatomically based concept. Reflex arcs have been identified at all levels in the nervous system. Most simply, a stretch receptor in a tendon excites a sensory neurone which connects to a motor neurone, causing the muscle to contract. This connection of sensory neurones to motor neurones underlies the reflex. When new reactions or reflexes are established, there is the development of connections between sensory and motor neurones. So if it is argued that the deficiency in receptors in the locus coeruleus is the anatomical basis for the conditioned reflex linking the stimulus of a supermarket to the response of avoidance, the likelihood of this being true is zero. A conditioned reflex is identified by its connections with stimuli and responses. Therefore, if some entity in the nervous system is to be identical to a conditioned reflex, it must have the same connections. But the instability of the locus coeruleus does *not* have the same connections. Therefore, it is not the neurological basis for any conditioned reflex.

Similarly, for the change in the locus to be identical to the cognition that one is going to have a heart attack, then changes in this belief alone should affect the locus, and people with such brain states should seek help from their doctors for their hearts. Similarly, if the defect in the locus is identical to the repression mechanism, it should occur in other cases where things are kept from consciousness and it should be reversed when insight is returned. But the defect in the locus coeruleus does not have the sort of connections to in-puts and out-puts required to qualify as reflexes, repressive mechanisms, intentions, or cognitions. Therefore the *specific* abnormality proposed by the biological theory is not what is postulated by the other theories – there is a conflict. There is also a conflict generated by the fact that genes predispose to and drugs treat the condition. If such facts are not to undermine the psychological theories, we have to show that they affect states with the right sort of in-puts and out-puts to qualify as psychological states.

The best explanation of agoraphobia incorporates elements of all theories. Because of the role of genetic factors and the responsiveness of the condition to drugs, it is reasonable to assume that there is some such biological abnormality in agoraphobics. Such an abnormality makes it more likely for those individuals to panic. This alone however cannot account for all the features of the condition, viz. the avoidance and the anticipatory anxiety. To account for the avoidance, the assumptions of the behavioural theory are needed. Respondent and operant conditioning explain why the person comes to avoid such situations. This modified theory cannot account for anticipatory anxiety. To explain this, the cognitive theory is required – it is the thought of experiencing panic that leads to anticipatory anxiety. In addition, the cognitive theory might help to explain why some people with the biological abnormality alone do not develop agoraphobia. It may be a combination of the heightened responsiveness of the locus coeruleus *plus* the misinterpretation of the bodily sensations of anxiety that leads to panic. To explain why agoraphobia occurs mostly in our culture (Littlewood and Lipsedge, 1987), we might have to invoke social factors which encourage dependency in women – these would operate as additional vulnerability factors. In order to explain the persistence of the disorder, we might invoke intentional factors – once the disorder is established, it might be the case that the rewards of the condition make the person perpetuate it intentionally. Finally, emotional conflicts may heighten autonomic arousal, making panic more likely, and past experience – e.g. abandonment – may lead to the attribution of a scary meaning to being left alone. In this way, psychodynamic theory can make a contribution to the aetiology of agoraphobia. In summary, then, the full explanation may require elements of *all* the different theories. Because the behaviour is abnormal, the process causing it will be abnormal. And because the process causes disability and distress, it counts as a disease. What we have here is a disease theory within a sophisticated medical paradigm.

In summary, the alternative paradigms are not really distinct paradigms at all. As they do not conflict with the medical paradigm, they are simply alternative theories *within* the medical paradigm. They all admit mental illnesses via other names, and therefore do not challenge the causal thesis. The medical paradigm does not have serious competitors, and reigns supreme in psychiatry. The theory most likely to succeed in explaining abnormal behaviour is one that refers to a number of different sorts of abnormal processes. It will be one that refers to behavioural, intentional, cognitive, psychodynamic, social and biological causes. This theory will occur within the (sophisticated) medical paradigm – there is no reason to abandon the medical paradigm, but only to broaden its conception.

This sophisticated medical paradigm can then explain why it is that psychiatrists use one or many of a whole range of therapeutic interventions. There are chemical treatments (drugs), physical treatments (ECT, psychosurgery), and a range of psychotherapeutic treatments from behaviour therapy to depth psychotherapy. But the use of these different therapies by different psychiatrists, and their use by a single psychiatrist, does not show that many paradigms exist in psychiatry. It does not show that psychiatrists are incorrigible pragmatists using different treatment modes simply because they work. It does not show that they lack a consistent theory to make sense of what they are doing. All it shows is that psychiatrists view abnormal behaviour as the consequence of some abnormal process going on in the brain of the patient – i.e. as the result of a disease – however that process is to be described (in terms of conditioned reflexes, inner conflicts, or depletion of neurotransmitters). Whatever treatment mode used, psychiatrists use a disease theory that gives their practice a unified theoretical foundation. After all, when psychiatrists use ECT, pharmacotherapy, psychosurgery or psychotherapy, they are trying to change the connections between various groups of neurones. When they use different therapies, they are trying to alter the same thing. That all effective treatments converge on the same process is supported by the observation that the same psychological traits of depression treated by cognitive therapy are treated equally well by drugs (Simons, Garfield and Murphy, 1984). Psychotherapy is none other than delicate psychosurgery, and psychosurgery is none other than crude psychotherapy.

10

THE NATURE OF MENTAL ILLNESS

The medical paradigm survives the onslaught from its competitors – the causal thesis remains intact. Here we must examine whether the conceptual thesis is true – whether diseases are malfunctions. I will first summarize the arguments showing that there is no fact of the matter whether some condition is a disease, and then defend an evaluative definition of mental illness. Finally, I will look at the boundaries of mental illness.

ETHICS AND NOSOLOGY

The medical paradigm assumes that the disease status of a mental condition can be settled by the facts – scientific methodology can be used to discover what conditions are mental illnesses. But this identification thesis is false – disease status cannot be settled by the facts. Instead, it is our values that determine the disease status of a condition. Ethics precedes nosology.

There are many examples from the history of psychiatry that appear to show that values influence the classification of a condition as a disease. Russian psychiatrists classified political dissidents as suffering from 'sluggish schizophrenia' and Dr Cartwright diagnosed runaway slaves as ill. In Victorian England, excessive sexual activity was classified as the disease 'spermatorrhoea' (Curling, 1856). Even criminal depravity was considered to be the disease of 'moral insanity' (Maudsley, 1874). It seems reasonable to conclude that these conditions were classified as diseases because political dissent, runaway slaves, sexual excess, and criminality were not valued by each society respectively. These examples appear to show that values influence the classification of a condition as a disease.

It is tempting, however, to suppose that such values simply distort the perception of the facts, and that a factual error has been made. It is tempting to suppose that Russians made a factual error in classifying political dissidence as a disease – if our nosology was purged of ethics, such a mistake would not be made. But this is wrong. Values determine disease status and not facts – it is because we do not agree with the values expressed in the classification of these conditions that they appear mistaken. I will defend this by showing that no factual error is made in classifying political dissidence as a mental illness.

We can argue that a factual error has been made in classifying political dissidence as a *schizophrenic* illness. But this is a mistake of disease identity and not disease status – i.e. a mistake over whether the condition is the same disease as schizophrenia and not a mistake over whether the condition is a disease at all. The former *is* partly a factual matter – to say that political dissidence is a schizophrenic disease is to assume that the same thing is going on in the brains of political dissidents as goes on in schizophrenics' brains, and this is a factual matter. But there is no evidence that they share the same underlying pathology – that political dissidents have increased dopamine receptors or increased cell loss in the dominant temporal lobe. So Russian psychiatrists *have* made a factual mistake in classifying political dissidence as a schizophrenic illness. However, this mistake is about the disease identity of the condition and not its disease status. It is open to Russian psychiatrists to concede this error, but submit that while this shows that it is not a form of schizophrenia, it does not show that it is not some distinct disease. We are still left with the question whether a factual mistake has been made in the classification of political dissidence as a different illness.

We cannot argue that the factual mistake of assuming that political dissidence is a disease is the factual mistake of assuming that political dissidence has the nature of a disease when it lacks it. This assumes that something is a disease if it has a certain underlying nature, which is the essentialist fallacy. Something is not a disease because it has a particular underlying nature. The infestation of our gastro-intestinal tracts by commensals is an 'infection' – i.e. has the same nature as many diseases, but is not a disease – on the contrary, it prevents diarrhoea. It is because we value the consequences of this infection that we do not take it to be a disease. Thus even if we discover that political dissidents have a slow viral infection of the brain, this does not mean that they are ill. They are only ill if we do not value the consequences of the viral infection. But because we value free political expression, we would not regard it as a disease.

We cannot argue that the factual mistake of holding political dissidence to be a disease is the factual mistake of assuming that there is some underlying abnormality when there is none. This assumes that something is a disease if it is due to an abnormality. But this assumption is wrong. There are many healthy conditions that have underlying abnormalities. We saw that Einstein's brain contained an abnormal number of glial cells which presumably was responsible for his genius. But we certainly would not regard this abnormality as a disease, and this because we value such consequences. Thus even if we discovered that political dissidents had an increased number of glial cells in their brains, this would not mean that they were suffering from some disease. And this is because the abnormality enables them to do something that we value – to express their political view.

We cannot argue that the factual mistake of holding that political dissidence is a disease is the factual mistake of assuming that there is some underlying biological malfunction when there is not. This argument assumes that something is a disease if it is a biological malfunction. But this is wrong. Many biological functions do not serve the good or well-being of the individual organism – e.g. there is a species of octopus where the female possesses an endocrine organ that comes into operation once she has laid her eggs. This organ has the function of shutting off her own appetite so that she guards her eggs while neglecting herself. She withers away, and dies soon after the eggs hatch, having thereby served her genes. However, if this organ is surgically removed, she tends to be a less than perfect mother, sometimes ignoring her eggs to satisfy her own needs. As a result, she lives to a ripe old octopus age (Barash, 1981, p. 95). While it is clear that this organ has a function, it is also clear that it is one that does not serve the good or well-being of the individual (mother) octopus.

There may be many such systems in man that have a function but which do not serve our individual good or well-being. Aging might be a self-destruct system that has the biological function of regulating population size. Suppose there is an infection that knocks out this system enabling us to live healthy and productive lives to the average age of 200. This infection causes a malfunction, but we would not classify it as a disease because we value its consequences. Thus it is a mistake to think that something is a disease if it is a biological malfunction. Even if we found that political dissidents had a malfunction of some 'conformity centre' in their brains, this would not mean that they had some disease, because we value this non-conformity.

We cannot argue that the factual mistake of holding that political dissidence is a disease is the mistake of assuming that political dissidence leads to reduced fertility and longevity (Kendell, 1975b). This assumes that something is a disease if it leads to reduced fertility and longevity, and this is wrong. Imagine a condition that enables us to be highly creative – affected individuals lead intense, productive, and fulfilling lives. However, instead of having the average of 2.2 children, such individuals have on average 2.1. In addition, instead of living the usual three score and ten, they live three score and nine. Thus the condition reduces fertility and longevity. But because we value the other consequences more highly than we disvalue the marginal decrease in fertility and longevity, we would not classify the condition as a disease. It is a mistake, then, to assume that something is a disease if it reduces longevity and fertility. Even if we were to discover that political dissidents had marginally reduced fertility and longevity, this would not mean that they were diseased as long as we valued their idealism more.

The fault with the last two accounts of disease is that they define disease in purely biological terms. Ultimate biological success is measured in terms of reproductive fitness, but disease cannot be understood as a condition reducing reproductive fitness. The gene for Huntington's chorea – a disorder characterized by late onset dementia and abnormal movements – might have persisted in the population because prior to the onset of the illness those with the gene are more promiscuous than average. But even if those with Huntington's chorea were reproductively fitter – i.e. left more offspring – this would not mean that it is not a disease! Similarly, we might discover that manic patients with their sexual disinhibition are reproductively fitter than most, but this does not mean it is not an illness. Conversely, we might find that brilliant individuals reproduce less than average. But this would not mean genius is a disease!

We cannot argue that the factual error of classifying political dissidence as a disease is the factual mistake of assuming that political dissidents are irrational when they are not. This makes two assumptions. First, that the notion of rationality is value-free, and second, that something is a mental illness if it produces a disturbance of rationality. Both assumptions are suspect. First, it can be argued that the notion of rationality is value-laden. While there is a narrow notion of rationality that is value-free – on this notion, someone is rational if he chooses the option most likely to maximize the satisfaction of his strongest desires – many argue that we need a broader notion of rationality which is value-laden. Certain desires seem to be irrational – the desire to mutilate oneself is such a candidate (Culver and Gert, 1982, p. 20). This makes rationality value-laden – only desires that serve valuable ends are rational, and since mutilating oneself is not a desirable end, it is irrational. This account is better able to explain why we judge that the drug addict, who maximizes the satisfaction of his strongest desire, is irrational. But in order to make such judgements, we have to introduce this evaluative element into the definition of rationality by judging such ends as irrational. Thus even if we could show that political dissidents were not maximizing the satisfaction of their strongest desires (because they discounted the negative utility of being sent to asylums), we would not take them to be irrational and mentally ill because we value such idealistic activity.

Second, whatever notion of rationality we select, it cannot provide an account of mental illness. While many symptoms of mental illness, like phobias, obsessions, and delusions, are defined in terms of rationality – phobias are irrational fears, obsessions are intrusive thoughts recognized as being irrational, and delusions are irrational convictions – there are other symptoms, like loss of drive, poverty of affect, poverty of thought, and anhedonia that are not. And hence there can be, and indeed are, mental illnesses that cannot be understood in terms of a disturbance of rationality. Simple schizophrenia (or the 'defect state') is characterized by such 'negative' symptoms as poverty of thought, anhedonia, poverty of affect, loss of drive, which involve no disturbance of rationality. But it is clearly a mental illness because such consequences are highly undesirable.

In addition, we have noted that some research suggests that it might be depressed patients rather than normal people that are 'truly' rational (Alloy and Abramson, 1979). We also argued that this might be beneficial – a positive mood ensures we realize our potentials. But if this is so, then on this definition, we are all mentally ill. However, making ourselves more rational (with depressant medication), and becoming unhappy, less productive, empty shells of ourselves, would not constitute an improvement in our health. And this because we value our normal 'good' mood and its consequent productivity even if this is sustained by the odd illusion or two. Thus even if political dissidents were being irrational, because we value such idealism (over being hopeless conformists), we would not consider dissidence to be an illness.

We have so far examined a number of candidates for the factual error allegedly made in classifying dissidence as a disease, and all fail to apply. As these are the most plausible candidates for the factual error, it seems reasonable to conclude that there is no factual matter at stake. While I recognize that this argument is inductive, and hence inconclusive, what makes it more powerful is that the best explanation for the failure to find the factual error is that the concept of disease is value-laden. It is because we value the consequences of certain underlying natures, abnormalities and malfunctions, because we value other consequences more than we disvalue the consequences of reduced fertility and longevity, and because we value certain irrationalities, that we do not consider certain conditions to be diseases. It is because the concept of disease involves values that no factual error is made in classifying political dissidence as a disease.

Does this mean that we cannot criticize Russian psychiatry for classifying political dissidence as a disease? Are we condemned to relativism? No. Certainly we cannot criticize Russian psychiatry for making a factual mistake. But this does not mean that we cannot object to their values. Just as we felt capable of criticizing Nazi values, and opposing them, so we should feel able to criticize the values implicit in classifying political dissidents as mentally ill. And of course we can criticize them for involuntarily treating political dissidents without evidence that they were incompetent. And we have already seen that we are not committed to relativism.

To conclude, no factual error is made in classifying a condition as a disease because being a disease is not a factual matter. This means that the conceptual thesis is false. And since the disease status of a condition cannot be settled by the examination of the facts, the identification thesis is also false. Instead, whether something is a disease is determined by our values. Ethics precedes nosology.

THE DEFINITION OF MENTAL ILLNESS

What, then, is mental illness? I suggest the following definition:

> Something is a (mental) illness if and only if it is an abnormal and involuntary process that does (mental) harm and should best be treated by medical means.

This definition incorporates a number of elements which I will discuss in turn.

First, a disease or illness must be a process. Static defects like cleft palate or Down's syndrome are not diseases because they do not evolve. Diseases are subject to change – they must have an onset and a natural history (Reznek, 1987).

Second, a disease must be an abnormal process. We must differentiate three sorts of norms – a statistical, an ideal, and a constructed norm. Something is a statistical abnormality if it departs from the average state (for that sex and age and species). But a disease cannot be understood in terms of a statistical abnormality because we can accept that a whole species can be ill. We can coherently imagine discovering we all suffer from a mild copper-induced dementia. And as Robert Kendell points out, if we were to discover that by the age of 90 over 50 per cent of the surviving population have the clinical deficits and neuropathology of Alzheimer's disease, this would not mean that it ceased to be a disease at this age. Something is an idealized abnormality if it falls short of the ideal for that species. But we are not ill simply because we are not supermen. I do not have (mild) mental retardation because I am less clever than others. The norm of health is in fact a construct. It is up to us where to draw it, and it is the consequences of any construct that influence this decision (Reznek, 1987). It is up to us whether to regard presbyopia – the universal hardening of the lens and consequent far-sightedness – as abnormal. Similarly, it is up to us whether to regard the menopause as an abnormality in view of its detrimental consequences – osteoporosis and heart disease.

The requirement that there be some abnormal process does not entail that this process be of a particular type – we must avoid the essentialist fallacy. The abnormal process can be a conditioned reflex, the transformation of libido, or a neurochemical depletion, etc. If one description, e.g. in terms of learning, does not refer to any abnormality, as long as there is a description at the biological level that does refer to an abnormality, then the process can be a disease.

Third, a disease must be an involuntary process – i.e. it must not be something that can be reversed at will. I have argued that if something is within our direct control, it ceases to be a disease and becomes instead a form of action. We do not judge that political dissidence, or drapetomania, or sexual excess, are diseases because we judge that such behaviour is voluntary (Flew, 1973). On the other hand, hysteria and schizophrenia are diseases because they cannot be reversed at will.

Fourth, mental illnesses do harm – i.e. they diminish our well-being by causing suffering and disability. This ensures that the concept of disease is value-laden – what counts as suffering and disability depends on our values (Reznek, 1987). For example, blindness is a disability because being able to see is desirable, while the inability to curl one's tongue is not because such a trait is not desirable. It is because we do not value the consequences of conditions that we classify them as mental illnesses. Schizophrenia is not a disease because it has some underlying nature, or underlying abnormality, or has a biological malfunction, or because it reduces fertility and longevity, or because it causes irrationality. It is a disease because we are better off without delusions, hallucinations, flattened affect, etc. It is because we value contact with reality, rationality, and emotional responsiveness that schizophrenia is a disease. Similarly, manic-depression is a disease because we are better off experiencing appropriate emotions rather than inappropriate highs and lows. And because we are better off without overspending, delusions, hallucinations, sexual disinhibition, etc. It is because we value being appropriately high (rather than unjustifiably euphoric), having some control of our sexual appetites, etc., that we consider mania to be a mental illness.

Finally, something is a disease only if it is best treated by medical means. There are many abnormal processes that make us worse off but are not mental illnesses. When we classify a condition as a disease, we not only judge that we ought to be without that condition, but also that we ought to remove it *in a certain way* – i.e. by medical means. Drug addictions are abnormal conditions that produce harm, but we might not wish to classify them as mental illnesses because we feel that the problem ought to be handled by the law. We might feel drug addicts are not victims of a disease, but slaves to be set free, and that the law is more likely to achieve this. If so, then a good argument can be made for not classifying drug addiction as a mental illness.

This explains the political dimension of the concept. A person with a black skin in a racist society might have an abnormal condition which makes him worse off. But he does not have a disease. And this is because we do not want to be the sort of people who would classify such a condition as a disease. Conversely, being psychopathic in a Nazi society might be advantageous, but because we do not approve of such a society, we do not judge that such personalities are healthy. In the extreme, a mystical culture might value individuals with hallucinations – being schizophrenic might carry social advantages there. But because we do not agree with such social values, we still judge schizophrenia to be a disease. Not only are we choosing what sort of people we would like to be when we judge that certain conditions are diseases, but we are also judging what sort of society we ought to create. If we do not want to live in a society where political dissidents are treated as ill, or where schizophrenics are not treated as ill, we must classify conditions accordingly.

Note that this definition does not define disease as what doctors treat (Kraupl-Taylor, 1979). A disease is not something a culture considers appropriate to treat because it prevents us from being able to say many things that we can say. We want to be able to say that Russian psychiatrists are mistaken in classifying dissidence as a disease – we want to be able to *contradict* them and assert that political dissidence is not a disease. But we can only do this if disease is not defined this way. If a disease is simply something that a culture treats, then the Russians are correct to treat it, and when we say that it is not a disease, we are simply saying that *we* don't treat it. But then there is no contradiction here as intended. However, we are able to make such contradictions, and to signal that particular cultures are wrong in the classifications of certain conditions as diseases. Therefore we cannot define disease in this way. By defining mental illness in terms of what doctors *ought* to treat, we avoid this objection.

Some argue that a disease must be a syndrome (Cavadino,

1989). However, we must make a distinction between cause, disease, and (clinical) syndrome. For example, the tuberculous bacillus and social factors cause an infective process (the disease) which in turn causes signs and symptoms (the clinical syndrome). Since we recognize that one agent, like streptococcus, can cause different diseases (rheumatic fever and pharyngitis), and different agents (radiation and chemicals) can cause the same disease (skin cancer), and that one disease (like polio) can be manifested by different syndromes (paralytic or meningitic forms), and that different diseases (gout and pseudogout) can cause the same syndrome, we must identify the disease not with the syndrome or the cause but with the underlying process.

CONTROVERSIAL CASES

(1) Grief

Any definition must be tested by difficult cases, and grief is one such case. Some psychiatrists argue it is a disease:

> As with classic diseases, ordinary grief constitutes a distinct syndrome with a relatively predictable symptomatology which includes both bodily and psychological disturbances. It displays the autonomy of disease; that is, it runs its course despite the sufferer's efforts to bring it to a close. A consistent aetiologic factor can be identified, namely, a significant loss.
>
> (Engel, 1961, p. 18)

> Illnesses are characterized by the discomfort and the disturbance of function that they produce. Grief may not produce physical pain, but it is very unpleasant and it usually disturbs function.
>
> (Parkes, 1986, p. 25)

However, the arguments they employ are mistaken.

First, it is wrong to argue that if something consists in a cluster of features (syndrome), it is a disease. Going through the changes of puberty consists in a cluster of features. But it is not a disease. Going into labour consists in a cluster of signs and symptoms, but it is not a disease. Second, it is wrong to argue that if something causes discomfort and dysfunction, it is a disease.

166

Pregnancy is a condition that causes relative dysfunction and considerable discomfort, but it is not a disease. Therefore, these arguments do not show that grief is a disease.

While it is true that those who are grieving have a process which they cannot voluntarily reverse and which causes considerable suffering, we do not think that we are better off without grief. This is true not only because those who are able to grieve achieve better psychological adjustment than those who do not (Parkes, 1986). Even if failure to grieve had no side-effects, we want to be beings that form attachments and who do not walk away from major losses without pain. Our relationships would be diminished if we were not able to grieve. Even if there were a drug that could cure us of our grief, we would not want to take it. This supports our view that we do not see it as a disease to be treated, and illustrates how our values about what sort of beings we ought to be influence disease classification.

(2) Homosexuality

Until recently, homosexuality has been seen as a mental illness. Edmund Bergler argues that it is a disease:

> Specific neurotic defences and personality traits . . . are specifically and exclusively characteristic of homosexuality and . . . these defences and traits put the homosexual into a special psychiatric category.
>
> (Bergler, 1956, p. 13)

He seems to argue that homosexuality is an illness because it is caused in a certain way – he commits the essentialist fallacy. A similar mistake is made by Irving Bieber – he sees homosexuality as the result of a close and sexually stimulating mother and a distant and threatening father. Women come to signify a threat from father, and men turn instead to other males for sexual gratification. In his study, 69 per cent of homosexuals had very intimate mother–son relationships, and only 32 per cent of heterosexuals did: 'Our findings point to the homosexual adaptation as an outcome of exposure to highly pathogenic parent–child relationships and early life situations' (Bieber et al., 1962, p. 173). But discovering that homosexuals are the product of certain parent–child relationships does not imply pathology unless we already judge that the consequence is pathological. One might just as easily argue that heterosexuality is a disease because it is the result of a distant and sexually unstimulating mother and a warm and unthreatening father! If we found that heterosexuality was a defence against the fear of losing one's masculinity, this would not prove it was a disease. We cannot discover the disease status of homosexuality by investigating its causes.

Others have argued that homosexuality is a disease because it is due to a biological malfunction. Gunter Dorner argues that the male homosexual's hypothalamus has failed to differentiate and behaves like a female's. He found that the hypothalami of 21 homosexuals functioned like female ones, responding with a rise of luteinizing hormone when injected with oestrogen, a response characteristic of women:

> The evocability of a delayed positive oestrogen feedback effect in the majority of. . . . homosexual men in contrast to . . . heterosexual men suggests that male homosexuals possess a predominantly female-differentiated brain.
>
> (Dorner, 1976, p. 205)

But being due to a malfunction does not make homosexuality a disease. We can imagine discovering that homosexuality has a biological function. Like worker ants, perhaps their function is to aid the reproduction of their relatives (Wilson, 1978). But this does not prove that homosexuality is not a disease. I do not care whether a condition serves the good of the genes – I am concerned whether it serves the good of the individual. Thus a condition's functional status is irrelevant to its disease status. Of course, this is a value judgement – someone may see the preservation of the species as more important than the individual, in which case he will classify different conditions as diseases.

Evelyn Hooker showed that homosexuals are not more disturbed than heterosexuals – most homosexuals are well-adjusted, most had long-lasting relationships, and similar psychological profiles to heterosexuals. So she concluded that it was not an illness (Hooker, 1957). But this commits the naturalistic fallacy – the facts cannot settle the disease status of a condition. Only if we judge homosexuals are worse off will it be a disease. One value judgement relevent to this classification is that homosexuals are worse off in being unable to have their own children. Homosexual couples are like infertile couples, and we classify infertility as a disease because we value being able to have our own children and because we value avoiding the distress infertility causes. Thus homosexuality is undesirable because they are infertile.

We can clarify matters by supposing that homosexuality is the result of some childhood endocrine abnormality or the failure of the foetal hypothalamus to differentiate. Let us also imagine a drug that can treat this, thereby preventing homosexuality. Would we prescribe the drug? *I* would, because heterosexuals are better off in being able to have their own children. But this does not mean that homosexuality is a disease – this is the treatment fallacy. We might be able to develop a drug that ensures that a foetus will be male. But this would not mean that being female is a disease!

But judging heterosexuals are better off does not mean that homosexuality is a disease. This is because in judging that a condition is a disease, we have to make a political judgement. We have to ask not only what sort of people it is worthwhile being, but also what sort of society we ought to create. A society where we stigmatize homosexuals is cruel and divisive. While there are conditions like AIDS that are diseases in spite of the stigma involved, they would still cause major suffering and disability without any stigma. The same is not true of homosexuality – most suffering comes from the label. Most homosexuals would choose to remain the way they are even if there was an effective 'treatment' – homosexuality is more like a choice than an illness, and it would be unjust to stigmatize a choice. Therefore I conclude that homosexuality is not a disease. This illustrates that the concept of disease has a political dimension.

(3) Alcoholism

For two centuries excessive alcohol consumption has been classified as a disease. The central twentieth-century exponent of this view is Edmund Jellinek:

> The disease conception of alcohol addiction does not apply to excessive drinking, but solely to the loss of control which occurs in only one group of alcoholics and then after many years of excessive drinking. The fact that this loss of control does not occur in a large group of excessive drinkers would point to a predisposing X factor in the addictive alcoholics.
>
> (Jellinek, 1952, p. 674)

His disease theory of alcoholism consists of a number of theses: first, alcoholism is a discrete entity – alcoholics differ qualitatively (the predisposing X factor) and not quantitatively from normality. Second, the alcoholic has impaired control over drinking. Third, if normal individuals drink excessively, they do not develop alcoholism. And fourth, once a (predisposed) person has become an alcoholic, he cannot return to moderate drinking without relapse. But the evidence does not support these claims.

First, if there was a special group of excessive drinkers called alcoholics, we would expect the distribution of alcohol consumption throughout society to be bimodal. However, it is not:

> Or to put it the other way about, consumption per head is the crucial variable determining the scale of the whole range of ill effects resulting from excessive drinking. Why should this be? The explanation is that the population is not composed of two separate groups, a large one of 'normal social drinkers' whose drinking habits are harmless and a much smaller one of 'alcoholics' who are responsible for all the trouble.
>
> (Royal College of Psychiatrists, 1986, p. 110)

It does not look like there is a qualitatively discrete group of alcoholics. In fact, different factors probably operate in different cases of excessive drinking: 'In short, there is no one cause of problem drinking; there are almost as many causes as there are problem drinkers' (Heather and Robertson, 1985, p. 224).

Second, if there were a discrete group with a special predisposition, we would expect alcoholism to have a hereditary component. Donald Goodwin has shown that the rate of alcoholism among adoptees who had an alcoholic biological parent was 3.6 times greater than that among adoptees whose biological parents were not alcoholic (Goodwin et al., 1973). However, this does not go very far in showing that alcoholics constitute a discrete group. 82 per cent of the sons who had an alcoholic biological parent did not become alcoholics, and while only 5 per cent of the sons of non-alcoholic biological parents became alcoholic, this group constitutes vastly more in numbers than the first group. This shows that the genetic component makes a difference in only a small minority.

Third, if alcoholics are unable to control their intake, we should not find experimental evidence that they can. But a number of studies show that if alcoholics are rewarded for simple tasks with alcohol, they resist becoming drunk, demonstrating significant control over their drinking:

> All these observations are inconsistent with the concept of loss of control in the sense of an inability to stop once drinking has commenced, and with the related concept of craving in the sense of an uncontrollable urge to consume more and more alcohol during a drinking session.
>
> (Heather and Robertson, 1985, p. 100)

Fourth, there is evidence that severe alcoholics *are* able to return to controlled drinking without a relapse of excessive and destructive drinking. In one follow-up study, 7 out of 93 alcoholics who were addicted to alcohol were able to return to at least five years' harm-free drinking (Davies, 1962).

In summary, the evidence does not support Jellinek's disease theory of alcoholism. But this does not mean that alcoholism is not a disease – there is more than one disease theory of alcoholism. The fact that alcoholism is not qualitatively distinct does not mean it is not a disease – many diseases are not qualitatively distinct from the norm. The fact that there is no single underlying cause for all cases of heavy drinking does not mean it is not a disease – many conditions, like anaemia, constitute a *group* of disorders. The fact that treated alcoholics can return to normal drinking does not mean that it is not a disease – all it means is that treatment can be curative. The fact that people without a genetic predisposition can become alcoholic does not mean alcoholism is not a disease. It just shows that the disease has environmental causes.

Robert Kendell argues that the disease theory has outlived its usefulness because the best way to reduce alcoholism is by such measures as increasing the price of alcohol:

> The conclusion seems inescapable. Until we stop regarding alcoholism as a disease, and therefore as a problem to be dealt with by the medical profession, and accept it as an essentially political problem, for everyone and for our legislators in particular, we shall never tackle the problem effectively. The medical profession and the caring professions in general are just as incapable of dealing effectively with the harm and suffering caused by alcoholism as the medical

services of the Armed Forces are incapable of dealing effec-
tively with the harm and suffering caused by war.

(Kendell, 1979, p. 369)

But Paul Harrison has pointed out that the best way to rid society
of lung cancer is to increase the price of cigarettes, and lung
cancer is still a disease.

What does seem relevant to the disease status of alcoholism is
the fact that alcoholics do have control over their drinking. If the
behaviour is fully voluntary (within the alcoholic's control), then
alcoholism is not a disease. However, the fact that alcoholics can
control the amount of alcohol they consume in experimental
conditions does nothing to show that in everyday circumstances
their behaviour is voluntary. Their behaviour is not fully voluntary because they are unable to do what they recognize (in the
cold light of day) they have most reason to do. In addition, there
is evidence that alcoholics suffer from a dependence syndrome
(Edwards *et al.*, 1977). They are physically addicted to alcohol
and this shapes their destructive behaviour. Because an addiction
is not something that can be voluntarily reversed, this supports
the view that alcoholism is a disease.

Two recent theories challenge the disease status of alcoholism.
One sees heavy drinking as the product of learning – 'problem
drinking is a consequence of faulty learning processes' (Heather
and Robertson, 1985, p. 10), and the other sees heavy drinking
as a 'way of life' (Fingarette, 1988, p. 100). But in both cases the
pattern of drinking is not something that can be reversed by a
simple act of will. An alcoholic cannot choose to unlearn his bad
programming, or disentangle himself by a simple act of will from
a way of life in which he has become stuck. Fingarette writes:

> The general truth is this: human beings do not always
> respond wisely and with foresight; we often drift, unwit-
> ting, into a tangled web of decisions, expectations, habits,
> tastes, fears, and dreams.
>
> (Fingarette, 1988, p. 103)

Just as we argued that becoming trapped in the social role of
madness is a *disease* process, so we can argue that becoming
entangled in a way of life can also be a disease process. If we are
to avoid the essentialist fallacy, we must acknowledge that adopting a way of life can be a disease process. Similarly for the social-

learning theory. Just as learning to become hypertensive is a disease process, so learning to be an alcoholic can be a disease process. Thus both these challenges propose a *disease* theory of alcoholism. Therefore I conclude that alcoholism is a disease. This illustrates that the disease status of alcoholism must not be identified with any particular disease theory and that alternative theories might be disease theories in disguise.

BOUNDARIES

There are three remaining questions to be answered. First, how do we draw the boundary between mental illness and normality? Second, how do we draw the boundary between mental illness and physical illness? And third, how do we draw the boundary between distinct mental illnesses? Let us answer these in turn.

The first problem is the problem of caseness – i.e. when does a condition become severe enough, or depart sufficiently from normality, to count as a case of some psychiatric disorder? To answer this, a number of points must be made. First, the problem arises because diseases can be quantitative as well as qualitative deviations from the norm. Similarly for mental illnesses. We all have various irrational fears, but not all amount to phobias. We all have bouts of low mood, but not all amount to depressive illnesses. Second, it is no good saying something becomes a mental illness when it is disabling because this concept too admits of degrees. Having an irrational fear that does not amount to a phobia is very mildly disabling. Third, this is another area where there is no fact of the matter at stake. If there is no qualitative difference between mentally ill and normal people, then there is no line in nature which our boundary can correctly reflect. And if there is no line in nature for the boundary to mirror, then there is no fact of the matter at stake. It is up to us exactly where to draw the line. Fourth, it is possible for most people in any given society to have one mental illness at a particular time. Normality does not mean simply what is typical (in a society at a given time) – if it were, then it would not be possible for most people in a given society to become depressed at one time. But it is possible – imagine all members lose a relative in a disaster. The notion of normality is constructed and may not mirror what is typical (Reznek, 1987). It is up to us when a condition is a case of psychiatric disorder and when it is sub-clinical distress. We should draw the line such that not everyone is turned into a psychiatric patient and only those who are more severely distressed and disabled are cases. But there is no fact of the matter which boundary line is correct.

The second boundary is between mental and physical illness. Here too we must make a number of points. First, we must not be misled by the distinction into thinking that mental illnesses are disturbances in some special mind stuff while physical illnesses are disturbances of the body. It is clear that mental illnesses like schizophrenia, obsessional neurosis and Alzheimer's disease have organic bases. So the distinction does not rest on the fact that mental illnesses involve no disturbance of the body. Second, some consequences of strokes, e.g. hemiplegia, are treated by neurologists and classified as neurological disorders, while other consequences, e.g. multi-infarct dementia, are treated as psychiatric disorders. Thus the basis for the distinction cannot be the sort of underlying process involved. Third, many physical illnesses have as part of their symptomatology a disturbance of mental functioning. For example, porphyria and hypothyrodism can cause psychoses, yet these conditions are classified as physical disorders. These points demonstrate again that there is no fact of the matter what disorders are mental illnesses. It is arbitrary to regard multi-infarct dementia as a psychiatric disorder while dysphasia from the same cause (stroke) as a neurological one. The most reasonable way to mark the distinction is to say that mental disorders are disorders that predominantly disturb mental functioning – viz. thinking, feeling, reasoning, etc. Where there is a disturbance of basic mental functions – e.g. in blindness – we do not take the person to have a *mental* illness. While the line between basic and higher mental functions is also arbitrary, the demarcation thesis remains plausible.

Finally, we must answer the question how to draw the line between individual mental illnesses. This question has three dimensions. First, whether mental illnesses now occurring in our culture, like anxiety neurosis and depression, are forms of the same disorder or distinct entities. Second, whether mental disorders existing at different times, like Hippocratic melancholia and contemporary depression, are variants of the same disorder or distinct entities. Third, whether disorders existing in different cultures, like panic in our culture and koro in Asia, are variants of the same disorder or distinct illnesses.

Let us take the historical example first. In medieval times, fasting was fundamental to the model of female holiness and expressed the religious ideal of suffering. There were some cases of women in the thirteenth and fourteenth centuries who refused food and became extremely thin – a condition described as anorexia mirabilis (Brumberg, 1988, p. 85). Nowadays, when the ideal of feminine beauty is on the malnourished side, the condition of refusing food, losing weight, and over-valuing being thin is called anorexia nervosa. Are these forms of the same disorder?

We might think that one disease is the same as another if and only if they have the same symptoms. But must disorders share *all* their symptoms, their *central* symptoms, or just a sufficient *majority* to be identical? And how do we count symptoms? In both anorexia mirabilis and anorexia nervosa the women feel that it is important to avoid food, they deliberately diet, they lose weight, and they stop menstruating. Does this mean the disorders are identical (because they share a majority of symptoms), or different (because they do not share all the symptoms)? Do the women share the same symptoms because they both think it is important to do without food, or do they have different symptoms because they think it is important for different reasons? What is the symptom – feeling that it is important to do without food, or feeling that it is important to do without food for specific reasons? If we decide that conditions must share their central symptoms to be identical, how do we decide what is central? Many might feel that the difference in reasons for doing without food are central enough to make the disorders distinct. There appears to be no non-arbitrary way of settling these questions.

The same problems arise in cross-cultural cases. South-east Asians suffer from a disorder called koro which is characterized by extreme anxiety, physical symptoms of autonomic arousal, and the belief that the penis is being withdrawn into the abdomen (Leff, 1988, p. 12). This latter belief is not delusional – others accept that it is a genuine fear and may even help to prevent the penis being retracted! In Chinese mythology, ghosts have no genitals, and so the fear that the penis is being retracted amounts to the fear that one is about to die. We suffer from a disorder known as panic disorder which is characterized by extreme anxiety, physical symptoms of autonomic arousal, and the belief one is having some serious physical disease like a heart attack. Are these two disorders cultural variants of the same mental illness?

The problem of symptom identity arises again. Do we say that the belief that one is having a heart attack is the same symptom as the belief that one's penis is being retracted because both are the belief that one is going die? And if we judge they are not the same symptom, do we decide this is not a central symptom, and therefore that the disorders are identical, or do we require that disorders must share all their symptoms to be identical, and conclude that they are not identical?

We can avoid these problems if disease identity is taken to consist in the identity of the same underlying process. Koro and panic disorder are the same disease if and only if the same underlying process is going on in both cases. Anorexia mirabilis and anorexia nervosa are identical if and only if they share the same underlying process. As I argued above, a disease must not be identified with a particular syndrome (cluster of signs and symptoms), but the underlying process. This is because we accept that more than one disease (schizophrenia, temporal lobe epilepsy and amphetamine psychosis) can cause the same syndrome, while the same disease (manic-depression) can cause distinct syndromes (mania and depression). This means that claims of identity among disease will be hypotheses because we know very little of the underlying processes that explain psychiatric symptoms.

Classificatory systems *are* hypotheses that can be tested by evidence. Cyclothymia is characterized by ups and downs and used to be classified as a personality disorder distinct from manic-depression. Then we discovered that the personality disorder occurred more commonly in relatives of manic-depressives, sometimes providing the genetic link across two non-successive generations with manic-depression. Also such personalities are vulnerable like manic-depressives to becoming manic when taking antidepressants. Because the disorders share the same causes and effects, it is likely that cyclothymia is in reality a mild form of manic-depression (Akiskal, Djenderedjian and Rosenthal, 1977). This led the American nosological system, DSM III-R, to classify cyclothymia as the same disease as manic-depression. This illustrates that classificatory systems are hypotheses tested by evidence from family studies and response to treatment. Such a responsiveness to the facts would be inexplicable unless classificatory systems were hypotheses about matters of fact – specifically, hypotheses about the identity of processes underlying syndromes.

Psychiatrists accept that claims of identity are hypotheses to be tested. They use such evidence as identity of clinical features, family history, prognosis, and response to treatment to support such claims (Robins and Guze, 1970). This data consists in evidence for the identity of the underlying process – it is data on the causes of processes (like genetic factors) and effects of processes (like the prognosis). Two processes will be identical if they have the same causes and effects. So taking this as evidence for disease identity only makes sense if disease identity consists in the identity of the underlying process.

Historical identity claims are difficult to settle because we have no access to past underlying processes. We have to see which hypothesis best explains the available data. Hippocratic melancholia looks clinically identical to depression. While there are some differences – melancholia supposedly afflicted the highly intelligent – these are not sufficient to undermine the claim that melancholia is depression. To suppose otherwise is to leave too many things unexplained – e.g. why did melancholia die out suddenly (in the nineteenth century) only to be replaced by an almost identical disorder? It is much neater to postulate that there is a single disorder existing at different times.

In cross-cultural psychiatry, we are faced with the issue of whether the cultural stereotype of illness so transforms the underlying biological events that different stereotypes create different disorders. For example, Arthur Kleinman studied one hundred patients in a psychiatry clinic in China with the diagnosis of neurasthenia. They met American diagnostic criteria for depression and so he treated them with anti-depressants. But they only responded partially and their somatic complaints persisted.

> Neurasthenia might represent culturally shaped illness experience underwritten by the disease depression. The biologically based disease responded to the 'therapeutic trial' of drugs; the illness experience ended only when powerful social contingencies 'conditioning' the sick role behaviour were removed.
>
> (Kleinman, 1988, p. 13)

Does the neurasthenic stereotype so transform the response to the biological events of what we call depression that it makes it a distinct disease from depression?

Similar issues arise in contemporary intra-cultural identifications. There is a current debate whether anxiety neurosis is a form of depression (Stavrakaki and Vargo, 1986). The evidence mustered to settle this debate is relevant to deciding the identity of underlying processes – studies of family history, stability of diagnosis, response to treatment, and clinical distinctness – which shows that psychiatrists take disease identity to consist in the identity of the underlying process. If we find that both conditions have the same underlying process, do we say that these are two forms of the same disease, or that the clinical features are so different that the diseases must be distinct? This is not settled by the fact that disease identity consists in identity of underlying process. For the underlying processes *must* be different in some way to explain the obvious clinical differences – if the underlying processes were identical in all respects, the clinical presentations would be identical, which they are not.

It is up to us whether to identify the disease with *part* of the whole underlying process or with *all* of it. The stereotype of madness may affect the prognosis of schizophrenia, implying that the total underlying process is altered by the adoption of a stereotype. But do we judge that schizophrenia affected by one stereotype is sufficiently different to count as a distinct disease from schizophrenia affected by a different stereotype? Here it makes sense to identify the disease with part of the underlying process. However, in the case of neurasthenia, the stereotype may so transform the underlying process that it makes more sense to see it as a distinct disease from depression. The postulation of a disease is supposed to explain all the clinical features of the condition. But if the disorder consists only in the biological process uncomplicated by psychological factors, we cannot explain why the clinical features vary.

Is disease identity then not a factual matter? Yes and no. It is partly a factual matter – while identity consists in the identity of the underlying process, this does not tell us *which* underlying process. In the case of depression and neurasthenia, they share the underlying changes in neuro-transmitters but not the process of adopting a stereotype. On a narrow view, they are identical. But if we consider the whole underlying process, they are not. So the facts cannot settle the identity of the disorders. But the facts can settle the non-identity of diseases – if there are *no* similarities between two processes (at any level), then the facts show that they are not identical.

Ultimately it is up to us what sort of nosological system to adopt. While there is no fact of the matter whether mental illness should be identified with part or all of the underlying process, various factors influence this decision. If it turns out that there are only one or two underlying biological defects, we may not want to conclude that there are only one or two mental illnesses! All phobias may share the same abnormality of limbic system, but what seems to make them different mental illnesses is that the learning involved is different – the fear is associated with different objects. And only if we allow disease identity to be determined by the whole underlying process, can mental illnesses explain all clinical features. If agoraphobia consists in only the biological defect, it cannot explain all the clinical features of the syndrome. On the other hand, if all differences in learning, cognitions, and adoption of stereotypes are taken as sufficient for transforming biological abnormalities into distinct diseases, then probably all instances of mental illness will count as distinct types of disease, which is absurd. I believe that the identity conditions for different disorders vary. While learning is an essential part of the phobias such that avoidance of different objects implies a distinct disease, it is not an essential part of schizophrenia – schizophrenics learning to adopt one stereotype do not have a distinct disease from those learning to adopt another.

In summary, it is our values and not the facts that settle the disease status of any condition. The conceptual thesis of the medical paradigm is false, and this has a number of implications for other theses of the medical paradigm. First, it means that the identification thesis is false. Because our values determine disease status, no scientific investigation of the facts can settle whether some condition is a disease. Many of the problems facing psychiatry are no longer easily soluble. Without the identification thesis, the problems of value relativity, disease status, and political abuse are more difficult to solve. Values are not facts that can be discovered, and so conflicts here cannot be settled by investigation of the world. Second, while the teleological thesis remains (trivially) true, the neutrality thesis is false. Because the concept of disease incorporates value judgements as to what sort of people we ought to be, and what sort of society we ought to create, the treatment of disease inevitably pursues moral and political goals as well. Finally, we have seen the boundaries existing around mental illnesses are largely a matter of convention. It is up to us

179

whether to regard a disease as identical to part or all of the underlying process, and our practice will vary depending on the disorder in question.

11

IS PSYCHIATRY A SCIENCE?

I will now investigate whether the epistemological thesis is true and whether psychiatry is a science. We have already seen that scientific method cannot be used to identify diseases – the identification thesis is false. Whether psychiatry is a science leaves untouched the question whether the practice of psychiatry is an art. Even if it is, this has no bearing on whether psychiatry acquires its theoretical knowledge scientifically.

WHAT IS A SCIENCE?

In order to decide whether psychiatry is a science, we need to understand what science is. I understand science thus:

> Science is the activity of formulating empirical hypotheses as substantive causal explanations of public and repeatable observations and the subjection of these hypotheses to empirical evaluation.

This definition makes a number of points.

First, science formulates empirical hypotheses. These are hypotheses that can, without contradiction, turn out to be false. '2 + 2 = 4' is not an empirical hypothesis because 2 + 2 cannot equal 5 without contradiction. 'Energy is conserved' is an empirical hypothesis because it could turn out to be false without contradiction. It is usually protected by *ad hoc* hypotheses – e.g. the violation of the conservation law by beta radiation led scientists to postulate the existence of neutrinos. But we have good reasons for protecting it – neutrinos were later discovered. But the law could still be false – we might discover that it is a statistical law holding only at the macroscopic level and that microscopic violations (which balance out because of the law of large numbers) occur all the time.

Second, the hypotheses must offer substantive explanations – they must not be tautologous. Molière pointed out that we cannot offer a substantive explanation for the fact that opium puts people to sleep by claiming that it has dormitive power – i.e. the power of inducing sleep. The explanation amounts to the claim that opium puts people to sleep because it puts people to sleep, which is empty of empirical content. To count as scientific, an explanation must make an empirical claim that goes beyond a restatement of the fact to be explained.

Third, the hypotheses must offer causal explanations. Scientific explanation has been characterized by the deductive-nomological model – to explain some event, we need to deduce a description of it from propositions describing a law of nature and initial conditions – e.g. we can explain the motion of the moon by deducing a description of it from a description of the masses involved and the law of gravitation (Hempel, 1965). But this model leaves out the important causal element – we cannot explain the height of a pole by reference to the length of the shadow and the law of rectilinear propagation of light, while we can explain the length of the shadow by reference to the height of the pole and the same law. This is because the height of the pole causes the length of the shadow and not the reverse. If someone was a 'shadow artist' and cut lengths of pole because of the length of shadow they cast (at a particular time of day), then we *could* explain the height of the pole by reference to the height of the shadow. But this is only because the explanation now has a causal element – the length of the shadow exerts a causal influence on the cutting of a particular length of pole. Genuine explanations, then, must involve a causal claim.

Fourth, science must purport to explain public and repeatable observations. Science is essentially a public and co-operative exercise, and the growth of knowledge has only been achieved by the fact that one experimenter's findings can be tested by others replicating them. If one cannot do this, the enterprise becomes essentially private and non-scientific – if one cannot repeat observations, then there would be no way of deciding between conflicting claims and making progress. A theory would then rest unchallenged on the authority of a single observation. For this reason, observations must be public and repeatable. Thus I cannot

182

develop a science about my own subjective experiences because any theory about this would have observational consequences that only I could observe. There would be no way others could verify it.

Fifth, science subjects its hypotheses to empirical evaluation. Causal claims are tested by subjecting them to Mill's Methods of Agreement and Difference (Mill, 1941), and hypotheses are tested by inferring observable consequences and verifying them. In order to establish that C is the cause of E, we have to establish that E follows from ABC, BCD, CDE, etc., showing that C is the only event regularly preceding E. This is the Method of Agreement. We also need to show that if C does not occur, E will not follow – that E does not follow on ABD, DFG, BFG, etc. This is the Method of Difference. The use of control groups embodies Mill's ideas – in order to see whether ECT treats depression we need to see whether improvement follows ECT and not placebo. Science tests its hypotheses by inferring and verifying observable consequences. Although scientific theories frequently refer to unobservable entities, such theories are tested by inferring observational consequences. Although physics postulates entities like magnetic fields, electrons, quarks, and other such unobservable things, this does not make the theories unscientific as long as the consequences of such assumptions *are* observable.

It has been the failure to use controls, i.e. Mill's methods, that has held back medical science for centuries. This was probably the result of the natural desire of doctors to 'do something' about their patients' suffering. Instead of holding back to observe the natural course of the illness *without* treatment so that therapy could be scientifically evaluated, they blundered in with untested theories, using such futile treatments as blood-letting. When the illness was short-lived, they congratulated themselves for using good therapy. And when the illness was unresponsive to blood-letting, they concluded the disease was too advanced for anything to work. Failures were discounted, and successes regarded as evidence in favour of the causal efficacy of the treatment. It was because Mill's methods were not used that medicine failed to progress.

Karl Popper has argued that the hall-mark of scientific theories is that they are falsifiable. But most theories are protected by *ad hoc* hypotheses until a better theory is found – if theories did not protect themselves in this way, no theory would receive a genuine test. Many *ad hoc* hypotheses turn out to be true, and if we rejected a theory without first trying to protect it, we would never save the right theory! In addition, most theories are 'born falsified' – at the time they are conceived, there are observational anomalies that refute them. If scientists took anomalies at face-value, no theory would ever get off the ground. While any theory can in principle be saved indefinitely from falsification, if it does so by becoming ever more complex, it is undermined by the observational consequences.

There is no reason why astrology, for example, cannot be a science. We could test the idea that Leos become leaders by seeing whether Leos are over-represented in groups of leaders such as a list of British prime ministers. If this observation fails to material-ize, the theory could be saved by some *ad hoc* hypothesis that only Leos born in certain phases of the moon become leaders. But as long as the *ad hoc* hypothesis is itself testable and subjected to test, astrology will not be unscientific. If *ad hoc* hypotheses are not testable, the methodology ceases to be scientific. Any theory can be protected by gremlin hypotheses – untestable assumptions like the existence of unobservable gremlins who secretly work to ensure that true theories look false. This illustrates that we must distinguish between theories that can in principle be scientific but which are not in practice developed scientifically.

Our definition shows that it is the logic of confirmation and not discovery that defines science. It is irrelevant how we arrive at a theory – if is subjected to empirical confirmation, it is scientific. Einstein remarked that while a theory could be tested by evidence, there was no path from evidence to theory. In fact, scientists can dream up their theories – in 1865 Kekule arrived at the structure of the 6–carbon atom benzene ring by dreaming of snakes form-ing themselves into a ring by biting one another's tails!

THE OBSERVATION BASE

If psychiatry is to be a science, then, it must have a public and repeatable observational base. But, at first glance, this seems far from the case. Essentially, psychiatrists postulate disease entities to explain the complaints of their patients. Most of these com-plaints are about subjective phenomena – hallucinations, intrusive thoughts, low mood, etc. But are these publicly observable? This is an important question because the whole edifice of psychiatric knowledge depends on the observation base of such symptoms – it is from these that we judge that someone is suffering from a psychiatric disorder, and it is from this that the search for the causes, underlying nature, and cure of psychiatric disorder can begin. In other words, psychiatry stands and falls with the detection of subjective symptoms.

Most text-books in psychiatry tell us that the foundation of psychiatry is phenomenology – the study of patients' subjective experience. The father of phenomenology, Karl Jaspers, wrote:

> This preliminary work of representing, defining and classifying psychic phenomena, pursued as an independent activity, constitutes phenomenology.
>
> (Jaspers, 1968, p. 1314)

While it is true that we have to begin with descriptions of the mental states of patients, can this be an observational base? These mental states clearly cannot be observed. We cannot observe someone else having an abnormal perceptual experience – we can only infer on the basis of his behaviour and reports that he is hallucinating. The 'observation' is a *hypothesis* invoked to explain the behaviour (verbal and otherwise) of the patient. So if psychiatry has an observation base, it cannot lie in the subjective phenomena reported by disturbed patients.

However, we do not have to find an observation base that is free of theoretical assumptions. All observational claims in science make theoretical assumptions. When scientists use measuring instruments, they hypothesize that these obey certain laws, thereby turning measurements into hypothesis. The simplest observation is a hypotheses that macroscopic physical objects (and not evil demons or holograms) explain our perceptual experience. But there is nothing viciously circular in this. As long as the theory to be tested is not presupposed by the theory needed to interpret the 'observations', there is no circularity. Thus the status of psychiatry is not undermined by the fact that its observational base actually consists of hypotheses.

The observational base in psychiatry must consist in the *behaviour* of patients (verbal and non-verbal). Although the observation of behaviour also requires us to make theoretical assumptions, these are no different from those needed to study macroscopic objects. And we often call hypotheses 'observations' – we speak of scientists observing electrons in cloud chambers when what they are doing is explaining the tracks in the chamber by hypothesizing electrons. Similarly, we speak of psychiatrists observing patients having hallucinations. This makes the observation base public – a hallucination is accessible to more than one observer because the behaviour is. And the observation is repeatable – others can make it at another time. But most importantly, just as scientists can be trained to observe electrons in cloud chambers, such that they can all agree when there is an electron there, so psychiatrists can be trained to agree when someone is hallucinating – i.e. such observations are reliable. Psychiatrists are able to achieve 80–90 per cent inter-rater agreement for diagnosing major psychiatric disorder from symptoms (Helzer *et al.*, 1977). This means that they are able to reliably identify such subjective phenomena as hallucinations.

The observation base in psychiatry rarely consists in behaviour in the sense of bodily movements – more often it consists in *meaningful* behaviour. But if the observation base consists of meaningful behaviour, this raises the problem of the hermeneutic circle. We have no access to the intentions of the agent apart from his behaviour. But in order to gain access to the intentions from the agent's behaviour, we must have access to his beliefs. But the same problem arises for the agent's beliefs. Suppose we are trying to understand what an agent is doing when he jumps off the Firth of Forth bridge. We can only infer his intention if we also know his beliefs. If we know that he believes he will kill himself, we can infer that he wants to die. Conversely, if we know he believes he can fly, we can infer the contrary desire. We can only get desires from behaviour if we also know the agent's beliefs. But the same problem arises for these beliefs. We are not aided by the fact that he can speak – if we ask him what he is doing, his reply 'I am trying to kill myself' is only evidence for this desire if we assume that he desires to communicate this desire to us, and believes that he will do this by uttering that sentence. But then we are caught in the hermeneutic circle again.

But the hermeneutic circle does not mean psychiatry cannot get off the ground. Assumptions about a patient's beliefs and desires are simply additional hypotheses needed to make observations. While it is correct that we can only get at intentions from behaviour if we already have beliefs, and vice versa, this does not mean that we cannot arrive at the best theory of what someone is doing. A bad theory about someone's beliefs and desires will rapidly become more and more complex and bizarre as it tries to save itself, and like any scientific theory, can be rejected on this basis. Thus if we stop our agent jumping off the bridge, only to find he tries to hang himself, we can only sustain the hypothesis that he did not want to kill himself by *ad hoc* hypotheses like he did not believe hanging would kill him, or that he wanted to fly so badly that our stopping him made him suicidal. A false theory becomes ever more complicated in order to defend itself and this counts as evidence against it. So we can have evidence in favour of one 'observation' and psychiatry can begin.

While the observation base in psychiatry is theory-laden, it is no different from other sciences. The important thing is that the terms in the observation base are reliable. This will imply that the scientific community shares the same underlying theory. If the terms are reliable, different psychiatrists will apply the term to the same events, and the same psychiatrist will apply the term to the same events at different times. And because terms like 'hallucinating' can be reliably applied, the science of psychiatry can get off the ground. Whether people are actually hallucinating when so judged does not really matter. If we can reliably detect abnormal (verbal or non-verbal) behaviour, psychiatry has a satisfactory observational base.

PSYCHIATRIC EXPLANATION

Some psychiatric explanations do not look scientific. Psychiatry purports to explain why certain people repeatedly break the law, develop little empathy with others, and have no conscience, by assuming they suffer from psychopathic personality disorder. But this does not appear to be a substantive explanation. Someone has psychopathic personality disorder if he has certain signs and symptoms like repeatedly breaking the law. But this explanation amounts to the claim that people break the law repeatedly because they repeatedly break the law! Such explanations do not specify the cause independently of the effect they are supposed to explain and hence are tautological and unscientific.

But this conclusion only follows if we define 'psychopathic personality disorder' as 'someone who breaks the law repeatedly, etc'. If we do, then the explanation is indeed tautologous. However, I have argued above that our terms refer to underlying explanatory natures. The term 'psychopathic personality disorder' refers to whatever it is in such people that explains their behaviour. Just as 'gold' refers to the atomic structure that explains the cluster of surface properties like colour, conductivity, etc., by which gold is recognized, so psychiatric terms have a similar meaning. This means that although the explanation does not qualify as a scientific explanation, it does provide us with a potential explanation. A psychopath is not someone who breaks the law repeatedly – this is merely how he is recognized. A psychopath is someone who has a particular underlying neurobiological nature that explains the way he behaves – he might be recognized by a cluster of psychological attributes and behaviours, but this is not what he is. Instead, he is someone with that underlying nature that causes such behaviours. While this underlying nature remains unspecified, the explanation is only a promise of an explanation. But some have tried to specify this nature – Jeffrey Gray has argued that a psychopath is someone whose physiology is bad at fear (Gray, 1971). This would explain why psychopaths have difficulty learning from experience, repeatedly risk punishment by breaking the law, and are difficult to discipline as children, etc. If a psychopath is someone with such an underlying physiological make-up, then this explanation is scientific.

While it is true that some explanations in psychiatry are not yet scientific, this does not mean that they are not crude scientific explanations. As most sciences begin with promises of explanations that are only later realized, it would be wrong to conclude that psychiatry is not scientific. This is like criticizing a branch of knowledge for not being advanced rather than unscientific. Provisional explanations must be made before they can be expanded into full-blown scientific explanations.

In any event, much of psychiatry does not explain symptoms or behaviour by reference to some disorder. Many theories explain why people acquire those personality disorders and mental illnesses – e.g. one theory explains (the symptoms of) depression by such social causes as stressful events, lack of support, early maternal loss, etc. (Brown and Harris, 1978). Another theory postulates that there is a genetic cause for schizophrenia (Kety, Rosenthal and Wender, 1971). These are genuine explanations in that they give causes which can be identified independently of their effects. Then there are other explanations that postulate that diseases consist of certain underlying processes – e.g. schizophrenia is explained in terms of an increased sensitivity of D2 receptors in the mesolimbic part of the brain (Crow *et al.*, 1976), and depression is explained by a cholinergic dominance in the limbic areas (Janowsky *et al.*, 1972). Such explanations are substantive and not tautological.

However, many explanations in psychiatry do not look like causal explanations. Instead, they explain behaviour in terms of reasons – i.e. an agent's desires and beliefs (conscious or unconscious). To explain the paralysis of a soldier, psychiatrists might postulate that he unconsciously desires to avoid battle, and that he believes that if he is ill, he will do so. What is seen as a symptom is reinterpreted as an unconscious action and explained by unconscious reasons. The issue here is whether explanations in terms of motives or reasons (conscious or unconscious) are or can be scientific. Many argue that explanations of behaviour in terms of reasons are neither causal nor scientific. Charles Rycroft writes:

> What Freud did here was not to explain the patient's choice causally but to understand it and give it meaning, and the procedure he engaged in was not the scientific one of elucidating causes but the semantic one of making sense of it. It can be argued that much of Freud's work was really semantic and that he made a revolutionary discovery in semantics, viz. that neurotic symptoms are meaningful disguised communications, but owing to his scientific training and allegiance, he formulated his findings in the conceptual framework of the physical sciences.
>
> (Rycroft, 1968, p. 13)

But rational explanations are causal. Let us look at an analyst who has two competing explanations for our soldier's symptom. He might explain his paralysis by the wish to avoid death or by his wish to avoid humiliation by his cowardice. While both explanations 'make sense' of the symptom, the analyst needs to know which is the correct one in order to treat him. But once we concede there is such a thing as the *correct* interpretation, there must be something in which this correctness consists apart from the fact that it 'makes sense' of the behaviour. It is plausible to argue that what makes one interpretation correct is that it tells us which motive or desire *caused* the behaviour – if the soldier's wish to avoid death caused his paralysis, then this is the correct meaning of his symptom, but if his wish to avoid humiliation caused his paralysis, then this provides the correct meaning. This shows that *meanings have to be causes*. Far from being different things, to give the correct meaning of the action is to give its cause. Freud cannot be construed as giving the meaning of the behaviour rather than the cause.

It may seem that explanations in terms of reasons are not scientific because the law that people are rational is unscientific. It seems unscientific because it cannot be tested or proved false, and hence is not scientific. In order to test the theory that agents act for reasons, we have to be able to test the following causal law: if an agent desires that p, and believes that by doing a, he will achieve p, he will do a (the law of rationality). But to test the law, we need to identify beliefs and desires independently of it. But this is impossible *without already assuming that people are rational*. If we wish to test the law of rationality with our agent jumping off a bridge, in order to see whether he is being rational, we need to identify his desires and beliefs. We might identify the desire to die and the belief that he will do this by jumping. But to identify these from his behaviour, we need to *assume* he is rational. And hence we cannot use these beliefs to test the law without circularity. If we see him on other occasions pulling children away from the edge of the bridge and scolding them, we might infer that he believes that people will kill themselves if they fall off the bridge. But we can only infer this if we assume this behaviour is rational (and that he does not want the children to die). If we see him try other methods of killing himself, we might infer that he wants to kill himself. But we can only infer this if we assume that this behaviour is rational (and he believes that these are methods of killing himself). In other words, we argue in a circle. In order to test the theory that people are rational, we have to identify someone's beliefs and desires. And in order to identify someone's beliefs and desires, we have to assume already that they act for reasons, i.e. they are rational.

But it is not true that we cannot identify beliefs and desires *without* assuming the truth of the law of rationality. Let us take the desire for water. We can identify this desire independently of behaviour by referring to states of the brain. If we assume that a cause of the desire for water is dehydration, we can identify the desire for water with the firing of the supraoptic nuclei. This identification is supported by the fact that this centre has osmoreceptors sensitive to dehydration of the blood. It might be argued that to support the claim that this brain state is identical to the agent's desire for water, we have to correlate this state with the agent's behaviour. But this correlation depends on assuming the law of rationality we hope to test. But we do not have to identify the desire this way. We simply assume that a cause of the desire is dehydration, and then formulate the hypothesis that firing of this centre is identical to the desire for water. With this theory-laden identification of the desire, we can test the law of rationality. This test also tests the identity between thirst and brain state, but since we cannot test any theory in isolation, there is nothing wrong here. Because we *can* identify desires and beliefs independently of the law of rationality, it is testable and scientific.

Others argue that the law of rationality cannot be false and so is not scientific. We cannot give up the law of rationality because it is a prerequisite to understanding one another and even ourselves. Unless we assume it, our speech will be nothing but empty noise (MacDonald and Pettit, 1981, p. 73). To take myself to be making meaningful utterances, I must assume that I intend the noises I make to communicate a certain message, and also that I believe this to be what it communicates – i.e. I must assume I am rational. Similarly for the speech of others. But if the law of rationality is false, this very proposition will become meaningless. And hence the law cannot be false.

However, we can have evidence for and against the theory that we communicate – i.e. that our utterances are meaningful, and therefore the law of rationality can be false. By and large, we have huge amounts of evidence for the success of communication – when we ask for a 'pen' we do not get a glass of wine, and hence we have evidence for the law of rationality. If all communication were to break down, and nobody were to get a single coherent message across to anyone, the chaos in our social lives would be vast. We can imagine that chaos, and hence we can imagine the underlying law being false. But this means that the law *is* a scientific law after all. And in the realm of explaining behaviour, we can also imagine particular breakdowns of the law. When subjects with post-hypnotic suggestions to open the window carried out this instruction, they claimed that they were doing this for 'reasons' – e.g. that the room was 'stuffy' (Hilgard, 1965). But we know that what caused their behaviour was *not* a reason but the post-hypnotic suggestion. But if we can discover that the law is false in a particular case, it is like any other scientific law. Thus there is nothing unscientific about psychiatric explanations.

METHODOLOGY

If psychiatry is to be a science, it must use the appropriate methodology. I will examine an example of the testing of a causal relationship and another of testing a hypothesis.

Let us see how psychiatry tested the causal claim that ECT treats depression and how it discovered the effective ingredient. Psychiatrists used Mill's methods as embodied in the use of control groups. Control groups work best if they resemble the experimental group in all respects besides the variable being tested – i.e. we can infer that C causes E if E follows ABCDF but not ABDF. If E follows ABCDF but not CDGH, we cannot know whether C or D is the cause. To show that ECT causes improvement, we must show that improvement does not follow some inactive treatment.

In 1965, the Medical Research Council ran a placebo controlled trial of ECT. They found that while 90 per cent of the ECT treated group improved in four weeks, only 30 per cent of the placebo group improved. This proved that ECT *is* causally effective in the treatment of depression. However, this does not identify the effective ingredient. ECT consists of giving attention, an anaesthetic, a muscle relaxant, a small current, and a seizure. In order to show that the seizure is the effective ingredient, Mill's methods dictate that the patient must be given everything *except* the seizure. In 1983 the Nottingham study compared real ECT with simulated ECT (Gregory, Shawcross and Gill, 1985). In the simulated group, the patient received everything that the real ECT group received except the electric current and seizure. There was a significant difference in the improvement rates, purporting to prove that the seizure causes the improvement. However, it might have been the electric current that was therapeutic.

This is where Mill's method of agreement comes in. There are other ways that seizures can be induced besides electricity – they can be induced by chemicals and by flashing lights. Patients receiving seizures from flurothyl improved as much as those receiving seizures from electric current (Laurell, 1970). In this way it was shown that it is the seizure and not the passage of electricity that is therapeutic – this is the only factor regularly preceding improvement. This example shows that psychiatry does employ scientific methods, viz. Mill's methods of agreement and difference, in proving its causal claims. While one swallow does not a summer make, a brief perusal of the leading journals of psychiatry will show the widespread use of controlled trials to (scientifically) prove the causal claims of psychiatry.

Scientific methodology does not only involve the use of Mill's methods. There is also the hypothetico–deductive method. This too is used in psychiatry. The following facts suggested a hypothesis to explain schizophrenia: drugs that stimulate dopamine receptors in the brain cause clinical syndromes indistinguishable from schizophrenia (Connell, 1958), and the drugs that are effective in the treatment of schizophrenia all block dopamine receptors (Crow et al., 1976). A hypothesis was constructed that schizophrenia was a disorder characterized by over-activity of the dopaminergic system of the meso–limbic part of the brain (Crow and Gillbe, 1974). Using the hypothetico–deductive method, it was predicted that we ought to be able to observe an excess of dopamine metabolites in the cerebrospinal fluid (CSF). But this was not observed (Bowers, 1974).

As we have been at pains to point out, it is *not* the mark of science that theories which have been falsified are rejected. The dopaminergic theory of schizophrenia still explained more than any other theory and was therefore modified rather than rejected. It was argued that the increased dopaminergic activity was a consequence not of the increased production of dopamine but of an increased number of dopamine receptors – this would explain why increased amounts of dopamine metabolites were not found in the CSF (Crow et al., 1976). Again, using the hypothetico–deductive method, it was predicted that we ought to observe an increased number of dopamine receptors in the brains of schizophrenics at post-mortem. This in fact has been observed, thereby supporting the theory (Owen et al., 1978). This is by no means the end of the story. There is more data to be evaluated, some of which is conflicting. But this example illustrates that the hypothetico–deductive method is alive and well in psychiatry. And like other branches of science, good theories are saved from falsification by internal alterations.

However, psychodynamic explanations are seldom tested in

the manner required to be scientific. Popper claimed that such explanations are not scientific because they are not falsifiable. But we have seen that the use of *ad hoc* hypotheses does not make a theory unscientific. There is nothing intrinsic to such theories that prevents them from being tested or falsified. Adolf Grunbaum showed that it is easy to test Freud's theory that paranoia arises from repressed homosexuality (Grunbaum, 1986). All we have to do is to find a paranoid homosexual and the theory is falsified! However, the question is not whether psychodynamic theories can be scientific – they can – but whether in practice they are tested in a scientific manner.

In practice they are seldom subjected to test. When they are, the reasoning is often circular – the interpretation of the data itself requires the assumption of the truth of the theory. For example, in a study of the Oedipal complex, with children interpreting figures of parents and children,

> more girls than boys – and this difference was highly significant – fantasized that the male figure mounted the stairs and entered the room. This, of course, is perhaps the strongest evidence for Freudian theory since in the theory mounting the stairs is symbolic of sexual intercourse and entering the room symbolizes the placing of the penis into the vagina.
>
> (Kline, 1984, p. 72)

Such 'evidence' is highly suspect because the sex difference can only be used as evidence for the Freudian theory if it adopts a 'symbolic interpretation' that implies that the girls are thinking of having sexual intercourse with their fathers – i.e. if it begs the question. The symbolic interpretation is a gremlin hypothesis preventing the theory from being tested – any result could be confirmatory given the right interpretation.

Psychodynamic theory is inherently self-protective – i.e. it has many built-in gremlin hypotheses that can explain away all contradictory data. Repression is another such gremlin hypothesis. If the patient agrees with an interpretation, this shows it was right. If the patient disagrees, he is simply repressing the truth. The existence of the repressing mechanism makes the theory too easy to save itself. While using *ad hoc* hypotheses to save theories is not inherently unscientific, if a theory lends itself too easily to such protectionism, in practice it will not be developed scientifically.

In addition, psychodynamic theories frequently lack genuine predictions. Because of the slack in the theory, they can be internally adjusted to fit with any observation – e.g. unconscious conflict over expressing aggression can lead to anger towards the self, a different person, total lack of anger, unrelated activity, depression, etc. According to Bayes' theorem, confidence in a theory is not increased if the predictions are as likely to occur if the theory is true as they are if it is not (Swinburne, 1973). But if Freudian theory predicts everything, it is not confirmed if anything is observed.

The other reason why there has been little rigorous testing of psychodynamic theories, from Freudian to Kleinian, is that such theories have led to religious movements, with proponents of each theory having a deep emotional commitment to the theory. There has therefore been a reluctance to expose the theories to scientific test, and anecdotal evidence gained from therapeutic sessions has been treated as confirmatory. But this is a hopeless way to do science. It is well known that Freudian patients produce Freudian dreams, Adlerian patients produce Adlerian dreams, etc. Patients, like anybody else, are eager to please, and what better than to give the therapist what he wants and confirm his beliefs.

In summary, psychiatry is a science – the epistemological thesis is true. There is room for improvement in many areas, but in most cases psychiatric research proceeds in a scientific way. Psychiatry has an observational base – the behaviour (verbal and non-verbal) of patients. Although its observational terms such as 'hallucinations', 'obsessions', 'delusions', etc., are inferences based on this behaviour, there is nothing unscientific in this. As long as the terms are reliable, and they are, psychiatry can be provided with empirical foundations. Psychiatry produces genuine explanations, and where it does not, it provides the sketch of a genuine explanation to be filled out by further investigation. Finally, the methodology used is scientific. In principle, there is nothing unscientific about all psychiatric theories, even psychodynamic ones. But in practice, some areas of psychiatry fall short of the scientific ideal.

12

PSYCHIATRY AND
RESPONSIBILITY

It is time to see whether the responsibility thesis is true – whether having a mental illness excuses a patient from being responsible for his actions.

MENTAL ILLNESS AND RESPONSIBILITY

When a psychotically depressed mother kills her children because she is convinced they are better off dead, we judge she is not responsible for her actions and excuse her from blame. Similarly for a schizophrenic who kills innocent people because he believes they are hostile Russian agents, for a kleptomaniac who steals a range of objects for which he has no conceivable use, and for an epileptic who strangles someone during a seizure. Can we justify these intuitions? Szasz argues not:

> If 'mental illness' is a bona fide illness, then it follows, logically and linguistically, that it must be treated like any other illness. Hence, mental hygiene laws must be repealed. There are no special laws for patients with peptic ulcer or pneumonia; why then should there be special laws for patients with depression or schizophrenia?
>
> (Szasz, 1974c, p. xii)

Since bodily diseases like pneumonia do not provide excuses for criminal actions like murder, Szasz argues that neither should mental illnesses. Having a disease *per se* seems unable to excuse someone from responsibility. Jennifer Radden argues that this is the major flaw in the medical paradigm:

> The failure of the medical model to accommodate our moral

196

intuition that insanity excuses wrong-doing is a neglected aspect of the standard critiques of that model. It is, moreover, the fundamental failing of a disease model. . . . We want to excuse the insane criminal or wrong-doer. Yet if we adopt a medical model we must explain why diseases constitute excuses – and they do not appear to do so.

(Radden, 1985, p. 42)

However, I will argue that the medical paradigm is not flawed in this way and that the responsibility thesis is defensible.

In considering whether someone is responsible for his actions, we are guided by the intuition that it is only just to punish those who are responsible for their actions. If our intuitions strongly suggest that we ought not to punish someone, this suggests we do not judge him responsible for his action. It is because we feel it would be unjust to punish the mentally ill offenders described above that we do not consider them responsible for their actions. What we need to do now is to explain why they are not responsible.

Our intuitions suggest that a person is only responsible for his voluntary actions. A voluntary action is an action performed intentionally, and a person is responsible for his actions if he 'could have done otherwise'. This latter idea is embodied in the policeman test – if a man would have done otherwise had there been a policeman at his elbow, he is responsible for his action. Conversely, a man is not responsible for involuntary actions – i.e. what happens to him. If he has a vaso-vagal attack at the wheel of his car and kills a pedestrian, we do not regard him as responsible because fainting is not a voluntary action. The law recognizes that we are only responsible for voluntary actions (Williams, 1983). If a person kills someone while sleep-walking, he is excused from responsibility because he is judged not to have formed any intent and thereby not to have acted voluntarily.

Our intuitions also suggest that ignorance and compulsion excuse a person from responsibility for his actions (Aristotle, 1955). If a man gives his wife her medicine, and unwittingly administers poison and kills her, he is not responsible for her death. And if a man acts under the threat of death to his family – i.e. under compulsion – then he is not fully responsible for his actions. We cannot expect a reasonable man to act otherwise.

On this basis, it can be shown that mental illnesses excuse.

The idea that mental illness excuses because it causes ignorance is reflected in the McNaughton Rules. In 1843, Daniel McNaughton shot and killed Edward Drummond, the private secretary to the prime minister, Sir Robert Peel, mistaking him for the prime minister. He was suffering from the delusion that Peel and others were persecuting him. At his trial, the defence of insanity was successfully used. The House of Lords justified this decision to Queen Victoria (whose would-be assassin had also recently been excused on such grounds) with the McNaughton Rules:

> To establish a defence on the grounds of insanity, it must be conclusively proved that, at the time of the committing of the act, the party accused was labouring under such a defect of reason, from the disease of the mind, as not to know the nature and quality of the act he was doing; or if he did know it, that he did not know what he was doing was wrong.
>
> (Regina v. McNaughton, 1843)

To be excused, the person must suffer from a disease of the mind which causes factual or moral ignorance.

In addition, a mental illness can excuse if it causes 'internal compulsion'. The law, at least in England and Scotland, admits that a person can have diminished responsibility:

> Where a person kills or is party to the killing of another, he shall not be convicted of murder if he was suffering from such abnormality of mind . . . as substantially impaired his mental responsibility for his acts and omissions in doing so or being a party to the killing.
>
> (Homicide Act, 1957)

If a person is compelled to do something because of some mental condition, then he is excused from full responsibility.

On this view, if a person acts because of ignorance or compulsion, and if mental illness is causally sufficient for this, then the agent is not responsible for his actions. Or if a person does something while failing to form an intent, he is not responsible. When a schizophrenic kills because of a delusion (ignorance), he is not responsible because he is ignorant of what he does. When a kleptomaniac steals because of some compulsion, he is not responsible because he would have stolen with security guards 'at his elbow' – he could not have done otherwise. When an epileptic kills because of a seizure, we excuse him because this was not a voluntary action.

There are a number of problems with this explanation. First, an epileptic may know he behaves violently in a psychomotor seizure, and may voluntarily induce a seizure by flicking his hand back and forth in front of his eyes in order to be violent. While it is true that, immediately before the violent act, he is unable to form an intent, he is nevertheless responsible for his violent action because he *did* form an intent to be violent in this way. Similarly, a schizophrenic may omit his medication knowing he will come to believe people are merely irritating insects to be killed. If he kills while labouring under this delusion, he is nevertheless still responsible because he is responsible for this ignorance.

Second, while the schizophrenic and depressive are ignorant – the former thinks that innocent people are Russian agents and the latter that life for his family will be an endless torment – and while they are not responsible for their illnesses, this ignorance is not sufficient to excuse. To count as an excuse, those actions must be justified if performed *without* ignorance. But if Russian agents had indeed infiltrated society intent on undermining it, killing them would not be justified – he ought to go to the police instead. Similarly, if life was going to be an endless torment for the depressive's family, killing them is not justified – she ought to discuss the matter with them and leave them the choice. Therefore, ignorance cannot provide an excuse here. But we still feel the schizophrenic and the depressive are not responsible.

Third, there are other cases where mental illness excuses but where no ignorance and compulsion can be found. In 1966 a sniper in the University of Texas killed several people. There was little evidence that he was suffering from ignorance or some irresistible impulse, but a brain tumour was found which presumably caused his actions. Jennifer Radden argues that the sniper was either ignorant of the source of his desire to kill, or he was not. If he was ignorant, this ignorance excuses and he was not responsible. If he was not ignorant, then assuming him to be of normal moral constitution, he would have refrained from acting unless the desire was irresistible (Radden, 1985, p. 36).

But this is wrong. First, the ignorance it supposedly causes cannot excuse. While it is true that the sniper does not know that the tumour caused his desire to kill, I am certainly unaware of the physical causes of my desires. But this does not make me ignorant in such a way that I am not responsible for my actions! On this criterion, we will *all* fail to be responsible for our actions. And second, the tumour may still excuse while not causing ignorance or an irresistible impulse. It may have caused personality changes making him have little respect for the lives of others. But Radden feels personality change cannot excuse:

> There is a good reason why we should be reluctant to excuse the criminal action of a person suffering long-term personality change. It is because the element of knowledge would appear to enter critically into this case. . . . Because with knowledge comes foresight and predictive and preventive powers, persons able to understand the disease's role in their motivation and action would be culpable in the same way as the alcoholic and drug addict. They could predict and thus would be held responsible for preventing the illegal actions by avoiding the occasion and means of criminality, or by actively seeking treatment and alleviation for that symptom of their condition.
>
> (Radden, 1985, p. 39)

But this is also wrong. A person who has undergone a personality change may not be ignorant of his new character – he may predict that he will kill. But as a result of the personality change, he may not care enough about others any more to be interested in preventing this. We do not regard the sniper as responsible because we feel that it was not *him* who committed these acts.

Another explanation why mental illness excuses argues it does so by causing a pervasive disturbance of rationality:

> Rationality is the fundamental premise by virtue of which we understand ourselves as human beings; that is, as creatures capable of adjusting their actions as reasonably efficient means to intelligible ends. Being mentally ill means being incapacitated from acting rationally in this fundamental sense. . . . Why does severely diminished rationality excuse? It is because our notions of who is eligible to be held morally responsible depend on our ability to make out rather regularly practical syllogisms for actions. One is a moral agent only if one is a rational agent.
>
> (Moore, 1980, p. 60)

This view has a prima facie plausibility because it can explain why rational agents are responsible for their actions. A person is rational if he is able to let good reasons determine his beliefs and his actions. The crude policeman test presupposes that if a person is given a sufficiently good reason, embodied in the presence of a policeman at his elbow, not to do something, he will behave otherwise – i.e. the test presupposes rationality. Let us see if this irrationality criterion can do better than the traditional view and show how mental illness excuses.

The criterion appears to do better than the reference to ignorance and compulsion. The schizophrenic with the delusion that Russian agents have infiltrated society ought not to have killed them even if his belief was true. Therefore, the ignorance criterion does not work. However, schizophrenia also serves to undermine the agent's reasoning powers such that he may well not have understood that there was any option. Therefore, we ought to excuse him. Similarly, we judge that the depressive ought not to have killed her family even if her belief in a bleak future was true. However, we ought to excuse her because severe depression distorts the agent's powers of reasoning such that she might well not have figured there was any alternative. If mental illness so undermines a person's rational faculty that he/she is unable to work out what he/she has most reason to do, then he/she is not responsible for those actions. We judge that the kleptomaniac is not responsible because rationality is undermined by the disorder – he recognizes that he has most reason not to steal, but finds he is unable to be rational. It is because the mental illness undermines his rationality so that he is no longer able to do what he has most reason to do, that we consider the mental illness to be an excuse. Someone is only responsible if he is rational, because only if he is rational is it the case that he could have done otherwise. So all in all, the criterion of irrationality appears to do quite well.

However, it comes into difficulties when it encounters the case of the personality change discussed above. The man undergoing the personality change should be excused from his crimes. However, this was not because the resultant personality was in any way irrational – he simply had radically different desires and concerns. We do not regard the sniper as responsible because he was not responsible for acquiring the tumour which gave him radically different desires and attitudes. While this different personality acted rationally (on the basis of these new desires and attitudes), we think the original person is innocent – it would be a travesty of justice if we were to excise the tumour and then convict him of murder. Therefore this explanation of how mental illness excuses also falters.

Any justification of the excusing property of mental illness must take account of the fact that not all mental illnesses excuse the sufferer from blame. Someone with hypochondriasis is not excused from defrauding an insurance company, and exhibition-ism does not provide an excuse for armed robbery. It seems reasonable to conclude that if a mental illness is to excuse, it must be causally related to the behaviour it is excusing. This suggests the following argument: from the conceptual premise that if an agent is not responsible for his disease, he is not responsible for the effects of that disease, and the factual premise that an agent is not responsible for his diseases, we can conclude that he is not responsible for any behaviour that is the effect of the disease. Is this argument sound?

The factual premise seems true. We are only responsible for voluntary actions and not for what happens to us. But diseases are by definition involuntary processes – i.e. not actions. If dis-abilities and symptoms were forms of action, being reproducible at will, they would not be symptoms of disease. But since they are not forms of action, we cannot be responsible for them. And hence it appears to follow that we cannot be held responsible for the diseases that we have.

However, the premise is false. There are cases where we *are* responsible for diseases we have. A man who knowingly goes to bed with a woman with gonorrhoea *is* responsible for getting the disease. The law recognizes this in its judgement on crimes committed under the influence of alcohol or drugs. Even though it may be the case that one is not responsible for one's actions while under the influence of alcohol or drugs, because one is responsible for putting oneself under the influence of alcohol or drugs, one is responsible for the crimes committed (Williams, 1983). Were this not the case, then a person wishing to commit violence could take a drug like PCP known to cause violent outbursts. But if we amend the factual premise to the assumption that an agent is not responsible for the diseases he has not know-ingly caused or failed to treat, then it is true.

The conceptual premise is also false. A man might not be responsible for acquiring diabetes mellitus, but whether he becomes symptomatic depends on whether he takes insulin.

Knowing that his symptoms depend on his taking insulin, if he refuses to take his insulin, becoming comatose at the wheel of his car and killing a cyclist, he *is* responsible.

It is only where diseases are not knowingly caused, and where the causal relationship between the disease and the effects is one of causal sufficiency, that the premise seems true. If the disease is causally sufficient for the behaviour, then the agent is not responsible for it. This is because there is no room for the agent to intervene to prevent the occurrence of this behaviour. In the diabetes case, there *is* room for this intervention – the diabetes is only necessary for a coma – and hence the agent remains responsible. Thus we have a justification why mental illness excuses – if a mental illness was not knowingly caused, and is causally sufficient for some behaviour, then the agent is not responsible for that behaviour.

But this requirement is too strong. The relationship between mental illness and the 'resulting' behaviour is not one of causal sufficiency. Rather, the disease in most cases is only necessary for the behaviour. For example, schizophrenia may be sufficient for abnormal beliefs, but is not sufficient for the resulting action – e.g. it may be sufficient for the belief that Russian agents have infiltrated society, but is not sufficient for the action – this depends on other factors like the desire to rid society of such agents. Because the mental illness is only a necessary condition for the behaviour, we cannot explain why it excuses with this argument. There may be mental illnesses, like temporal lobe epilepsy, where the disorder is sufficient for the automatic behaviour during a seizure, and where such a justification applies. But there are many more where this justification will fail to apply.

We need an explanation why the schizophrenic is responsible while the diabetic is not when in both cases the disease is necessary for the behaviour. We need an explanation why a disease that causes a new desire (to kill) in the sniper undermines his responsibility, but the disease of TB that causes anger towards the state for not improving living standards (responsible for the disease) and subsequent terrorist activity does not undermine responsibility. We also need an explanation why the man who induces a psychomotor seizure is responsible. Finally, we need an explanation why the kleptomaniac who acts irrationally is not responsible, while someone who chooses irrationally to fulfil a dare to steal is responsible.

The explanation lies with the notion of autonomy. Someone is responsible only if he is autonomous – if his actions are *fully* voluntary – and diseases can undermine autonomy. Someone is autonomous if he determines his own life without interference. To expand, we must understand what it is for *him* to determine his life. For the self to determine his life, he must act rationally in accordance with his own desires. If a man acts because of a post-hypnotic suggestion, we do not think that he acts autonomously – it is not *him* who acts. Generalizing, we regard alien desires – i.e. desires acquired in abnormal ways, like hypnosis or disease – as undermining autonomy. If a man acts in a drugged state with his rational faculty undermined, we do not take him to be autonomous. In addition, factors that undermine the agent's rationality, such as impulse disorders or addictions, also undermine autonomy. Finally, outside pressures such as coercion undermine autonomy. Any notion that hopes to explain why an agent is responsible must explain why we should only praise or blame him. And the notion of autonomy does just this. If an agent acts because of alien desires, or because his rationality is undermined, or because he is being coerced, it is not *him* who is acting. Only when the self determines his actions do we consider it fair to praise or blame him.

Thus we can hypothesize that it is only where disease undermines autonomy that it can excuse the person from responsibility. In the TB case, the formation of the new desire (for justice) occurs in the normal way – the agent perceives that someone has caused his TB and desires retribution. Although the disease causes the desire, it does so *in a normal way* – the new desire is not alien and therefore autonomy is not undermined. But in the case of the sniper, the new desire (to kill others) is *not* caused in a normal sort of way – the disease directly causes the desire without the agent accurately perceiving he has a new need – his new desire is alien. For this reason his autonomy is undermined. In fact, the change most calculated to undermine autonomy is personality change – if an alien process produces a new set of desires and attitudes, then it is no longer the (original) self who determines his future. In the case of the schizophrenic, the new belief is caused in an abnormal way – it is not acquired on the basis of the available evidence because the disease has undermined rationality.

Hence autonomy has been undermined. While in the diabetes case, the desire (to acquire symptoms) *is* formed in a normal way, and hence he is responsible for the death. Similarly for the epileptic who induces his seizure. The kleptomaniac has his rationality undermined by his illness in that he is unable to stop himself doing what he recognizes he has most reason not to do – his action is not determined by normal rational deliberation and autonomy is undermined. While the person acting on the dare, though irrational, is acting after rational deliberation (to take the risk). To illustrate:

Epilepsy Case:
Disease —A→ Action   Not autonomous
                                                            Not responsible

Self-induced Epilepsy Case:
Desire + Belief —N→ Disease —A→ Action   Autonomous
                                                            Responsible

Sniper Case:
Disease —A→ Desire, + Belief —N→ Action   Not autonomous
                                                            Not responsible

TB Case:
Disease —N→ Desire, + Belief —N→ Action   Autonomous
                                                            Responsible

Schizophrenia Case:

Disease —A→ Belief, + Desire —N→ Action   Not autonomous
                                                            Not responsible

Kleptomania Case:
Desire + Belief + Disease —A→ Action   Not autonomous
                                                            Not responsible

Dare Case
Desire + Belief —N→ Action   Autonomous
                                                            Responsible

—N→   =   causes in normal way
—A→   =   causes in abnormal way

While this is probably an oversimplification, it illustrates that only if behaviour is determined in a certain way (by rational deliberation on desires and beliefs normally formed) will the agent be responsible.

It might be considered odd that one sort of cause undermines responsibility while another does not. But this is the only reasonable position to take. Being responsible is not a matter of actions being uncaused – if they had no causes, we would have no control over them. We would find ourselves stealing when we had no good reason, and this would hardly be a state of affairs where we would be responsible. Being responsible is a matter of one's actions being caused *in a certain way* – by reasons caused in the right sort of way. Only if our actions are under the control of reasons normally formed are we responsible. This entails that if our actions fall under the control of other sorts of processes, we cease to be responsible. And this is precisely the position we have arrived at.

Thus the responsibility thesis is defensible. And there *is* a logical connection between mental illness and responsibility. Diseases can undermine autonomy, and autonomy is required for responsibility. Hence we can explain why diseases excuse a person from responsibility. QED.

THE EXISTENCE OF EVIL

It seems natural to assume that some people are evil – i.e. there are people who voluntarily perform evil acts. It is also natural to assume that once our values have determined what are evil acts, it is a factual matter whether or not someone is evil. But whether we regard someone as responsible depends on whether their behaviour is the product of a disease, and since this depends on our values and not on the facts, a person's responsibility is not a factual matter. This means that whether someone is evil depends on our values and not on the facts.

This seems unpalatable. There appears to be a danger of inventing labels for deviant behaviour which excuse that behaviour in a circular fashion. Barbara Wootton warns:

> The psychopath is a critical case for those who distinguish between the mad and the bad. He has no symptoms of mental disorder independent of objectionable behaviour. Mental abnormality is inferred from behaviour while anti-social behaviour is explained by mental abnormality.
>
> (Wootton, 1959, p. 11)

She argues that only if disease is defined in an objective way will this problem be avoided.

> Definitions of mental health merely reflect their author's personal conception of the Good Life or the Good Citizen in the frame of his own particular culture. No matter how widely they may be endorsed, they lack any scientific foundation. . . . I would express the hope that psychiatrists will resist the temptation to dress up moral judgements in medical clothing.
>
> (Wootton, 1980, p. 527)

But there *is* no objective definition of disease, and hence we cannot avoid the problem in this way.

If some harmful act is to count as evil, it must be voluntary. It might seem that there is a fact of the matter whether some behaviour is voluntary. But whether behaviour is voluntary or involuntary is partly an evaluative matter. Let me illustrate. Suppose we discover that deeds of great self-sacrifice – for children or comrades in arms – are all preceded by an unusual brain state which can be recorded on an electroencephalogram (EEG). Suppose too that if this electrical pattern is artificially reproduced, acts of self-sacrifice are performed. The question arises whether the condition producing this brain state is a disease. Would we judge that the brain state is pathological, and hence conclude that his behaviour is involuntary? I think not. Even if we discovered a new anti-convulsant which could prevent such electrical abnormalities, thereby preventing acts of self-sacrifice, we would not want to treat the condition.

Let us compare this to the discovery that motiveless murderers have abnormal EEG recordings. In fact, it has been found that 73 per cent of men who committed apparently motiveless murders had abnormal EEGs (Stafford-Clark and Taylor, 1949). Let us suppose too that such abnormalities are also reversible with anti-convulsant treatment, thereby inhibiting acts of impulsive violence. Would we regard conditions producing such abnormalities as diseases, and the behaviour as involuntary? I think we would. And the reason for the asymmetry here is clear. We value acts of self-sacrifice whereas we do not value acts of impulsive violence. It is because we value the consequences of the one condition that we do not regard the behaviour as involuntary, while it is because we do not value violence that we regard the violent behaviour as involuntary.

Given our account of disease, once we decide on the disease status of some condition, we *automatically* decide the involuntary status of the 'symptoms'. If the symptoms are behaviour, it follows that the behaviour is not voluntary. What comes first is the decision whether some condition is a disease, and then it follows by definition that the behavioural consequences are involuntary. We decide the boundaries between voluntary and involuntary behaviour by first deciding the boundaries between disease and normality. And since disease status is determined by our values, the voluntary status of behaviour is also determined by our values.

If voluntariness consists in some fact, it is difficult to find. Voluntariness of some behaviour cannot consist in the fact that the behaviour is reproducible on demand. This is because it is open for us to argue that the desire that motivates such reproducible behaviour is so perverse as to be the consequence of some disease. And hence that this behaviour is not fully voluntary. For example, we are liable to suspect that someone who can mutilate himself on request is disturbed and that his behaviour is not fully voluntary. Hence voluntariness cannot consist in this fact.

Voluntariness cannot consist in the fact of being able to do otherwise – i.e. behaviour being subject to influence from other incentives. Consider this example. A woman raided the fridge to have binges in her sleep. However, she did not do so when she knew before retiring that her husband had left out a toy snake for which she had a phobia – when she had a good reason for not bingeing, she did not (Roper, 1989). Does this mean that she was responsible for her somnambulant bingeing? No. For we can argue that one of the causes of her involuntary sleep-walking was the belief that there was no snake near the fridge. Some people with hay fever and asthma may have attacks induced by the belief that there is a cat in the room. But this does not mean that hay fever is not an involuntary process. The fact that beliefs (and desires) are causally instrumental in causing some occurrence does not mean that the process is under voluntary control and therefore not a disease. This shows that it is open to us to interpret the policeman test – only certain behaviour which can be modified by incentives is voluntary, and it is up to us to decide what behaviour.

Voluntariness cannot consist in the fact of being able to do otherwise because we are forced to say that actions for which we cannot provide good reasons to desist are by definition involuntary. But this cannot be right. If behaviour is directed to the most desired goal of the agent (at that time), it follows that it is not subject to influence from other incentives – i.e. is involuntary. But acts of self-sacrifice are not involuntary simply because they are strongly motivated.

Voluntariness cannot consist in the fact that the person does not suffer from any culpable ignorance or compulsion because these are not facts. When we say that someone was suffering from culpable ignorance, rather than ignorance *per se*, we are implying that *he ought to have known better*. But when we judge this, we are not describing what is the case, but prescribing what should be the case – it is not a factual matter, but an evaluative one. And as regards the question of compulsion, I think that this too involves an evaluative component. If I place a bomb in a busy restaurant because a mob threatens to kill my kidnapped family, I am judged to be acting under compulsion. This is because of the value judgement that the death of one's family is an awful enough consequence to force me to comply with the mob. However, if I place the bomb in the restaurant because a mob threatens to cut off the ear of my pet gerbil, I am not judged to be acting under compulsion. This is because of the value judgement that the mutilation of my pet gerbil is not an awful enough consequence to force me to comply with the mob. This is in spite of the fact that I might want to save my gerbil from mutilation more than I want to save the people in the restaurant. So if voluntariness consists in this, it is not a factual matter.

Voluntariness cannot consist in the fact of not being the consequence of an irresistible impulse. It is not a factual matter whether a desire is irresistible. In fact, the very idea of an irresistible impulse is suspect (Kenny, 1984). For to decide whether some desire is irresistible, we have to be able to distinguish a person of normal strength of will succumbing to an abnormally strong desire and a person of abnormal weakness of will yielding to a normal desire. Past actions cannot help us decide. If he acted similarly in the past, does this mean he always suffers from abnormally strong desires, or that he is usually unwilling to control himself? And if he has acted differently in the past, does this mean that he has newly acquired a weakness of will, or that the new desire must have to have been abnormally strong to make him act out of character? We might think that some desire is irresistible if the agent's actions are irrational – i.e. if he does not do what he has most reason to do. But how do we judge that an agent has not at the moment he acts changed his values such that his action becomes what he has most reason to do? We cannot avoid this difficulty by arguing that someone suffers from an irresistible impulse if *he* judges that he had more reason to do otherwise but failed to do so. Frequently we allow ourselves to act on impulse when we know we have more reason to desist, but we are not thereby suffering from an irresistible impulse. Similarly, what do we say of someone who repeatedly is altruistic, doing things that he has more reason not to do? Do we say he suffers from altruistic impulse disorder? Again we see the role of values. Because we value the occasional ability to act on impulse and not be constrained by reason, and because we value altruism, we would not consider such cases examples of irresistible impulse.

Voluntariness cannot consist in being the product of the machinery of the (free) will. There is nothing in the brain that fits the description of this free will. In addition, to postulate such an entity to explain behaviour lands us into difficulties. First, we have to accept that physical laws of nature are violated every time free will interferes with the workings of the brain to determine an action. Second, if free will is not determined by antecedent causes, then it cannot be determined by antecedent reasons either, and our behaviour will end up being spontaneous and out of our (rational) control – hardly what we would regard as responsible action! And third, even the machinery of the will is made compatible with the laws of nature by arguing that the laws of nature are indeterministic (Eccles, 1970), this does not help matters – our actions are not voluntary if they are determined by randomness (Ayer, 1954). The difference between voluntary and involuntary behaviour does not consist in the difference between behaviour that is caused and behaviour that is uncaused. Instead, the voluntariness of behaviour consists in having one sort of a cause rather than another.

This illustrates that there is no fact of the matter as to whether some behaviour is voluntary. Whether there is evil or not does not depend on the facts. Instead, it is up to us whether to see certain behaviour as bad or mad. Let us look at it a different way. Suppose we undertake an empirical study of evil. We study men like Hitler, Eichman, Cesare Borge, and other men who are unequivocally evil. Suppose that we find that all such men have abnormalities in their brains – their amygdalas are abnormally large. Then we have a choice – are they all diseased, or have we identified the neurological basis of evil? In this case, the choice is inextricably related to the issue of how we feel such men should be treated. If we feel that we should punish them, then we will admit the existence of evil and regard them as bad. If we feel that we should treat them, then we will deny the existence of evil and regard them as mad. If we regard all wrong-doers as ill, we should be treating and not punishing them. We have to ask whether we want to live in a world where wrong-doers are incarcerated in prisons and punished for their wickedness, or in a world where they are treated in mental asylums for mental illness and restored to their normal moral state. And this is exactly the decision that is needed to decide whether some condition is a disease. This decision will be heavily influenced by the existence of some treatment – if there is a drug that causes the atrophy of the amygdala, and reverses the evil behaviour, we would be more inclined to think of the condition as a disease.

So where does failure of responsibility end and evil or wickedness begin? Radden argues that failure of responsibility ends and wickedness begins with personality disorder:

> Legal hesitation in classifying character disorders as criminal insanity (and thus as exculpating conditions) seems to rest on the impulse to separate mad from bad. A condition characterized by nothing but aberrant desires to harm others cannot be adequately distinguished from sheer evil. . . . For most deviance – both that associated with cognitive and with affective states – is also defective: the states reflect unreason. When they do not – that is, when there are psychiatric conditions characterized solely by their deviance, like sadism and psychopathic personality – the intuition to judge them as excuses for wrong-doing seems also to be more equivocal and so less reliable as a guide to their treatment.
> (Radden, 1985, pp. 116–19)

Let us examine this issue in more detail.

We have argued that the sniper is not responsible for his actions. Suppose that there is a type of tumour which, like many actual frontal lobe tumours, produces a psychopathic personality change

211

– i.e. a lack of concern for others and a failure to learn from experience. Let us also suppose that the tumour is self-limiting and does not cause any other symptoms. We would certainly regard such changes as a tragedy, and for this reason we would classify it as a disease. Once it is classified as a disease, we then come to see the agent as mad rather than bad.

If we decided to punish him, we would in effect be saying that the original person had ceased to exist, and that a new person had been created who was evil, and that this new person ought to be punished because he is responsible for his actions. We might mourn the passing of the original person, but argue that the new person should be punished because he is evil. But this makes it logically impossible for someone to undergo a change in personality, which is common enough. Hence this description is not correct – the change is not the creation of a new (and evil) person who should be punished, but the acquisition of a disease. Therefore, we ought to treat him, removing the tumour to restore him to his old self. It would be unjust to punish him.

Turning now to the actual personality disorders, why should they be treated any differently than the fantasy example of the tumour? Since we then regard the tumour as a disease because of its undesirable effects, by parity of reasoning, we ought to regard any condition with similar effects as a disease. We ought (if we are not to be inconsistent) to regard psychopathic personality disorder as a disease. As long as personality disorders are valid entities, and have some underlying physical basis, then there is no reason to think that they do not excuse in the same way that the tumour does. And there is some evidence that they have an underlying physical basis – personality disordered patients with impulsive aggression have lowered serotoninergic functioning (Coccaro *et al.*, 1989). Therefore personality disorders diminish responsibility. The physical state causing the personality disorder prevents the normal person emerging and, as in the case of the tumour-induced personality, we ought to try to restore his normal personality rather than punish him.

In the end, it is up to us whether to view such conditions as alien factors outside the self which undermine autonomy, or as an integral part of the self not undermining autonomy. It is up to us where to draw these boundaries around the self and which factors to regard as alien influences – i.e. diseases. Again, this is something that is dependent on our values.

There is thus a natural tension between the law and the medical paradigm over the existence of evil. Where the law is likely to see serial killers as evil, psychiatry is likely to suspect that such individuals are mentally ill and not responsible for their actions. The very existence of such categories as psychopathic personality disorder which is recognized by anti-social and aggressive behaviour attests to the tendency of psychiatry to 'explain away' evil acts as symptoms of disease. In this way, the class of evil acts shrinks. At the limit, and certainly there is no sight of this at present, there is the fear or hope (depending on your point of view) that psychiatry will eliminate the category of evil by showing that all acts of evil are in fact symptoms of disease. But what I have argued is that this is not something that depends upon the facts. Whether someone is mad or bad depends on whether they are suffering from a disease, and this depends on our values.

In conclusion, mental illness does excuse by undermining our autonomy – the responsibility thesis is true. Because what counts as a disease and voluntary action depends on our values, what conditions count as excusing also depends on our values. Whether evil exists is up to us, and whether we ought to punish serial killers or treat them is not something that depends on the facts. Ultimately, it is the decision whether we ought to treat or punish – i.e. the decision whether they have a disease, that determines whether they are responsible. If we feel we ought to treat psychopaths, then they are ill. If we feel they should be punished, they are not. We do not first decide that they are not responsible, and then conclude that they are therefore ill. The conceptual dependence proceeds in the opposite direction. It is our intuition that we ought to be treating depressives and schizophrenic murderers that leads us to classify them as ill and therefore not responsible. On the other hand, it is because of our intuition that we ought to be punishing Nazis that we do not classify them as ill.

13

THE PRACTICE OF PSYCHIATRY

We must now look at the practice of psychiatry, especially those aspects that raise ethical problems. In this chapter, I will concentrate on the guardianship thesis, asking whether we are justified in treating patients against their will. And more generally, whether psychiatrists are justified in imposing their values on their patients. I will look at these issues not only in cases where patients are involuntarily hospitalized and treated, but also in those cases where treatment is allegedly voluntary.

INVOLUNTARY HOSPITALIZATION

Hospitalizing and treating a patient against his will is an example of paternalism. A psychiatrist acts paternalistically towards a patient if he benefits the patient but does so by violating a moral rule (Culver and Gert, 1982, p. 130). If a psychiatrist hospitalizes and treats a patient against his will, he acts paternalistically because he benefits the patient by violating the moral rule that a person has the right to determine his own future. According to English law, such paternalistic intervention is legally justified if, first, the person is suffering from a treatable mental illness, second, the mental illness puts the patient at some risk of either harming himself or others, and third, the patient refuses treatment. Such a situation obtains if someone is so severely depressed that he is determined to kill himself. Szasz argues such paternalistic intervention is never justified:

> The hypothetical suicidal patient is not ill: he has no demonstrable bodily disorder; he does not assume the sick role – he does not seek medical help. In short, the physician uses

the rhetoric of illness and treatment to justify his forcible intervention in the life of a fellow human being – often in the face of explicit opposition from his so-called patient. . . . A person's life belongs to himself. Hence, he has the right to take his own life, that is, to commit suicide.

(Szasz, 1979b, p. 72)

I will argue that paternalistic intervention is justified here and that the guardianship thesis is correct.

We cannot justify intervening to prevent suicide against a person's will by arguing that he will in the future (after treatment) give his retrospective consent. This is because of the existence of brainwashing. We could change someone's sexual orientation or political affiliation by aversive conditioning such that he expresses his approval afterwards for being 'treated'. But this would not justify such treatment.

We cannot justify treating a suicidal patient against his will by arguing he has given his consent in a 'living will'. If a person has requested ECT for future illnesses, we cannot conclude we are not treating him against his will because he may have changed his mind. People change – they acquire new interests and consequently new reasons for doing things. Someone may refuse to give consent to ECT for some future illness, and we may therefore feel duty-bound not to give it to him when he is next ill even if he asks for it. However, he may have genuinely changed his mind, and if we follow his living will, we cannot give it to him. It is because the use of living wills does not take this into account that they cannot be used to justify involuntary hospitalization.

We cannot justify intervention to prevent suicide by arguing that the behaviour is caused by a disease. Suppose that someone with cancer knows that a painful and protracted death awaits him. While the physical disease is causally responsible for his wanting to kill himself – if he were not physically ill, he would not be trying to kill himself – we do not think that we have the right to interfere. The reason for this is because we consider such a person competent to make such decisions. A person is competent to make certain decisions if and only if he is able to understand what the different options entail and is able to make a rational choice among these alternatives. Since he both understands what the options entail and is rational – his choice of a death with dignity over a long, painful decline is rational – he is competent. We have no right to interfere because the person is competent to make this decision.

We cannot justify intervening to prevent suicide by arguing that suicidal behaviour is caused by a mental illness. Suppose that someone discovers he has Huntington's chorea or Alzheimer's disease at a stage when he is still lucid. Recognizing that his future consists of a slow deterioration of his mental (and physical) powers, he may rationally choose an early but more dignified death by suicide. Because this choice is competent, we have no right to interfere. Here a mental illness is causally responsible for his wanting to kill himself – if he did not have the mental illness, he would not want to kill himself – but this does not justify our intervention against his will because the person is competent to make this decision.

It is because we value autonomy that we only feel justified in treating incompetent patients against their will. As I argued, someone is autonomous if he determines his life by competent decisions without outside or inside interference. A typically autonomous person is someone who understands the choices facing him, who is rational, who acts on the basis of desires and beliefs normally formed, and who is free from coercion. We are reluctant to interfere with autonomous agents. On the other hand, when someone is so depressed that he ceases to understand fully what he is doing and ceases to be rational, he ceases to be autonomous. It is usually argued that our respect for autonomy should prevent us treating someone against his will (Culver and Gert, 1982). But a real respect for autonomy demands we intervene to restore it.

A necessary condition for the justification of involuntary intervention is that the person be incompetent and not autonomous. While there are no doubt some cases of rational suicide, there must be a presumption that potential suicides are not rational. A number of studies have confirmed that the vast majority of suicides – over 90 per cent – are mentally ill and probably not competent (Barraclough et al., 1974). This suggests we are justified in intervening in all cases of suicide until its rationality is proven. The irreversibility of suicide and the reversibility of the intervention reinforces this policy (Heyd and Bloch, 1984). We are also justified in intervening to treat psychotic illnesses. Whenever a patient is psychotic and fails to perceive reality clearly, he inevitably fails to understand the alternatives facing him and is incompetent to make decisions about his future – a psychotic patient thinks the alternatives open to him are being the way he is (in touch with reality), or being 'brainwashed' by treatment to think differently, and this amounts to a failure to understand his options.

We are not justified in intervening to treat someone against his will simply because he is incompetent – his irrationality or failure to understand must be due to a mental illness. Someone may wish to become the latest person to survive Niagara Falls in a barrel. Because the benefit of surviving Niagara Falls in a barrel is so outweighed by the potential harm, such an action is irrational. But this does not entitle us to intervene and 'treat' his absurd desire. Similarly, suppose someone with a dreadful and terminal illness refuses to give up his positive view of things. We may consider that he is being irrational because he chooses a painful protracted death over a dignified painless one. But we are not justified in forcing him to take depressant medication to cure his optimism! In spite of the fact the optimism may make him irrational, it is not a disease. Optimism is desirable because, even if it is misplaced, it enables us to attain a happier and more fulfilled life. Only at the extreme, where optimism so distorts reasoning as to cause grandiose delusions, does it become undesirable and pathological. These examples show that involuntary intervention is only justified if incompetence is caused by mental illness.

But while having a mental illness is necessary for involuntary treatment to be justified, this does not mean that we are entitled to treat all mentally ill patients against their will. Someone with a spider phobia might be better off treated, but we are not entitled to drag him from his home and subject him to systematic desensitization because he is competent to refuse treatment.

In addition to being mentally ill and incompetent, paternalistic detention is only justified if the benefits of detention outweigh its harms. However, this does not imply that we are only justified in cases of potential suicide (Culver and Gert, 1982). Intervention is also justified in other cases of potential self-harm. A manic patient may harm himself by overspending, disinhibited sexual behaviour, etc. Such harms are also sufficient to justify involuntary hospitalization and treatment. Indeed, I would argue that the mere continuation of the mental disease itself constitutes sufficient harm to justify intervention. We have seen that disease is defined in terms of harm – something is a disease only if it causes suffering and disability – i.e. harm. Thus it follows by definition that a person is harmed by the continuation of any mental illness.

The only reason why it is thought that the treatment of a mental illness is not a sufficient benefit to outweigh the harm of the loss of liberty is that this latter value is over-inflated. But it is not liberty, or freedom from outside interference, that we value, but autonomy. It is because we value the ability of the individual to determine his own life rationally in accordance with normally acquired desires that we consider such intervention justified. If a patient is not autonomous, such intervention does not diminish autonomy – it enhances it.

> The truly incompetent lack full autonomy, and so that quality cannot be violated by imposing treatment. If there is a reasonable likelihood that their autonomy can be preserved or restored by medication, then forced treatment of such patients is warranted.
>
> (Macklin, 1982, p. 340)

In other words, if it is autonomy rather than the simple freedom to be, amongst others things, mentally ill, that we value, then this demands that we ignore rather than respect the wishes of the incompetent mentally ill patient. Freedom to choose is hardly desirable if the patient is unable to understand and reasonably assess the alternatives open to him. Thus there will hardly be a situation where the benefits of hospitalization will not greatly outweigh the evils of the loss of liberty.

This justification presupposes that we can benefit the patient by treating him – i.e. that effective treatment exists. It would make a patient worse off if in addition to his illness he were also incarcerated in a hospital with little hope of a cure. We can only justify doing something unpleasant if there is a reasonable chance of a greater benefit in return. For this reason British law requires someone to suffer from a *treatable* mental illness before he can be involuntarily hospitalized and treated.

In order for involuntary hospitalization and treatment to be justified, then, a patient must be suffering from a mental illness causing incompetence to determine his future such that the benefit of involuntary detention outweighs the harm. This illustrates how psychiatrists impose their values on their patients. Whether involuntary hospitalization is justified depends on the value judgement that such-and-such a condition is a disease. When the patient refuses to acknowledge that what he has is a disease, the psychiatrist imposes his values on the patient in the first instance by declaring him ill. For example, a manic patient may deny that he is ill, arguing that he cannot be ill if he is enjoying himself so much. It is because we only value appropriate emotional highs that we consider mania to be a disease, and we impose this value on the patient. And it is because of our values that we consider suicidal behaviour to be prima-facie evidence of disease. We do not consider self-destruction desirable and therefore take it to be evidence of mental illness, arguing that only a mental illness would make someone want to do that. Because we value life (or a certain quality of life), we are inclined to see the pursuit of death as irrational and inexplicable without reference to some disease.

A psychiatrist also imposes his values on the patient by judging that the harm done by the loss of liberty is less than the harm done by his being psychotic. I judge it is preferable to be returned to sanity again than left in a psychotic and 'free' state. This implies a value judgement – that the harm of being psychotic is greater than the temporary harm of losing one's liberty. Whether a psychiatrist considers involuntary treatment justifiable will depend on his value judgements – on his weighing the values of sanity and liberty. Here we use the maxim of Hillel, the great Jewish patriarch, as a guide: do not do unto others as you would not have them do unto you. If you do not want to be left in a psychotic but free state, then do not leave your patients untreated. Using this maxim, we conclude that sanity is more valuable than a temporary loss of liberty.

Competence to consent to treatment admits degrees. One can understand to a greater or lesser extent the implications of the options open to one, and one can reason more or less rationally. Someone is minimally competent if he understands that, by accepting treatment, he will have to take some drug, and that, by refusing, he will remain in his present mood. On the other hand, if he understands more of the likely consequences of treatment and more of the consequences of the untreated disorder, he understands more about the alternatives and is more competent. If someone reasons that he likes being high, and does not like being normal, and concludes he ought to refuse treatment, we may judge him minimally rational and competent. On the other hand, if someone accepting treatment weighs up other relevant factors, he is more rational and competent. Where we set the level of incompetence required for involuntary hospitalization to be justified is an arbitrary matter, and will be influenced by our values. If we value freedom highly, we may set a high threshold, ensuring that few patients are incompetent to consent to treatment. On the other hand, if we value autonomy more than mere freedom, we will set a low threshold, ensuring that more mentally ill patients are incompetent and can be involuntarily treated.

Finally, the psychiatrist imposes his values on the patient by his judgement as to what is rational (i.e. competent). To be competent one must be rational. But the judgement whether someone is rational is a value judgement. Suppose someone suffering from a depressive illness refuses to take his tablets because he dislikes swallowing them. He judges it is worth enduring his agitated state to avoid the discomfort of having to swallow tablets. We are tempted to judge that such a decision is irrational because being depressed for so long is a much greater evil than the discomfort of taking tablets, and therefore judge the person is incompetent to refuse treatment. Similarly, because we judge that a potential suicide's life is worth living, we conclude he is being irrational. And if someone prefers being psychotic to being sane, we are apt to see such a desire as irrational, and conclude that the person is not competent to refuse treatment. This shows that being rational is an evaluative matter, and is another area where we impose our values on our patients. Our values influence how we weigh competing desires and which desires we consider irrational, and this influences what patients we see as competent to refuse treatment.

There are many cases where a psychiatrist will have to make a value judgement. A person may refuse treatment on religious grounds, saying that God would not have asked him to endure such suffering if there was not a reason. He may refuse treatment on ideological grounds, saying that psychiatrists are simply trying to make him better adjusted to a sick society. He may refuse treatment on the grounds that he enjoys being mad, and prefers it to boring sanity (one of my patients once offered this argument to me). He may refuse treatment because he dislikes the side-effects of the treatment more than he values his sanity. In judging whether such people are rational (and hence competent), we are inevitably committed to making value judgments, and hence inevitably committed to imposing values on our patients.

This does not mean that we can intervene to treat every irrational person. It is only where someone is suffering from a mental illness that this is justified. But the existence of profound irrationalities may influence us into thinking that the person *does* have a disease. Suppose there is a sort of person who indulges repeatedly in games of Russian roulette. We consider this activity irrational – the benefits of the game are outweighed by the obvious risk of harm. We are therefore inclined to consider this activity as a behavioural addiction – as in some way involuntary – and therefore as a disease. This classificatory move might then enable us to treat such people against their will. Of course, this does not mean all behavioural addictions are diseases. We might find that mountaineers are 'addicted' to the challenge of climbing. In spite of the fact that it seems irrational to value reaching the summit over life, because we value such achievements, we would not classify it as a disease.

Unfortunately, the current trend in society is to value hollow liberty over substantial autonomy, and therefore to restrict the powers of the psychiatrist to intervene against the patient's will. As Paul Chodoff comments:

> I believe that we are witnessing a pendular swing in which the rights of the mentally ill to be treated and protected are being set aside in the rush to give them their freedom at whatever cost. But is freedom defined only by the absence of external constraints? Internal physiological or psychological processes can contribute to a throttling of the spirit that is as painful as any applied from the outside.
>
> (Chodoff, 1976, p. 501)

If my arguments are correct, it is this restriction of the powers of psychiatrists that is unjustifiable. A society where I could not receive treatment for a psychosis if I refused it, and where psychiatrists could only treat me if there was a reasonably high probability of harming myself or others, would be inhumane.

Not all acts of involuntary hospitalization are paternalistic. Potential harm to others is also regarded as justifying involuntary hospitalization, but not because the benefit to the *patient* outweighs the harm to him. But potential harm to others is not sufficient to justify intervention. We cannot hospitalize just any dangerous person. We know the son of a mafia boss is almost certainly going to harm someone, but this does not give us the right to hospitalize him against his will and 'treat' him with a frontal lobotomy. This is because he is not mentally ill. But having a mental illness and being dangerous are not sufficient to justify involuntary treatment. Someone may have a spider phobia and, because of this, seek help. He may enter years of psycho-analysis only to discover that his therapist is a charlatan. Because of this, he may conspire to kill his analyst. While it is true that he is plotting to kill his therapist because of his mental illness – if it were not for the spider phobia, he would not be plotting to kill his analyst – we are not justified in hospitalizing him against his will.

It is only where the mental illness undermines autonomy that we are justified in intervening against a person's will. If someone is autonomous, he will be responsible for his actions – his actions will be voluntary. I argued above that if dangerous behaviour is caused by a disease *in an abnormal way*, the person is not fully responsible for his actions. We are happy to let legal sanctions influence a person's behaviour as long as he is not suffering from any mental illness undermining his autonomy. However, as soon as there is evidence that such sanctions are failing to influence the person and that he is no longer responsible for his actions, we feel justified in intervening to treat him. In other words, when the person is suffering from a mental illness that undermines his responsibility for his actions, then we ought to stop him from doing the harm. If we value autonomy rather than mere freedom, it follows we ought to interfere in behaviour that is not fully voluntary to restore autonomy.

Being mentally ill such that autonomy is undermined is not sufficient to justify non-paternalistic involuntary detention. The benefit of the policy to society must in addition outweigh the harm done. Suppose one in a thousand persons will commit an act of violence that warrants involuntary detention. Suppose that our ability to predict whether some person will be violent is 90 per cent accurate – i.e. for every one hundred people, ninety will be correctly identified as either potentially violent or harmless, and ten will be incorrectly identified. This is probably over-optimistic – a forensic psychiatrist once said that he could tell that half of his patients were dangerous, but that he could not tell which half (Scott, 1977)! Suppose that our society consists of one million people. Then it follows that 900 of the 1,000 potentially violent people will be identified (90 per cent accuracy), but also that 99,900 harmless people will be identified as potentially violent out of the remaining 999,000 harmless people (90 per cent accuracy). Thus to protect society from 900 violent people, we have to involuntary commit 99,900! Even if the accuracy were increased to 99 per cent – more than we could ever ask for – 9,990 harmless people would be hospitalized (Livermore, Malmquist and Meehl, 1982, p. 256). Though some might see the deprivation of liberty of 99,900 as being justified by the prevention of 900 murders, many would argue that involuntary hospitalization is not justified here.

However, we are not talking of involuntarily hospitalizing any person. We are only talking about detaining those who are dangerous because of mental illness. Let us suppose that 10 per cent of the population is mentally ill, and that one in five hundred of them are potentially violent – the figure is known to be higher than in the general population (Lagos *et al.*, 1977). If our ability to predict violence was 90 per cent accurate, we would identify 180 out of the 200 dangerous mentally ill patients. We would also identify 9,980 harmless mentally ill patients as dangerous. Thus we are really looking at the temporary detention of 9,980 being justified by the prevention of 180 murders. Since the benefit to the 9,980 of restoring their autonomy almost certainly outweighs the harm done to them by temporarily depriving them of their liberty, everybody benefits by the policy. Thus we can argue that where we have effective treatment, the policy of involuntarily detaining dangerous mentally ill patients is justified.

However, our treatments are not 100 per cent effective. As a result, the 9,980 harmless mentally ill patients might seldom be released, and hence their loss of liberty would not be temporary. Thus we have to balance the prevention of 180 deaths with the variable loss of liberty in 9,980 mentally ill patients. This makes the justification of the policy less convincing. However, I think the policy is still justified for two reasons. First, death is a far greater evil than the loss of liberty, and therefore the prevention of the deaths of a few members of society does outweigh the harm done to more members by periods of loss of liberty. And second, someone's death is irreversible, but the loss of liberty is not. With improvements in treatment and prediction, there is a good chance that such patients will be helped as well as quickly released when no longer dangerous.

Thus the guardianship thesis is defensible. Psychiatrists are justified in hospitalizing and treating incompetent and dangerous patients against their will. It is their loss of autonomy and our true respect for it that makes it justifiable.

IMPOSING OUR VALUES

A frequent accusation levelled against psychotherapists and psychiatrists is that they impose their values on their (voluntary) patients. They do so in three ways. First, by coercing their patients to varying degrees. Second, by defining what counts as normal – this determines what are mental illnesses, who needs treatment, and what are the goals of therapy. And third, by failing to provide their patients with the information necessary to make an informed decision about treatment. In this section I will discuss to what extent this occurs and whether it is justified.

We have seen that with involuntary hospitalization, the psychiatrist imposes his values. First, he defines the patient as ill – a definition with which such patients disagree. Second, he defines the threshold of competence at such a level so as to enable him to treat such patients, thereby enabling him to impose his values. Third, he defines certain desires as irrational so that he will be entitled to regard such patients as incompetent and requiring involuntary treatment. Fourth, he assigns certain weights to reasons such that if a patient refuses treatment, he is *ipso facto* irrational and incompetent. In these ways, the psychiatrist imposes his values on the patient.

Just as I have argued that competence admits of degrees, so involuntary hospitalization also admits of degrees. While the vast majority of hospitalized psychiatric patients are voluntary, many have been coerced by family, friends or employers into coming into and remaining in hospital, and many of these have been coerced into accepting treatment. Psychiatric patients are under the threat of becoming involuntary patients. They know that if they refuse treatment, they may become involuntary, and this creates sufficient threat to coerce many into accepting treatment – they cease to be voluntary patients and hence they also have values imposed upon them.

It is difficult to say how extensive this coercion is. In one study, limited by the fact that the researcher did not have access to all interactions, only 76 per cent of 'voluntary' patients agreed to come into hospital. In 73 per cent of 'voluntary' admissions, it was the doctor who recommended admission, thereby creating a very real pressure, and in 15 per cent there was evidence of coercion from relatives. Once in hospital, 14 per cent of 'voluntary' patients were detained in hospital against their will (Cavadino, 1989). Another study showed that 4 per cent of 'voluntary' patients were given Hobson's choice – either come into hospital voluntarily or compulsorily (Bean, 1980)! Thus, even on conservative estimates, coercion of voluntary patients exists on a significant scale.

Second, psychiatrists impose their values on their patients by operating with the concept of normality which they impose, by their authority and prestige, on their patients. We have seen that the history of psychiatry is full of examples where psychiatrists achieve social control by imposing their values on others. Soviet psychiatrists imposed their value of not favouring free political expression by classifying political dissidents as mentally ill. The slave-owning society imposed their value of not favouring disobedient slaves by classifying runaways as mentally ill. Victorian society imposed their puritanical values by classifying sexual excess as the disease of spermatorrhoea and classifying masturbation as pathological. This imposition also occurs in everyday clinical settings:

> From this position of relative power, the therapist has to consider to what extent he is imposing his own values on the patient. . . . One example concerns the individual who presents with low sexual interest or drive. . . . In such circumstances, we encourage conformity to a norm of sexual activity. A comparable and perhaps more contentious issue concerns female orgasm. While it is relatively unusual for an adult male to be non-orgasmic, it is far from rare among women. There seems little doubt that many women have become orgasmic with help, realizing the potential that had lain dormant. But a corollary of this has been the growing expectation that every woman should be orgasmic, yet there is no evidence or even likelihood that this is possible. . . . It is difficult to avoid the process of reinforcing 'norms' and the consequent pressure to conform to them.
>
> (Bancroft, 1984, pp. 165–71)

By insisting on what is normal, psychiatrists make value judgements. With the authority of the medical profession behind them, pressure is exerted on patients to define themselves as ill.

With the definition of normality, psychiatrists determine the goals of psychotherapy. This means that the assessment of the progress a patient makes is value-laden. A patient may consult a psychotherapist complaining that he is frightened to leave his house. If the therapist is a Freudian analyst, he may judge that the patient has some repressed wish which is being transformed into symptoms. Progress in therapy will consist in developing insight into this repressed wish and *not* in the disappearance of the original symptom. In fact, 'progress' can be made in therapy while the symptoms get worse! As Paul Kline writes:

> The aims of psychoanalysis are different from those of, say, behaviour therapy. In behaviour therapy, a method of treatment purportedly based upon learning theories, the aim is the remission of symptoms. In psychoanalytic therapy, however, the aim is far more than this. It is nothing less than to produce a change in the dynamic balance of id, ego and superego. Where id was, there shall ego be. Thus to be freed of symptoms for a psychoanalyst would not be a sign of therapeutic success. Indeed Freudian theory has a notion of the flight into health (where symptoms do indeed disappear), but which is by no means regarded as recovery.
>
> (Kline, 1984, p. 120)

This is important for it means that psychiatrists can impose their values on their patients by deciding what the goals of therapy consist in. A patient may enter therapy with the goal of getting rid of his symptoms, and be persuaded to accept different goals. He is taught to see the growth of insight as more important than the removal of symptoms. For many patients, 'personal growth' or 'insight' is not what they valued when they came to see the psychiatrist. By changing the goal posts, the psychiatrist can subtly impose his values on the patient.

Different psychotherapists will have different goals:

> While broadly recognized goals include Freud's 'love and work', and variants of growth, self-realization, self-sufficiency, security, and freedom from anxiety, all of which may be noble aspirations, ethical issues are inherent in the practices which are conducted in their name. . . . A funda-

mental ethical dilemma related to these various models is whether to encourage the patient to rebel against a repressive environment or to adjust to his current condition.

(Karasu, 1984, p. 94)

The different goals of the therapist influence whether he sees adjustment to his circumstances as the goal of treatment, or holds some more lofty ideal of healthy functioning in mind. And by persuading the patient to accept treatment, he is thereby imposing his values on the patient.

Third, psychiatrists frequently do not give patients enough information to enable them to make an informed decision about treatment. Instead, the information is selected, and negative information is played down, manipulating the patient into making a decision. For example, when the patient is told about ECT, he is seldom told that he has a 4–7 chance per 100,000 of dying from the procedure. It is argued that such information will put patients off a procedure with benefits that outweigh the risks. All this presupposes a certain evaluation of the options, with the psychiatrist arguing that recovery is worth such a lot that it outbalances what small risk there is of death. In this way, the psychiatrist imposes his own values on the patient.

Similarly, when a schizophrenic patient is prescribed neuroleptic medication, he is usually too psychotic to understand the long-term risks, the most important of which is tardive dyskinesia (TD) – a condition characterized by involuntary bodily movements. Even when well, he is seldom told that one third of all patients on long-term treatment acquire TD, and is seldom shown graphically (*in vivo* or on video) what the disorder is like. But psychiatrists may often show patients a video of what they are like when psychotic so they can make an informed decision about taking medication! The psychiatrist attaches a certain value to being insane, which is an extremely high negative value, and a value to having TD, which is negative but much less so. Because the psychiatrist values being sane with TD over being insane without TD, he manipulates the information in such a way that the patient is forced to share his values and make the same decision.

It is obvious, then, that psychiatrists impose their values even on voluntary patients. Is this justified? It might be argued that it is justified because it would be absurd to let patients impose their values on the psychiatrist. Suppose it were left to the patient to decide what is normal – what is and is not a symptom. Then an anorectic could come to the psychiatrist complaining that she is obese and demand appetite suppressants. If a psychiatrist was not imposing his own values, he would prescribe amphetamines, or suggest that she undergo psychosurgery to knock out the 'appetite centre' in the hypothalamus. It would not be up to the psychiatrist to suggest that the patient had a distorted image of herself, or an over-valuation of appearance – normality would be determined by the patient. But if normality was determined by the patient, this leads to such absurdities.

Absurdities would also result if patients decided the goals of therapy. A businessman could consult a psychiatrist saying that he could not progress in his career because he was too compassionate, and that he wanted to become heartless and cruel. If the patient could determine the goals of therapy, the psychiatrist would then devise some 'treatment' which might involve torturing animals during 'therapy' sessions for rewards, role-playing firing employees ruthlessly, etc. Similarly, a hit-man could consult a psychiatrist saying that he was troubled by his conscience, and the psychiatrist would then have to treat him by getting the 'patient' to work through a hierarchy of evil acts thereby habituating him to the pricks of his conscience. But this is absurd. It is not up to the patient to determine the goals of therapy.

These cases appear to work because such goals of therapy are immoral. However, someone might wish to become free of any jealous feelings whatsoever, or wish to enjoy pain so as to rid himself of the fear of it, or wish to become a shoe fetishist – because shoes are more easily available for dates! If the patients determined the goals of therapy, the psychiatrist would have to devise treatments to create such abnormal individuals as shoe fetishists and masochists. But this is absurd. Therefore, patients should not determine the goals of therapy.

However, these examples only show that psychiatrists should not become mechanics to serve whatever ends their patients demand – that they should not let patients impose their values on their psychiatrists. They do not show that we should let psychiatrists impose their values on their patients. If patients define normal traits as symptoms, then the psychiatrist should not treat them. He is not duty-bound to do what the patient asks, but to do what he sees as benefiting the patient. If he does not judge that he is improving the well-being of the patient, then he ought not to embark on treatment. To this extent, he has to be true to his own values. But in either event, we have not produced a justification for psychiatrists to impose their values.

We can argue that psychiatrists should impose their values because this leads to greater benefit for the patient. If the psychiatrist conveyed all the information in a vivid way, thereby making informed consent possible, this would deter patients from the treatment they need. A depressed patient might be agitated, seeing everything as terrifying. He might need ECT, but might refuse if told that there is a 4–7/100,000 risk that he will die each time he receives it. This will mean that the patient will not receive adequate treatment and remain depressed. However, given that competence admits of degrees, we can argue that some degree of coercion is justified. We can argue that illness often distorts the patient's perception of the facts and makes him less able to rationally evaluate the options. The agitation makes him irrationally fearful of ECT, and therefore less competent than usual to consent to treatment. Thus we are justified in talking of the risks in broad and less informative terms, saying that every anaesthetic procedure carries a risk but that this is no more than crossing a busy street, in order to get the patient to agree to treatment. The justification here is thus the same as for involuntary hospitalization. Inevitably the psychiatrist will be imposing his values to some extent, but this is justified when the patient is incompetent to that same extent.

The fact that psychiatrists impose their values to a greater or lesser extent on their involuntary and voluntary patients might seem to many that psychiatry is an instrument of social control. But this conclusion is unwarranted for a number of reasons. First, when psychiatrists impose their values, they are only preventing suffering in patients not competent to help themselves. They are not taking competent political radicals and treating them against their wills. Second, it is far more likely that *treated* schizophrenics and depressives will present a challenge to the social order than severely ill individuals. Far from protecting the social order, by restoring sanity, psychiatry is making revolution possible. Third, contrary to Foucault, restoring rationality is not tantamount to shoring up bourgeois capitalism:

More fundamentally, it seems likely that there is at least a minimum of rational functioning which is necessary or at least desirable for individuals in *any* society. . . It seems unlikely that much of what is dealt with as 'mental illness' would really be regarded as an equally valid and desirable way of perceiving the world in any conceivable society.

(Cavadino, 1989, p. 14)

Fourth, while it might be true that psychiatrists diagnose mental illness when patients deviate from social norms (with bizarre behaviour or beliefs) and treat such deviance, it does not follow that they are agents of social control. It is only where deviation results from disabilities that psychiatrists diagnose mental illness – eccentrics who deviate from social norms are not classified as ill. And it is only where competence is impaired that psychiatrists impose treatment. And fifth, while Lucy Johnstone argues that the adoption of the medical paradigm commits psychiatrists to diagnosing faults in individuals rather than society at large – e.g. diagnosing depression in women when it is their social role or circumstances that is at fault – this does not mean that psychiatrists are agents of social control:

What most women in psychiatric hospitals need is first, to be helped to see that they are only part of the problem, and second, to get angry enough about it to make real changes. The medical model cannot allow for this. Diagnoses are attached to individuals – there is no such thing as a medical diagnosis that includes a husband, children, parents, or wider society as an equal part of the problem.

(Johnstone, 1989, p. 120)

However, the adoption of the medical paradigm does *not*, even in physical medicine, preclude the recognition and correction of social causes. To treat TB or schizophrenia, social intervention is needed. And contrary to her critics, psychiatry does not treat depression to restore women to servile roles – it does its best to enable them to lead more fulfilling lives. If anything, psychiatry is liberating rather than repressive.

While it is true that the concept of disease is not ethically and politically neutral, this does not mean that psychiatry is an agent of social control. In theory, any politically offensive behaviour can be labelled as an illness. But this does not entitle the psychiatrist to conclude that such people 'lack insight' because they refuse to believe they are ill, that they are therefore incompetent and can be treated against their will. Incompetence *cannot* be judged on the 'lack of insight' into being ill – since judgements of illness are essentially value judgments, disagreements over this imply only a difference in values and *not* a psychosis and hence a failure of competence and loss of autonomy. Therefore, even if politically offensive behaviour can theoretically qualify as a disease, this does not entitle psychiatrists to treat it involuntarily. And in practice, the definition of politically offensive behaviour as an illness is *extremely* rare – the examples of sluggish schizophrenia and drapetomania are striking because they are so uncommon. Political abuse and social control remain a theoretical risk, it is true, but given the good moral sense of psychiatrists, it is thankfully not a real danger. Schizophrenia and manic-depression are the disorders most likely to be involuntarily treated, but their treatment hardly involves a dimension of political control.

In conclusion, a psychiatrist is justified in imposing his values on incompetent patients and treating them against their will – the guardianship thesis is true. In addition, since not all patients are fully competent, lesser degrees of coercion are justified in cases with lesser degrees of incompetence. Once again, we see how value-laden the whole enterprise of psychiatry is. Values play a role in deciding the disease status of a condition, the goals of therapy, and the competence of patients. But this does not mean that the aim of psychiatry is to secure social control. For fully competent and autonomous patients, no imposition is justified. Such patients should receive the information necessary to make an informed decision and be left free to make it.

CONCLUSION:
THE NATURE OF
PSYCHIATRY

We started with the knowledge that psychiatry is committed to the medical paradigm. However, we saw that there was a crisis in psychiatry. The medical paradigm was threatened by competitors that challenged its causal thesis and denied the existence of mental illness. Many other theses of the medical paradigm were also questioned.

However, the crisis in psychiatry was in appearances only. The alternatives to the medical paradigm are competitors in name only – although they purport to replace the causal thesis, denying the existence of mental illness, they admit mental illnesses via the back door. They are all committed to postulating that abnormal processes lead to suffering and disability. But this means they are committed to the existence of mental illnesses – something is a mental illness if it is an abnormal process leading to mental suffering and disability. It was because these 'alternative paradigms' committed the essentialist fallacy that they denied the existence of disease. But because a disease can be any sort of (abnormal) process, there is nothing to stop us saying that the process of acquiring certain conditioned reflexes is identical to the phobic disease process, or that unconsciously playing at being physically ill is identical to the hysterical disease process, or that the transformation of frustrated libido into symptoms is identical to the neurotic disease process, or that unconsciously playing the social role of madness is identical to the schizophrenic disease process. To deny that these are diseases is to commit the essentialist fallacy – to be a disease, a process does not have to be an infection, or a tumour, or even something qualitatively distinct from normality. This means that the other paradigms do *not* dispense with the category of mental illness and therefore they are not compet-

232

ing paradigms. Because they do not deny the causal thesis, they cease to be distinct from the medical paradigm and lose their paradigmatic status, collapsing into different disease theories *within* the medical paradigm.

Only if we assume that our terms have a descriptive meaning will we conclude that other paradigms are distinct from the medical one. But if the terms refer, they can refer to the same thing. If 'conditioned reflex' refers to whatever explains the stimulus-response association, 'repression' refers to whatever explains the failure to acknowledge some obvious fact, 'faulty cognition' refers to whatever explains the person's mistaken belief, there is nothing to stop us saying that these terms are referring to the same thing as our disease terms. Since we do not accept that there is some additional mind-stuff that they can be referring to, they must be referring to physical processes – i.e. exactly what our disease terms refer to. But this means that if these psychological factors explain some abnormal behaviour, then it follows that some theory referring to an abnormal physical process explains it, and hence no competing non-disease theory has been formulated. The competing paradigms reduce ultimately to theories that can be couched in biological terms – since they refer to diseases (under a different name) to explain abnormal behaviour, they become theories within the medical paradigm.

But all this does not mean that psychological and social factors do not explain abnormal behaviour, or that the mind does not exist. All that follows from the fact that the mind is not a distinct substance from the brain is that psychological and social factors are physical processes – not that they do not exist or do not exert an influence on behaviour. The reduction of the alternative paradigms to the medical paradigm does not mean that there are no such things as conditioned reflexes, or unconscious conflicts, or intentional strategies. Abnormal behaviour might be explained by conditioned reflexes, but this simply means that it is explained by one sort of abnormal physical process rather than another.

But the medical paradigm does not survive all challenges intact. The most important change to the medical paradigm comes from the rejection of the conceptual thesis. A process is a mental illness only if it has undesirable consequences, and this means that values and not facts determine what counts as a mental illness. This change requires further modifications to the medical paradigm. First, it means that psychiatry cannot be ethically and politically neutral – the neutrality thesis is false. When we decide what is a disease, we are deciding what sort of people we ought to be, and what sort of society we ought to live in. When we decide that sexual sadism is a disease, we are deciding that we ought not to be beings that derive sexual pleasure from torturing and mutilating others. When we decide that homosexuality is not a disease, we are deciding that we ought not to be a society that stigmatizes such a sexual variation. Second, the identification thesis is false – we cannot rely on scientific methodology to identify diseases. Because the facts do not determine disease status, an investigation of the facts will not enable us to discover what conditions are diseases. Third, the teleological thesis must be modified. The goal of psychiatry might be the prevention and treatment of mental illness, but because the definition of mental illness requires us to judge what sort of people we ought to be, and what sort of society we ought to live in, by serving the goal of treating mental illness, we are also serving ethical and political goals. But we have seen that this does not mean that psychiatry is an agent of social control – if anything, the practice of psychiatry makes revolution more likely!

It might be felt that this new medical paradigm is less able to settle debates over disease status, and to solve the problems of value relativity and political abuse. Hitherto, such debates were settled by the facts – it was the facts that prevented us calling any political nuisance a disease, or calling anything some psychiatrist did not like a disease. But while the facts cannot help us solve these problems, as long as we are clear that the issue is an evaluative one, and we are clear what we value, we can solve these problems. As soon as we know what we value, we will have decided what are and are not diseases. And we do not have to embrace relativism. If different psychiatrists or cultures have different values, we do not have to concede that they are correct to classify the conditions differently. If Nazis classify psychopaths as healthy, we do not have to agree. If one psychiatrist values loss of contact with conventional reality, we do not have to agree. This is tantamount to endorsing inconsistent values.

The universality thesis does not survive intact. Some mental illnesses can be time- or culture-bound. An illness is the same as another if it shares the same underlying process, and some diseases are identified with the whole underlying process. This entails that if this process involves the adoption of a stereotype, then it can only exist where we find that stereotype – i.e. in that culture. Such diseases will be culture-bound, and if such stereotypes occurred in the past, time-bound. Other mental illnesses will not be culture- or time-bound because their identity consists only in part of the underlying process – the biological defect. Disease identity is partly a factual matter, partly a matter of convention. The facts can settle that two illnesses are *not* identical because the underlying processes do not share anything in common. But they cannot settle that two illnesses are identical – it is up to us *which* process to regard as an essential part of the disease.

Other theses of the medical paradigm have remained intact. The demarcation thesis survives – mental illnesses are those that cause predominantly a disruption of mental functions. The entitlement thesis still holds – having a mental illness entitles a patient to enter the sick role, but this role does not consist in being totally passive. The epistemological thesis also remains intact – scientific methodology enables us to discover the causes and cures for diseases. We have seen that psychiatry is a science. Psychiatric theories are formulated to explain publicly observable phenomena and evaluated on the basis of scientific criteria. While there are clearly areas of psychiatry, like psychodynamic psychiatry, where practitioners do not go to proper lengths to subject their theories to empirical test, this does not mean that such theories are intrinsically unscientific.

The guardianship thesis is also true. We are justified in treating incompetent patients against their will. Such a justification comes from a real respect for their autonomy. A society where seriously disturbed patients cannot get help would be awful. The responsibility thesis also survives intact. If someone has a mental illness that undermines autonomy, then he is not fully responsible for his actions. If a disease determines behaviour by causing desires and beliefs in an abnormal way, or undermines rationality, then the agent cannot be held responsible for his actions. Whether someone is mad rather than bad depends on our value judgement that we ought to treat him in a medical manner rather than punish him – i.e. on the value judgement that he is suffering from a disease and hence that his behaviour is not fully voluntary.

While the new medical paradigm appears less able to solve many problems facing psychiatry, it is nevertheless more powerful. The old paradigm's solution to the problem of disease status, of value relativity, of political abuse, was illusory – it was based on an incorrect conception of mental illness that was its source of weakness. The new paradigm rests on a better understanding of mental illness and has a better chance of success.

Psychiatry is clearly value laden. It is influenced by our conception of what sort of people we ought to be, and also by our conception of what society we ought to aspire towards. Whether we treat someone depends on what we find undesirable. It is because we consider grieving after a major loss desirable that we do not judge it to be a disease. And it is because we judge becoming depressed as undesirable that we judge it to be a disease. It is because we take some areas of irrationality to be desirable that we do not try to force people to be sadder but wiser. And it is because we consider delusions undesirable that we treat them.

All this does not mean that psychiatry is any different from the rest of medicine. It is because we value intelligence that increased glial cells in the brain is not a disease. And it is because we do not value idiocy that phenylketonuria is a disease. It is because we value muscular strength that we take muscular dystrophy to be a disease and do not take an abnormal preponderance of slow muscle fibres to be a disease. It is because we value the changes of puberty that we do not treat it, while it is because we do not value the changes following the menopause that we treat it with HRT. All medicine is value-laden and psychiatry is no different. This value-laden nature of psychiatry (and medicine) may be regarded by many as its major weakness. It exposes the practice of psychiatry to many moral dangers, not least of which is its use to repress political dissent and individuality, and to impose values on competent patients and secure social control. But like any powerful tool, the morality of its use will ultimately depend on the morality of its practitioners.

REFERENCES

Akiskal, H., Djenderedjian, A. and Rosenthal, R. (1977), 'Cyclothymic disorder: Validating criteria for inclusion in the bipolar affective group', *American Journal of Psychiatry,* 134: 1227–33.

Alloy, L. and Abramson, L. (1979), 'Judgement of contingency in depressed and nondepressed students: Sadder but wiser?', *Journal of Experimental Psychology*, 108: 441–85.

Aristotle (1955), *Ethics*, Harmondsworth, Penguin.

Ayer, A. (1954), *Philosophical Essays*, London, Macmillan.

Bancroft, J. (1984), 'Ethical aspects of sexuality and sex therapy', in S. Bloch and P. Chodoff (eds), *Psychiatric Ethics*, Oxford, Oxford University Press, pp. 160–84.

Barash, D. (1981), *Sociobiology: The Whisperings Within*, Glasgow, Fontana.

Barraclough, B. *et al.* (1974), 'A hundred cases of suicide', *British Journal of Psychiatry*, 125: 355–73.

Bateson, G., Jackson, D., Haley, J. and Weakland, J. (1956), 'Towards a theory of schizophrenia', *Behavioural Science*, 1: 251–64.

Bayer, R. (1987), *Homosexuality and American Psychiatry*, Princeton, Princeton University Press.

Bean, P. (1980), *Compulsory Admissions to Mental Hospitals*, Chichester, John Wiley & Sons.

Beck, A., Rush, A., Shaw, B. and Emery, G. (1979), *Cognitive Therapy of Depression*, New York, Guildford.

Begleiter, H. *et al.* (1984), 'Event-related brain potentials in boys at risk for alcoholism', *Science*, 225: 1493–6.

Behan, P., Behan, W. and Bell, E. (1985), 'The postviral fatigue syndrome', *Journal of Infection*, 10: 211–22.

Bergler, E. (1956), *Homosexuality: Disease or Way of Life?*, New York, Hill & Wang.

Bieber, I. *et al.* (1962), *Homosexuality: A Psychoanalytic Study*, New York, Random House.

Bloch, S. and Reddaway, P. (1977), *Psychiatric Terror*, New York, Basic Books.

Boorse, C. (1976), 'What a theory of mental health should be', *Journal of Theory of Social Behaviour*, 6: 61–84.

Bowers, M. (1974), 'Central dopamine turnover in schizophrenic syndromes', *Archives of General Psychiatry*, 31: 50–4.

Braginsky, B., Braginsky, D., and Ring, K., (1969), *Methods of Madness*, New York, Holt, Rinehart & Winston.

Brown, G. (1989), 'Depression: a radical social perspective', in K. Herbst and E. Paykel (eds), *Depression: An integrative approach*, London, Heinemann, pp. 21–44.

Brown, G. and Birley, J. (1968), 'Crises and life changes in the onset of schizophrenia', *Journal of Health and Social Behaviour*, 9: 203–14.

Brown, G. and Harris, T. (1978), *Social Origins of Depression*, London, Tavistock.

Brown, G., Bhrolchaim, M. and Harris, T. (1975), 'Social class and psychiatric disturbance among urban populations', *Sociology*, 9: 225–34.

Brown, R. (1976), 'Psychosis and irrationality', in S. Benn and G. Mortimor (eds), *Rationality and the Social Sciences*, London, Routledge & Kegan Paul.

Brown, R. *et al.* (1986), 'Post mortem evidence for structural brain changes in schizophrenia', *Archives of General Psychiatry*, 43: 36–42.

Brumberg, J. (1988), *Fasting Girls*, London, Harvard University Press.

Calhoun, J. (1977), *Abnormal Psychology*, New York, Random House.

Cartwright, S. (1851), 'Report on the diseases and physical peculiarities of the negro race', *New Orleans Medical and Surgical Journal*, 7: 707–9.

Cavadino, M. (1989), *Mental Health Law in Context*, Aldershot, Dartmouth.

Charney, D., Heninger, G., and Redmond, D. (1983), 'Yohimbine induced anxiety and increased noradrenergic function in humans', *Life Sciences*, 33: 19–29.

Chodoff, P. (1976), 'The case of involuntary hospitalization of the mentally ill', *American Journal of Psychiatry*, 133: 496–501.

Churchland, P. (1986), *Neurophilosophy*, London, MIT Press.

Clark, D. (1988), 'A cognitive model of panic attacks', in S. Rachman and J. Maser (eds), *Panic: Psychological Perspectives*, New Jersey, Lawrence Erlbaum, pp. 71–90.

Clark, D. Salkovskis, P. and Chalkley, A. (1985), 'Respiratory control as a treatment for panic attacks', *Journal of Behaviour Therapy and Experimental Psychology*, 16: 23–30.

Coccaro, E. *et al.* (1989), 'Serotonergic studies in patients with affective and personality disorders', *Archives of General Psychiatry*, 46: 587–99.

Connell, P. (1958), *Amphetamine Psychosis*, Oxford, Oxford University Press.

Crow, T. (1985), 'Integrated viral genes as the cause of schizophrenia: a hypothesis', in S. Iversen (ed.), *Psychopharmacology: Recent advances and future prospects*, Oxford, Oxford University Press, pp. 228–42.

Crow, T. and Gillbe, I. (1974), 'Brain dopamine and behaviour', *Journal of Psychiatric Research*, 11: 163–72.

Crow, T., Deakin, J., Johnstone, E. and Longden, A. (1976), 'Dopamine and schizophrenia', *Lancet*, 2: 563–6.

REFERENCES

Crowe, R. (1974), 'An adoption study of antisocial personality', *Archives of General Psychiatry*, 31: 785–91.

Culver, C. and Gert, B. (1982), *Philosophy in Medicine*, Oxford, Oxford University Press.

Curling, T. (1856), *A Practical Treatise on Diseases of the Testis*, London, Churchill.

Davidson, D. (1980), 'Mental events', in D. Davidson, *Actions and Events*, Oxford, Clarendon Press, pp. 207–28.

Davidson, D. (1984), 'Radical interpretation', in D. Davidson (ed.), *Inquiries into Truth and Interpretation*, Oxford, Clarendon Press, pp. 125–40.

Davies, D. (1962), 'Normal drinking in recovered alcohol addicts', *Quarterly Journal of Studies in Alcohol*, 23: 94–104.

Dilman, I. (1984), *Freud and the Mind*, Oxford, Blackwell.

Dorner, G. (1976), *Hormones and Brain Differentiation*, Amsterdam, Elsevier.

Dubos, R. (1965), *Man Adapting*, London, Yale University Press.

Duhem, P. (1962), *The Aim and Structure of Physical Theory*, New York, Atheneum.

Eccles, J. (1970), *Facing Reality*, Heidelberg, Springer-Verlag.

Eccles, J. (with K. Popper) (1977), *The Self and its Brain*, London, Routledge & Kegan Paul.

Edwards, G., Grossman, M., Keller, M., Moser, J. and Room, R. (1977), *Alcohol-related Disabilities*, Geneva, WHO.

Eisenberg, L. (1988), 'The social construction of mental illness', *Psychological Medicine*, 18: 1–9.

Ellis, A. (1980), 'On the Freudian theory of speech errors', in V. Fromkin (ed.), *Errors in Linguistic Performance*, London, Academic Press, pp. 123–31.

Engel, G. (1961), 'Is grief a disease?', *Psychosomatic Medicine*, 23: 15–27.

Engelhardt, T. (1975), 'The concepts of health and disease', in T. Engelhardt and S. Spicker (eds), *Evaluation and Explanation in the Biomedical Sciences*, Dordrecht, Reidel.

Eysenck, H. (1952), 'The effects of psychotherapy: an evaluation', *Journal of Consulting Psychology*, 16: 319–24.

Eysenck, H. (1970), 'Learning theory model', in W. Sahakian (ed.), *Psychopathology Today*, New York, Peacocke, pp. 73–85.

Eysenck, H. (1973), 'Learning theory and behaviour therapy', in T. Millon, *Theories of Psychopathology and Personality*, London, Saunders, pp. 338–49.

Eysenck, H. (1975), *The Future of Psychiatry*, London, Methuen.

Eysenck, H. (1978), *You and Neurosis*, Glasgow, Fontana.

Eysenck, H. (1985), *Decline and Fall of the Freudian Empire*, Harmondsworth, Penguin.

Fingarette, H. (1988), *Heavy Drinking: The Myth of Alcoholism as a Disease*, Berkeley, University of California Press.

Fisher, S. and Greenberg, R. (1977), *The Scientific Credibility of Freud's Theories and Therapy*, Hassocks, Harvester Press.

Flew, A. (1973), *Crime or Disease?*, London, Macmillan.

239

Foucault, M. (1971), *Madness and Civilization*, London, Random House.

Freud, S. (1950), 'Analysis terminable and interminable', in S. Freud, *Collected Papers*, 5: 330–47.

Freud, S. (1973), *Introductory Lectures on Psychoanalysis*, Harmondsworth, Penguin.

Freud, S. (1975), *The Psychopathology of Everyday Life*, Harmondsworth, Penguin.

Freud, S. (1979), *On Psychopathology*, Harmondsworth: Penguin.

Freud, S. (1985a), *Civilization, Society and Religion*, Harmondsworth, Penguin.

Freud, S. (1985b), *The Origins of Religion*, Harmondsworth, Penguin.

Freud, S. (1986), 'Neurosis and psychosis', in A. Freud (ed), *The Essentials of Psychoanalysis*, Harmondsworth, Penguin, pp. 557–72.

Fromm, E. (1955), *The Sane Society*, New York, Rinehart.

Gelder, M., Marks, I. and Wolff, H. (1967), 'Desensitization and psychotherapy in phobic states: a controlled enquiry', *British Journal of Psychiatry*, 113: 53–73.

Gelder, M., Gath, D. and Mayou, R. (1984), *Oxford Textbook of Psychiatry*, Oxford, Oxford University Press.

Goldberg, D. (1972), *The Detection of Psychiatric Illness by Questionnaire*, Oxford, Oxford University Press.

Goldberg, E. and Morrison, L. (1963), 'Schizophrenia and social class', *British Journal of Psychiatry*, 109: 785–802.

Goodwin, D. *et al.* (1973), 'Alcohol problems in adoptees raised apart from alcoholic biological parents', *Archives of General Psychiatry* 28: 238–43.

Gray, J. (1971), *The Psychology of Fear and Stress*, London, Weidenfeld & Nicolson.

Gregory, S., Shawcross, C. and Gill, D. (1985), 'The Nottingham ECT study', *British Journal of Psychiatry*, 146: 520–4.

Grunbaum, A. (1986), 'Precis of "The foundations of psychoanalysis" ', *The Behavioural and Brain Sciences*, 9: 217–28.

Healy, D. (1990), *The Suspended Revolution*, London, Faber.

Heather, N. and Robertson, I. (1985), *Problem Drinking*, Harmondsworth, Penguin.

Helzer, J. *et al.* (1977), 'Reliability of psychiatric diagnosis', *Archives of General Psychiatry*, 34: 136–41.

Hempel, C. (1965), *Aspects of Scientific Explanation*, New York, Free Press.

Hernandez-Pion, R. *et al.* (1963), 'Somatic evoked potentials in one case of hysterical anaesthesia', *Electroencephalography and Clinical Neurophysiology*, 15: 889–99.

Heyd, D. and Bloch, S. (1984), 'The ethics of suicide', in S. Bloch and P. Chodoff (eds), *Psychiatric Ethics*, Oxford University Press, pp. 185–202.

Hilgard, E. (1965), *Hypnotic Susceptibility*, New York, Harcourt Brace Jovanovich.

Hooker, E. (1957), 'The adjustment of the male overt homosexual', *Journal of Projective Techniques*, 21: 18–30.

Jackson, S. (1986), *Melancholia and Depression*, London, Yale University Press.

Janowsky, D., El-Yousef, M., Davis, M. and Sekerke, H. (1972), 'A cholinergic–adrenergic hypothesis of mania and depression', *Lancet*, 2: 632–5.

Jaspers, K. (1968), 'The phenomenological approach in psychopathology', *British Journal of Psychiatry*, 114: 1313–23.

Jellinek, E. (1952) 'The phases of alcohol addiction', *Quarterly Journal of Studies on Alcohol*, 13: 673–84.

Johnstone, E., Crow, T., Johnson, A. and McMillan, J. (1986), 'The Northwick Park study of first episodes of schizophrenia', *British Journal of Psychiatry*, 148: 115–20.

Johnstone, L. (1989), *Users and Abusers of Psychiatry*, London, Routledge.

Karasu, T. (1984), 'Ethical aspects of psychotherapy', in S. Bloch and P. Chodoff (eds), *Psychiatric Ethics*, Oxford, Oxford University Press, pp. 89–116.

Karmel, M. (1969), 'Total institution and self-mortification', *Journal of Health and Social Behaviour*, 10: 134–41.

Kendell, R. (1975a), *The Role of Diagnosis in Psychiatry*, Oxford, Blackwell.

Kendell, R. (1975b), 'The concept of disease and its implications for psychiatry', *British Journal of Psychiatry*, 127: 305–15.

Kendell, R. (1979), 'Alcoholism: a medical or a political problem?', *British Medical Journal*, i: 367–71.

Kenny, A. (1984), 'The psychiatric expert in court', *Psychological Medicine.*, 14: 291–302.

Kety, S., Rosenthal, D., Wender, P. (1971), 'Mental illness in the biological and adoptive families of adoptive schizophrenics', *American Journal of Psychiatry*, 128: 302–12.

Kleinman, A. (1988), *Rethinking Psychiatry*, New York, Macmillan.

Kline, P. (1984), *Psychology and Freudian Theory*, New York, Methuen.

Kraupl-Taylor, F. (1979), *The Concepts of Illness, Disease and Morbus*, Cambridge, Cambridge University Press.

Kreitman, N., Smith, P. and Eng-Seong, T. (1970), 'Attempted suicide as language', *British Journal of Psychiatry*, 116: 465–73.

Kuhn, T. (1970), *The Structure of Scientific Revolutions*, University of Chicago Press.

Lagos, J., Perlmutter, K. and Saexinger, H. (1977), 'Fear of the mentally ill, *American Journal of Psychiatry.*, 134: 1134–7.

Laing, R. (1965), *The Divided Self*, Harmondsworth, Penguin.

Laing, R. (1967), *The Politics of Experience*, Harmondsworth, Penguin.

Laing, R. (1983), *The Voice of Experience*, Harmondsworth, Penguin.

Laurell, B. (ed.) (1970), 'Flurothyl convulsive therapy', *Acta Psychiatrica Scandinavia*, supp. vol. 213.

Lee, S. (1958), 'Social influences in Zulu dreaming', *Journal of Social Psychology*, 47: 265–83.

Leff, J. *et al.* (1982), 'A controlled trial of social intervention in schizophrenic families', *British Journal of Psychiatry*, 141: 21–34.

Leff, J. (1988), *Psychiatry Around the Globe*, Plymouth, Gaskell.

Leifer, R. (1969), *In the Name of Mental Health*, New York, Science House.

Lewinsohn, P., Youngren, M. and Grosscup, S. (1979), 'Reinforcement and depression', in R. Depue (ed.) *The Psychobiology of the Depressive Disorders*, New York, Academic Press, pp. 300–25.

Lewis, A. (1955), 'Health as a social concept', *British Journal of Sociology*, 4: 109–224.

Littlewood, R. and Lipsedge, M. (1987), 'The butterfly and the serpent', *Culture, Medicine and Psychiatry*, 11: 289–335.

Livermore, J., Malmquist, C. and Meehl, P. (1982), 'On the justifications for civil commitment', in R. Edwards (ed.) *Psychiatry and Ethics*, New York, Prometheus, pp. 252–72.

MacDonald, G. and Pettit, P. (1981), *Semantics and Social Science*, London, Routledge & Kegan Paul.

McEvedy, C. and Beard, A. (1970), 'Royal Free epidemic of 1955: a reconsideration', *British Medical Journal*, i: 7–11.

McGarry, L. and Chodoff, P. (1984), 'The ethics of involuntary hospitalization', in S. Bloch and P. Chodoff (eds), *Psychiatric Ethics*, Oxford University Press, pp. 203–19.

McGinn, C. (1978), 'Mental states, natural kinds, and psychophysical laws', *Proceedings of the Aristotelian Society*, supp. vol.: 35–58.

McHugh, P. and Slavney, P. (1986), *The Perspectives of Psychiatry*, London, Johns Hopkins University Press.

McKeown, T. (1979), *The Role of Medicine*, Oxford, Blackwell.

Macklin, R. (1982), 'Refusal of psychiatric treatment: Autonomy, competence, and paternalism', in R. Edwards (ed.), *Psychiatry and Ethics*, New York, Prometheus, pp. 331–40.

Maher, B. (1988), 'Anomalous experience and delusional thinking', in T. Oltmanns and B. Maher (eds), *Delusional Beliefs*, New York, John Wiley & Sons.

Maher, W. and Maher, B. (1982), 'The ship of fools: *stultifera navis* or *ignis fatuus*?', *American Psychologist*, 37: 756–61.

Margolis, J. (1966), *Psychotherapy and Morality*, New York, Random House.

Marks, I. (1986), 'Genetics of fear and anxiety disorders', *British Journal of Psychiatry*, 149: 406–18.

Mathew, R., Weinnman, M. and Mirabi, M. (1981), 'Physical symptoms of depression', *British Journal of Psychiatry*, 139: 293–6.

Maudsley, H. (1874), *Responsibility in Mental Disease*, London, Henry King & Co.

Medical Research Council Clinical Psychiatry Committee, (1965), 'Clinical trial for the treatment of depressive illness', *British Medical Journal*, i: 881–6.

Meissner, P. (1964), 'Family psychopathology', *Family Process*, 3: 1–40.

Mendelwicz, J. and Rainer, J. (1977), 'Adoption study supporting genetic transmission of manic-depressive illness', *Nature*, 268: 327–32.

Mill, J. (1941), *A System of Logic*, London, Macmillan.

Miller, J. (1978), *The Body in Question*, London, Macmillan.

Miller, N. and DiCara, L. (1967), 'Instrumental learning of heart rate changes in curarized rats', *Journal of Comparative Physiology and Psychology*, 63: 12–9.

Moore, G. (1903), *Principia Ethica*, Cambridge, Cambridge University Press.

Moore, M. (1975), 'Some myths about mental illness', *Archives of General Psychiatry*, 32: 1483–97.

Moore, M. (1980), 'Legal conceptions of mental illness', in B. Brody and T. Engelhardt (eds), *Mental Illness: Law and Public Policy*, Dordrecht, Reidel, pp. 25–69.

Moran, C. and Andrews, G. (1985), 'The familial occurrence of agoraphobia', *British Journal of Psychiatry*, 146: 262–7.

Murphy, J. (1976), 'Psychiatric labelling in cross-cultural perspective', *Science*, 191: 1019–28.

Nemiah, J. (1981), 'A psychoanalytic view of phobias', *American Journal of Psychoanalysis*, 41: 115–20.

Owen, F. *et al.*, (1978), 'Increased dopamine receptor sensitivity in schizophrenia', *Lancet*, 2: 223–6.

Parkes, C. (1986), *Bereavement*, Harmondsworth, Penguin.

Parry-Jones, W. (1972), *The Trade in Lunacy*, London, Routledge & Kegan Paul.

Parsons, T. (1951), *The Social System*, Illinois, The Free Press.

Paykel, E., Myers, J. and Dienelt, M. (1969), 'Life events and depression', *Archives of General Psychiatry*, 21: 735–41.

Penfield, W. (1975), *The Mystery of the Mind*, Princeton, Princeton University Press.

Phillips, D. (1982), 'The impact of fictional television suicide stories on US fatalities', *American Journal Sociology*, 87: 1340–59.

Pickering, G. (1962), 'The nature of hypertension', *Lancet*, i: 1296–304.

Pinel, P. (1962), *Treatise on Insanity*, New York, Hafner.

Platt, S. (1990), 'The social transmission of parasuicide: Is there a modelling effect?', *Crisis*, forthcoming.

Popper, K. (1963), *Conjectures and Refutations*, London, Routledge & Kegan Paul.

Putnam, H. (1975), *Mathematics, Matter and Method*, Cambridge, Cambridge University Press.

Putnam, H. (1976), *Mind, Language and Reality*, Cambridge, Cambridge University Press.

Quinton, A. (1984), 'Madness', *Proceedings of the Aristotelian Society*, supp. vol.: 17–41.

Rack, P. (1982), *Race, Culture and Mental Disorder*, London, Tavistock.

Radden, J. (1985), *Madness and Reason*, London, George Allen & Unwin.

Rakusin, J. and Feinin, L. (1963), 'Five assumptions for treating chronic psychosis', *Mental Hospitals*, 14: 140–8.

Rapoport, J. (1989), 'The biology of obsessions and compulsions', *Scientific American*, 260: 82–9.

Ratna, L. (1978), 'Crisis intervention in psychogeriatrics', in L. Ratna (ed.), *The Practice of Psychiatric Crisis Intervention*, Napsbury Hospital, League of Friends.

Redmond, D. (1977), 'Alterations in the function of the nucleus locus coeruleus: a possible model for studies in anxiety', in I. Hanin and E. Usdin (eds), *Animal Models in Psychiatry and Neurology*, New York, Pergamon Press, pp. 67–87.

Redmond, D. and Huang, Y. (1979), 'New evidence for a locus coeruleus–norepinephrine connection with anxiety', *Life Sciences*, 25: 2149–62.

Regina v. McNaughton (1843), *English Reports*, 718: 722–3.

Reich, W. (1984), 'Psychiatric diagnosis as an ethical problem', in S. Bloch and P. Chodoff (eds), *Psychiatric Ethics*, Oxford, Oxford University Press, pp. 61–88.

Reiman, E. *et al.* (1989), 'Neuroanatomical correlates of a lactate–induced anxiety attack', *Archives of General Psychiatry*, 46: 493–500.

Reznek, L. (1987), *The Nature of Disease*, London, Routledge & Kegan Paul.

Robins, E. and Guze, S. (1970), 'Establishment of diagnostic validity in psychiatric illness', *American Journal of Psychiatry*, 126: 983–7.

Roper, P. (1989), 'Bulimia while sleepwalking – a rebuttal for sane automatism?', *Lancet*, ii: 796.

Rosenhan, D. (1973), 'On being sane in insane places', *Science*, 179: 250–8.

Roth, M. (1980), 'Senile dementia and its borderlands', in J. Cole and J. Barrett (eds), *Psychopathology in the Aged*, New York, Raven Press, pp. 30–47.

Roth, M. and Kroll, J. (1986), *The Reality of Mental Illness*, Cambridge, Cambridge University Press.

Roy, A. *et al.* (1988), 'Pathological gambling: A psychobiological study', *Archives of General Psychiatry*, 45: 369–73.

Royal College of Psychiatrists (1986), *Alcohol: Our Favourite Drug*, London, Tavistock Publications.

Rycroft, C. (1968), 'Causes and meaning', in C. Rycroft (ed.), *Psychoanalysis Observed*, Harmondsworth, Penguin, pp. 7–22.

Sartorius, N. *et al.* (1986), 'Early manifestations and first contact incidence of schizophrenia in different cultures', *Psychological Medicine*, 16: 909–28.

Sartorius, R. (1980), 'Paternalistic grounds for involuntary civil commitment', in B. Brody and T. Engelhardt (eds), *Mental Illness*, Dordrecht, Reidel, pp. 137–46.

Schatzman, M. (1971), 'Paranoia or persecution: The case of Schreber', *Family Process*, 10: 177–207.

Scheff, T. (1966), *Being Mentally Ill: A Sociological Theory*, London, Weidenfeld & Nicolson.

Scheff, T. (1975), 'On reason and sanity: some political implications of psychiatric thought', in T. Scheff (ed.), *Labelling Madness*, New York, Prentice Hall, pp. 12–20.

Schrag, P. and Divoky, D. (1975), *The Myth of the Hyperactive Child*, Harmondsworth, Penguin.

Scott, P. (1977), 'Assessing dangerousness in criminals', *British Journal of Psychiatry*, 131: 127–42.

Sedgwick, P. (1973), 'Illness – mental and otherwise', *Hastings Centre Studies*, 1: 19–40.

Sedgwick, P. (1982), *Psycho Politics*, London, Pluto Press.

Seligman, M. (1975), *Helplessness: On Depression, Development and Death*, San Francisco, Freeman.

Shapere, D. (1974), *Galileo: A Philosophical Study*, Chicago, University of Chicago Press.

Shapiro, D., Tursky, B. and Schwartz, G. (1970), 'Control of blood pressure in men by operant conditioning', *Circulation Research*, 26: 127–32.

Siegler, M. and Osmond, H. (1980), *Models of Madness: Models of Medicine*, New York, Macmillan.

Siegler, M., Osmond, H. and Mann, H. (1972), 'Laing's models of madness', in R. Boyers and R. Orrill (eds), *Laing and Anti-Psychiatry*, Harmondsworth, Penguin, pp. 99–122.

Simons, A., Garfield, S. and Murphy, G. (1984), 'The process of change in cognitive therapy and pharmacotherapy for depression', *Archives of General Psychiatry*, 41: 45–51.

Skultans, V. (1979), *English Madness*, London, Routledge.

Stafford-Clark, D. and Taylor, F. (1949), 'Clinical and electro-encephalographic studies of prisoners charged with murder', *Journal of Neurology, Neurosurgery and Psychiatry*, 12: 325–30.

Stavrakaki, C. and Vargo, B. (1986), 'The relationship of anxiety and depression', *British Journal of Psychiatry*, 149: 7–16.

Swinburne, R. (1973), *An Introduction to Confirmation Theory*, London, Methuen.

Szasz, T. (1972), *The Myth of Mental Illness*, London, Paladin.

Szasz, T. (1974a), *The Second Sin*, London, Routledge & Kegan Paul.

Szasz, T. (1974b), *Ideology and Insanity*, Harmondsworth, Penguin.

Szasz, T. (1974c), *Law, Liberty, and Psychiatry*, London, Routledge.

Szasz, T. (1979a), *Schizophrenia*, Oxford, Oxford University Press.

Szasz, T. (1979b), *Theology of Medicine*, Oxford, Oxford University Press.

Szasz, T. (1987), *Insanity*, New York, John Wiley & Sons.

Taerk, G. *et al.* (1987), 'Depression in patients with neuromyasthenia', *International Journal of Psychiatry and Medicine*, 17: 49–56.

Temerlin, M. (1968), 'Suggestion effects in psychiatric diagnosis', *Journal of Nervous and Mental Disease*, 147: 349–58.

Thoresen, C., Telch, M. and Eagleston, J. (1981), 'Altering type A behaviour', *Psychosomatics*, 8: 472–82.

Torrey, F. (1980), *The Death of Psychiatry*, Radnor, Chilton Books.

Torrey, F. (1986), *Witchdoctors and Psychiatrists*, New York, Harper & Row.

Tyrer, P. and Steinberg, D. (1987), *Models for Mental Disorder*, Chichester, John Wiley & Sons.

Varma, L., Srivastava, D. and Sahay, R. (1970), 'Possession syndrome', *Indian Journal of Psychiatry*, 15: 59–70.

Vaughn, C. and Leff, J. (1976) 'The influence of family and social factors on the course of schizophrenic illness', *British Journal of Psychiatry*, 129: 125–32.

Veith, I. (1965), *Hysteria: The History of a Disease*, Chicago, Chicago University Press.

Watson, J. (1930), *Behaviourism*, London, Kegan Paul.

Wessely, S. (1987), 'Mass hysteria: two syndromes?', *Psychology Medicine* 17: 109–20.

Williams, G. (1983), *Textbook of Criminal Law*, London, Stevens & Son.

Wilson, E. (1978), *On Human Nature*, Cambridge, Mass., Harvard University Press.

Wing, J. (ed.) (1975), *Schizophrenia from Within*, London, National Schizophrenia Fellowship.

Wing, J. (1978), *Reasoning about Madness*, Oxford, Oxford University Press.

Wing, J. and Brown, G. (1970), *Institutionalism and Schizophrenia*, Cambridge, Cambridge University Press.

Wootton, B. (1959), *Social Science and Social Pathology*, London, George Allen & Unwin.

Wootton, B. (1980), 'Psychiatry, ethics and the criminal law', *British Journal of Psychiatry*, 136: 525–32.

World Health Organization (1973), *The International Pilot Study of Schizophrenia*, Geneva, WHO.

Yarrow, M., Schwartz, C., Murphy, H., and Deasy, L. (1955), 'The psychological meaning of mental illness in the family', *Journal of Social Issues*, 11: 12–24.

Zealley, A. (1983), 'Mental handicap', in R. Kendell and A. Zealley (eds), *Companion to Psychiatric Studies*, London, Churchill Livingstone.

Zitrin, C., Klein, D. and Woerner, M. (1978), 'Behaviour therapy, supportive psychotherapy, imipramine and phobias', *Archives of General Psychiatry*, 35: 307–16.

INDEX